A NEW IRELAND

A NEW IRELAND

How Europe's Most Conservative Country
Became Its Most Liberal

NIALL O'DOWD

Skyhorse Publishing

Skyhorse Publishing books may be purchased in bulk at special discounts for sales promotion, corporate gifts, fund-raising, or educational purposes. Special editions can also be created to specifications. For details, contact the Special Sales Department, Skyhorse Publishing, 307 West 36th Street, 11th Floor, New York, NY 10018 or info@skyhorsepublishing.com.

Skyhorse® and Skyhorse Publishing® are registered trademarks of Skyhorse Publishing, Inc.®, a Delaware corporation.

Visit our website at www.skyhorsepublishing.com.

10 9 8 7 6 5 4 3 2 1

Library of Congress Cataloging-in-Publication Data is available on file.

Cover design by Daniel Brount
Cover photo credit: Getty Images

Print ISBN: 978-1-5107-4929-0
Ebook ISBN: 978-1-5107-4930-6

Printed in the United States of America

TABLE OF CONTENTS

To Elsa, Sonny, Patrick, Fionn, Katie, Phoebe, and Ciara,
Grow Up Big and Strong

ACKNOWLEDGMENTS

The origins of this book occurred because of the sheer number of interested Americans who asked me what on Earth had gone on in Ireland with so much radical change in recent years.

I decided to tell the story and put the remarkable events such as the massive vote for same-sex marriage, a gay *taoiseach* (prime minister), and passage of abortion rights in political and historical context.

To do so involved going back to the very root of Christianity, politics, and society in Ireland and following it through to its modern transformation when all changed utterly.

This book had many champions, not least my former editor, Michael Campbell; current editor, Yezanira Venecia; and Skyhorse publisher, Tony Lyons, whose insights were truly invaluable. Special thanks to Dermot McEvoy for his usual wise counsel.

Special thanks to Donal and Mary in Ireland for grammar, proofing, and support, and to Fergus who read and advised. As always, love to Debbie for all her support and calmness, and to Alana for always encouraging her dad.

SECTION ONE

INTRODUCTION

"Walk on air against your better judgment," Irish Nobel poet Seamus Heaney urged as his final epitaph. The Irish people took Heaney's advice and transformed a country that had long been a bastion of theocracy, so much so that the Church wrote significant parts of the 1937 Irish Constitution.

How narrow was their thinking? In April 1944, Archbishop John McQuaid, the "Catholic Ruler of Ireland," as his biographer tagged him, wrote to an Irish minister in the Department of Health and informed him the bishops had met to discuss the arrival of Tampax into Ireland and wanted the product banned on the grounds that insertion might stimulate women sexually. The government agreed and banned Tampax. McQuaid was obsessed with female genitalia. Shortly after, he used a magnifying glass to show a newspaper proprietor that the mons veneris of a woman was visible in a ladies' underwear advertisement.

This was the man who set the tenor of the times in Ireland for generations.

Yet side by side with the prudish Victorian morality existed a heart of darkness in church-run schools and orphanages that would shock the world.

The state could not claim innocence, as they were willing participants in the ghastly tableaux. There was a vicious war against "fallen women" and their helpless offspring that defied all rational explanation. There was a separate dirty war against children by priest pedophiles, protected by the hierarchy as they ran amok, knowing their activities would be covered up.

Gay people were targets, too. Queer-bashing had become a popular sport for young thugs, with no recourse for the bashed.

Women's rights were almost nonexistent, with the very words of the constitution militating against them. Each year thousands fled to Britain for terminations, often as a result of rape and incest.

And yet, somehow, despite the sepulchral gloom, Irish people found a way to transform and illuminate their society, which amazed the watching world. No people had ever done something quite like it. Seamus Heaney would have approved. It is a story for the ages.

This is how they did it.

CHAPTER 1

The Sins of the Fathers

"He talked about the Irish institutions as being like concentration camps for children."
Tom Lynch, Boys Town archivist, on Father Flanagan's
view of Irish industrial schools and orphanages

Those looking for the seeds of what later became the near destruction of the Irish church over child mistreatment and abuse would have found it in the clarion voice of Monsignor Edward Joseph Flanagan—the founder of Boys Town, made famous by the Spencer Tracy movie of the same name. The Irish-born Flanagan, though an international figure and beloved by all for his amazing work, found himself a forlorn voice when he traveled to Ireland to inspect their facilities for treating orphans and needy children.

Flanagan's connection to Ireland was deep, and he knew what he spoke about. He was born on July 13, 1886, in the townland of Leabeg, County Roscommon, to John, a herdsman, and Honoria Flanagan. In 1904, he immigrated to the United States, entered the priesthood, and, in 1917, created Boys Town in Omaha, Nebraska.

From the start of his ordination, Flanagan made clear he would be a social reformer with special emphasis on children. At a time when child labor was common, he felt it was his mission to ensure that kids would be valued by the adult world and that those kids who were most in need were looked after.

The Boys Town center was open to all. There were no fences to stop the boys from leaving. Father Flanagan said he was "not building a prison."

"This is a home," he said. "You do not wall in members of your own family." The 1938 movie *Boys Town* made a national hero out of Father Flanagan.

In 1946, Father Flanagan decided to return to his birthland to visit his family and the "so-called training schools" run by the Christian Brothers. He wanted to see if they were truly a success.

With the success of the film *Boys Town*, Flanagan was treated like a celebrity upon his arrival back home. The *Irish Independent* wrote that Flanagan had succeeded "against overwhelming odds," spurred on by the simple slogan: "There is no such thing as a bad boy."[1]

As quoted in *History Ireland* magazine in 2004, according to Flanagan expert Doctor Eoin O'Sullivan of the Department of Social Studies in Trinity College Dublin, Flanagan was not home to take a victory lap:

> . . . The priest had a deep-rooted abhorrence of the institutionalisation of children. His unique legacy was that Boys'[sic] Town and the various projects that he initiated were to divert children away from punitive carceral institutions, which he believed damaged children, to self-regulating, empowering, open communities for young people of all creeds and races.[2]

Flanagan had made clear his problems with incarceration of children, which he believed was a traumatic experience that scarred them for life.

He wrote to a fellow priest:

> I am particularly interested in the juvenile problem. I would like to get their [Irish welfare department] reaction as to

whether these so-called training schools conducted by the Christian Brothers are a success or a failure. My memory—and it is not very clear—is that they have not been very successful in developing individuality, Christian character, and manliness, because they are too much institutionalised. This, as you know, helps the good Brothers and makes it easier for them.[3]

But Flanagan was plunged into despair about what he found in Ireland, especially the Victorian orphanages and reform schools where young offenders were sent. He found them "a scandal, un-Christ-like, and wrong."

He spoke to a large audience at a public lecture in Cork's Savoy Cinema and, according to Irish media reports, said:

You are the people who permit your children and the children of your communities to go into these institutions of punishment. You can do something about it. . . . I do not believe that a child can be reformed by lock and key and bars, or that fear can ever develop a child's character.[4]

He even attacked the Christian Brothers—the teaching order founded in Ireland to educate the masses and revered as an institution.

Tom Lynch, Boys Town archivist, told the late Mary Raftery, a journalist, who herself did incredible, groundbreaking work on church scandal: "It was very well known that he was shocked by what he discovered in Ireland. He talked about the Irish institutions as being like concentration camps for children."[5]

As Raftery subsequently wrote in the *Irish Times* in 2004, "[Flanagan] had a profound sense of outrage at how children were treated within these institutions."

His own words, written in 1947, summed up Flanagan's thoughts on Ireland and were repeated by Father Val J. Peter, one of his successors at Boys Town, in a letter to the *Irish Times* in 2002 on the topic of child abuse:

. . . [U]njust incarceration, unequal distribution of physical punishment both inside and outside the prisons and jails, and the institutionalisation of little children, housed in great big factory-like places, where individuality has been, and is being, snuffed out with no development of the personality of the individual, and where little children become a great army of child slavery in the workshops, making money for the institutions which give to them a little food, a little clothing, very little recreation, and a doubtful education.[6]

As Raftery noted, it was this view of the institutions that had prompted Father Flanagan to describe them publicly as "a disgrace to the nation," which received widespread press coverage.

Father Flanagan was also supplied with documentation confirming the savage flogging of a child by Christian Brothers at the industrial school in Glin, County Limerick. This material was sent by a deeply courageous local representative, Martin McGuire, who at the time demanded a public inquiry into the treatment of children in industrial schools.

Gerard Fogarty, the child at the center of the case, died in 2007 at the age of seventy-seven. As reported by the Alliance Victim Support Group, Martin McGuire told Fogarty's story:

He was flogged by a Christian Brother for escaping from St. Joseph's Industrial School after being committed there for skipping school.

The youngster ran away again the night of the flogging and walked through fields for 32 miles until he returned to his mother in Limerick City.

[Fogarty himself remembered,] "By the time I got home, the bleeding on my back had stopped and the blood had dried into my shirt. I must have been a terrible sight. My mother nearly tore the hair out of her head when she saw me."

The Fogartys along with almost 100 of their neighbours, arrived into Cllr McGuire's offices at his mill and bakery business on Francis Street.

The councillor was so shocked by the boy's injuries that he wrote a letter to the Minister for Education just two days later in which he stated that it was his "distasteful duty to draw your attention to what I consider is a matter of paramount public importance."

He demanded to know if such a form of punishment was "prescribed by law."

The councillor was relentless in his demands for a public enquiry into industrial schools and Borstal institutions. . . .[7]

The Christian Brother was quietly transferred, and McGuire was publicly denounced.

Father Flanagan detested the same Christian Brothers, the organization that educated almost every young male in Ireland. He compared them to Nazis.

In 1947, he wrote in private correspondence:

[We] have no Christian Brotherhood here at Boys Town. We did have them for five years, but they left after they found out that they could not punish the children and kick them around[.] We have punished the Nazis for their sins against society. We have punished the Fascists for the same reason. I wonder what God's judgment will be with reference to those who hold the deposit of faith and who fail in their God-given stewardship of little children?[8]

The reaction to Flanagan from the powerful leaders of the theocratic state was as expected. Despite Flanagan's profile and the worldwide respect for his work, his words were utterly ignored. He was vilified and asked how dare he cast doubt on Ireland's leaders—both of church and state—who were fine upstanding men (and they were all men). They batted away Flanagan's broadside.

The reaction in political Ireland was especially bilious. According to the parliamentary record, then-Minister for Justice Gerald Boland said in the *Dáil* (Ireland's parliament) that he was "not disposed to take any notice of what Monsignor Flanagan said while he was in this country because his statements were so exaggerated."[9]

Flanagan, appalled by the reception and hostility he faced, struck back, but it would be over fifty years before his words were borne out.

He wrote an open letter to the Irish clergy and political leaders:

What you need over there is to have someone shake you loose from your smugness and satisfaction and set an example by punishing those who are guilty of cruelty, ignorance, and neglect of their duties in high places. . . . I wonder what God's judgment will be with reference to those who hold the deposit of faith and who fail in their God-given stewardship of little children.[10]

That judgment day was indeed coming. One could only imagine from his perch in Valhalla what Flanagan's reaction would have been as the scandals rolled by like tumbleweeds in a gale.

"Told you so" would surely have been on the tip of his tongue. But not even he could have imagined the incredible scale and mountainous waves of change that would come rolling in, transforming his native country from theocracy to one of the most liberal thinking in the Western world.

CHAPTER 2

The Son of the Bishop Shows Up

> "We've had a call from a man who says he wants to tell us about a boy in America who's the son of Bishop Eamonn Casey."
>
> *News Editor,* Irish Times

The beginning of the end that Flanagan predicted crept in decades later rather than announcing itself.

January 1992 was a very busy month in Irish news. On the 30th of January, the *Taoiseach* (Prime Minister) Charles Haughey announced his resignation after it was proven he had tapped two Irish journalists' phones a decade before.

Haughey had overcome several heaves to get rid of him, both from within his own party, Fianna Fáil, and from opposition benches. But the bugging scandal proved to be the end of a political Houdini.

It should have been no surprise when news broke that his former Justice Minister Sean Doherty admitted he was not acting alone when bugging the phones of the journalists but had kept Haughey informed, but it could never be proven unless Doherty came clean. Now Doherty had finally told the truth, thus ending the leadership of the most controversial Irish leader since Eamon de Valera.

It was not the only major story. British Secretary of State Peter Brooke, one of the more enlightened and sympathetic proconsuls sent to Belfast, set in motion his April resignation after bizarrely singing the music hall ditty "Oh My Darling Clementine" on Irish television's top-rated program, *The Late Late Show*, just hours after a deadly IRA bombing had killed seven Protestants.

Unionists were outraged at the perceived failure to show proper respect, and his relationship with them suffered irretrievably. Brooke was clearly on borrowed time thereafter.

Meanwhile, in Áras an Uachtaráin, the stately home of the Irish president in the Phoenix Park, Mary Robinson was finalizing plans in 1992 to become the first-ever Irish head of state to visit Belfast in early February. Her visit, she knew, would be a prelude to other trips there. In June 1993, she would meet and shake hands with Sinn Féin leader Gerry Adams in a move that infuriated the British. They tried everything to prevent it, but, like Margaret Thatcher, Mary Robinson was not for turning.

Both were momentous stories, and they were soon to be joined by the beginning of the biggest story of all in the era of modern Catholic Ireland.

In his excellent memoir, *Up with the Times*, former *Irish Times* Editor Conor Brady remembers the day the Catholic Church showed its first signs of collapse. He writes how the quiet newsroom of the *Irish Times* on a gunmetal-gray January day, usually a month when the news was scarce, suddenly came to life with a once-in-a-lifetime scoop.

The duty editor picked up a ringing phone and heard an American voice on the other end. The man refused to identify himself but stated he wanted to discuss the matter of a prominent bishop who had a son by an American woman who was now the caller's partner.

The duty editor passed the story onto the news editor, John Armstrong. An hour or so later, Brady recalls Armstrong came to see him wearing a grim expression.

According to his book *Up with the Times*, he said, "We've had a call from a man who says he wants to tell us about a boy in America who's the son of Bishop Eamonn Casey . . .

"This man's name is Arthur Pennell. He's the partner of a woman called Annie Murphy. She claims she had an affair of several years with the Bishop of Galway, Eamonn Casey, and that he's the father of her child, Peter, who's now 17 years old. She wants to tell us the whole story . . .

"I had the impression that he wanted to get all this out into the open. He seemed under pressure himself."

As Brady relates it, the American had put the woman on the phone.

A check of the American address given by her worked out. An Annie Murphy lived at the Ridgefield, Connecticut, address.

The two editors agreed it was a case for their newly arrived US correspondent, Conor O'Clery, a legendary figure known for getting it first and getting it right.

Bishop Eamonn Casey, too, was a legend. He first became known for his dedicated work with poor Irish immigrants in London, where a "No Irish Need Apply" mentality still existed.

He was now sixty-five and a beloved figure who had always spoken out on Third World issues. In 1986, he was caught drunk driving and issued a frank apology, which only increased his popularity.

As his *Irish Times* obituary noted:

His social conscience and work rate, evident in Limerick, soon became apparent in London as he immersed himself in emigrant life. He became active in the Catholic Housing Aid Society, moving to London in 1963 to place it on a national footing at the invitation of Cardinal Heenan, then Archbishop of Westminster.

He participated in a powerful BBC documentary, *Cathy Come Home*, highlighting homelessness, and in an RTÉ

Radharc documentary which featured his work in London. He was a church star, and a hero among the Irish in London, when, aged 42 years, he was made bishop of Kerry in 1969.[11]

The obituary was also notable for the fact that its closing line was "[Bishop Casey I] is survived by his son Peter."

CHAPTER 3

Casey at the Bat for Pope

"Young people of Ireland, I love you."
Pope John Paul II in Galway September 1979

Tellingly in 1979, Casey had been one of two clerics who were chosen to speak before the pope's arrival in Galway. Picked to stand alongside him was Father Michael Cleary, a Dublin pastor renowned for his communication skills. He had written a book titled *The Singing Priest*, which outlined his love of singing and music and his ability to charm young people back to God.

Both men, though of different vintage, had many similar pronouncements on the sacredness of marriage and the battle against those seeking divorce or legal abortion and were seen as the most presentable among the Irish clergy on the pope's visit.

Both men also held dark secrets. All along they were breaking those same rules with utter abandonment, preaching about the evils of sex outside marriage while conducting secret affairs and molesting children themselves.

The shocking news about Casey the molester was not made public until 2019. The beloved pastor who erred because he was human with Annie Murphy and who had every major dignitary, including the Irish president, at his funeral was an accused child molester.

In addition to fathering a child with Annie Murphy, it has been revealed that he also allegedly abused three young girls, including his niece.

Even in a country swamped with exposés of clerical abuse, the Casey case was astonishing. He has long been held in sympathetic regard because of his love affair, which was widely accepted as human foible. But raping young nieces was a different matter.

But there was his niece, Patricia Donovan, telling the *Irish Daily Mail* that she was raped by Casey when she was just five years old and was sexually assaulted by the bishop for years to come.

Donovan, now fifty-six, said, "It was rape, everything you imagine. It was the worst kind of abuse, it was horrific. I stopped being able long ago to find any words in the English language to describe what happened to me. It was one horrific thing after another."[12]

Both Casey and Cleary were fathers, not the ecclesiastical kind either, and both covered up scandalous relationships that would blow the Catholic Church apart in Ireland when their stories and others were told.

Father Cleary was a twisted soul, too. *The Singing Priest* built a wonderful façade, a Father Trendy figure who made a huge name for himself as an entertainer and cleric seen as being in touch with young people. Just how much he was in touch came out later.

Cleary also led from the front on the 1983 abortion referendum, promising fire and brimstone and hell against anyone who went against the church's wishes. He was to be a leading church figure in the battle against divorce, which would lead to a referendum in 1995. Trendy, godly, a pathfinder to the Church for young men and women, Cleary was a real star in the eyes of the hierarchy.

After all that, he went home to his rectory—a handsome brick house on Mount Harold Terrace near fashionable Rathmines, where he had commenced an illegal affair with the housekeeper, Phyllis Hamilton. She was just seventeen years old—Cleary was thirty-four—when the affair started. Abused by her father, Phyllis was an easy mark for the smooth-talking celebrity padre.

He had his own call-in radio show, had a TV interview program, and he was famous—all reasons why Phyllis was swept off her feet.

She cooked for him, cared for him, slept with him, and bore him at least two children. (A third child, a woman now living in Florida who is Hamilton's third child, was conceived from a rape by another priest.)

The unnamed third priest had found out about the relationship with Cleary and blackmailed her according to her psychiatrist, Doctor Ivor Browne, to whom she gave permission to reveal the truth, but only after she died in 2001.

Browne also revealed that despite desperate entreaties, Cleary refused to come clean that his housekeeper was the mother of his children and insisted it be kept secret. But fellow clergy soon understood what was really going on in the rectory.

The Church surely knew toward the end. A friend of Hamilton and Cleary said:

> In October 1993 I met with [Monsignor] Alex Stenson at the archbishop's house, who agreed to meet in confidence. I told him about Michael, Phyllis and their two sons and their fears of public exposure. His view was that until Michael told the Church directly, they could not offer him, or anyone else that may be involved, any support.[13]

And there the matter rested.

Those were the two men of all the clerics in Ireland handpicked to perform on stage and meet and greet Pope John Paul II on his historic trip to Ireland in 1979. As hundreds of thousands waited at Galway racetrack for the arrival of the first-ever pope to come to Ireland, it was the Casey and Cleary Show, both in full flight, singing, praying, swaying to the gospel music and then embracing the pontiff when he arrived.

As journalist Kim Bielenberg wrote in the *Irish Independent*:

Like his friend Fr Michael Cleary, who joined him as the warm-up act at the Papal Mass in Galway in 1979, Casey was the bridge between the fusty and reserved old world of the hierarchy, stuck in the 1950s, and the modern media world of soundbites, chat shows, and talk radio. Casey and Cleary, with their populist touch and crowd-pleasing manner, were seen at the time as standard-bearers for the more youthful Church of the future. But this was to unravel in spectacular fashion when news emerged much later of their sons and lovers.[14]

Galway was the site where John Paul bellowed out what became the meme of his visit: "Young people of Ireland, I love you." But his speech echoed the uneasiness among church leaders that the vice-like grip on the young would loosen in an age of materialism, exploding technology, and failures to remember the unbroken bond with the past. John Paul had come for a reason—to prop up the conservative faith and doctrine that had ruled for centuries.

His speech went directly at that theme:

The religious and moral traditions of Ireland, the very soul of Ireland, will be challenged by the temptations that spare no society in our age. Like so many other young people in various parts of the world, you will be told that changes must be made, that you must have more freedom, that you should be different from your parents, and that the decisions about your lives depend on you, and you alone. . . . The lure of pleasure, to be had whenever and wherever it can be found, will be strong and it may be presented to you as part of progress towards greater autonomy and freedom from rules.

The desire to be free from external restraints may manifest itself very strongly in the sexual domain, since this is an area that is so closely tied to a human personality. The moral standards that the Church and society have held up to you for so long a time, will be presented as obsolete and a hindrance to the full development of your own personality. . . .

Yes, dear young people, do not close your eyes to the moral sickness that stalks your society today, and from which your youth alone will not protect you. How many young people have already warped their consciences and have substituted the true joy of life with drugs, sex, alcohol, vandalism and the empty pursuit of mere material possessions.[15]

Ironically, the moral sickness he feared was flanking him on the podium by the showrunners Bishop Casey and Father Cleary, who were among the cast of characters for the dreadful and seemingly never-ending scandals to come.

CHAPTER 4:

A Dead Pope and a Mystery Irishman

"I want the Irishman; get me the Irishman."

Pope John Paul

In 1979, the Church seemed resurgent. John Paul II, young at fifty-nine years old and, by papal standards, vigorous and relentless, cut a mighty dash in Ireland.

He was the 263rd pope and the first pontiff since Peter founded the Church in AD 33 and since St. Patrick brought Catholicism in the fifth century to visit Ireland. He represented a huge tradition and fealty that the modern Vatican believed could not be allowed to slip away.

It was noticeable that everywhere he went in Ireland his private secretary, Monsignor John Magee, followed, keeping pace like a silent shadow. It was a big occasion for him, too.

He had played a huge role in delivering the pope to his native Ireland. Standing beside the first non-Italian pope since the sixteenth century, Magee's story was an incredible one, too. He was a mysterious private secretary to three popes and accused of helping to kill one. He was known to some as the "Pope's Apprentice."

When it came to the Vatican intrigue, there was no one as prepared for the dark side as Magee. The fact he was at John Paul's side was proof of that. John Paul II, a.k.a. Karol Wojtyla, had just been declared pope in October 1978 when he urgently sought Monsignor Magee, son of a dairy farmer from Newry, County Down. "I want the Irishman; get me the Irishman," he told his secretary according to an interview Magee gave to British journalist and author John Cornwell.

It was a curious request. Magee was at the center of an international storm of intrigue and sensational accusations charging him with involvement in killing the previous pope, John Paul I, who died on September 28, 1978, after just thirty-three days in office. Magee was among the very last to see him alive, if not the last. He had even been interviewed by Interpol.

Magee had originally stated it was he who found the pope dead, but later it turned out to be Sister Vincenza, a member of the pope's household, who found the deceased pope. The idea of a nun being in the pope's private bedroom unnerved the Vatican Press Office, who manufactured the story that Magee found him.

It issued the fake statement: "This morning, September 29, 1978, about 5:30 a.m., the private secretary of the pope, contrary to custom, not having found the Holy Father in the chapel of his private apartment, looked in his room and found him dead in bed with the light on . . ."[16]

It was actually Sister Vincenza who had come to the papal chambers to give him his morning coffee and found him sitting up in bed with the documents he had been reading beside him, glasses still perched on his nose, allegedly with a smile on his face. Sister Vincenza thought he was sleeping, then realized he had expired.

That was the Vatican story at least, even though it had holes deeper than the Grand Canyon.

Once he was called to the scene, Magee immediately alerted the Vatican secretary of state and senior officials. Soon the sensational story broke.

It did not take long for a conspiracy theory to take hold, one with Magee smack in the middle of it. "Who ever died sitting upright in bed with a smile on their face?" asked the conspiracy theorists who included many senior Vatican figures.

The body must have been placed there, they alleged. "The pope was poisoned" was the narrative because he was threatening to unveil a huge financial scandal around the Vatican Bank.

Why was there no autopsy? What about the embalmers who were allegedly told to show up at 5:00 a.m., before the pope had even been discovered? (It turned out they had actually been booked at 5:00 p.m., not 5:00 a.m.)

Autopsy experts agreed there was no way the pope could have died sitting up in bed smiling. His jaw, for instance, would have slackened, making a smile impossible. Someone had propped him up on the bed or perhaps lifted him from the floor.

John Cornwell, called in by the Vatican to investigate when the speculation about poisoning was rampant, dismisses every conspiracy with convincing authority—all except one.

Cornwell assumes that the pope was found dead much earlier by Magee, who checked on the pope on his way to his own room, saw the light on, and walked in. It was then very likely that he found the pope dead from a heart attack on the floor. He called for Pope John Paul's personal secretary, Father Diego Lorenzi, who served the pope in Venice and had moved to Rome with him. Together they propped the pope up on his bed with pillows and left him as if reading.

The hue and cry was understandable. It was the era of the scandal behind the Banco Ambrosiano, a corrupt bank funded in part by the Vatican. Its chairman, Roberto Calvi, had hanged himself from Blackfriars Bridge in London. There were allegations about the American Bishop Paul Marcinkus, who ran the Vatican Bank, and the fears he had that the new pope would fire him because of the scandals.

Magee was the obvious media target, and rumors spread quickly and viciously that he was somehow involved.

His backstory made him even more interesting. He was plucked from obscurity as a missionary priest in Africa by a visiting cardinal who was deeply impressed by him.

From there he rose to be private secretary to three popes: Pope Paul VI, Pope John Paul I, and Pope John Paul II.

His proximity to the popes was impressive. According to an article in the *Irish Central*:

> John Cooney, an Irish-based journalist covering religious affairs, wrote how "Magee proudly boasted that Pope Paul VI treated him like a son, and that John Paul II treated him like a brother.
>
> According to Cooney, he was considered the "most handsome man" in the Vatican and had incredible access to the Popes. He lived in a wonderful villa on the Vatican grounds.
>
> It even had a private chapel, and he loved to entertain friends from Ireland and arrange meetings with the Pope for a chosen few.[17]

In *Angels & Demons*, Dan Brown's prequel to *The Da Vinci Code*, an ambitious Irish priest close to the pope almost becomes pope himself by plotting and eliminating enemies during a papal conclave. The book's Rev. Patrick McKenna would seem to have been based on Magee. His fame as secretary to the popes was known far and wide.

Magee told confidants he was not surprised the pope had died. The previous night he had asked if he should call a doctor, as John Paul seemed unwell. The pope refused. After the pope retired, Magee sat with the household nuns in the kitchen and expressed his fear the pontiff was ailing.

Then he said he had an eerie premonition and went looking up the shortest reign of popes. Given the time of death was placed at about 11:00 p.m., the pope was already dead as Magee discussed his health and looked up the record of popes who died soon after taking office. John Paul had the eleventh shortest reign as pope.

He subsequently told journalist John Cornwell that the new pontiff had been deeply traumatized by winning the job. He suffered from edema, which led to severe swelling of his ankles, and complained of pain in his heart area the night before he died. The stress of the job was weighing heavily on him. He had not wanted to be pope, but the Italians in the conclave were desperate to hang on to the papacy.

Now Magee was under suspicion of poisoning the pope, implicated utterly by innuendo. Nonetheless, Magee had to flee the Vatican and landed at his sister's house in Manchester, England, until the hue and cry faded.

Now back in Rome with a new pope, Magee expected to be blotted out permanently from the landscape and sent to some obscure parish given the notoriety that now surrounded him.

But then came the surprise summons from Karol Wojtyla. We can only surmise the new pope wanted the real story, whatever it was, about the demise of his predecessor. Then, to everyone's astonishment, he hired Magee as his private secretary. Did he fear what Magee knew and decide to keep him close?

Magee was once again ensconced as the closest of all in terms of physical proximity to his third pontiff and no doubt first implanted the idea of the pope's visit to Ireland, a historic first.

The two men became close for a time, but there was no major promotion, merely as bishop to Cloyne encompassing parts of County Cork, one of the lesser dioceses after Armagh and Dublin. John Paul II consecrated him as Bishop of Cloyne in Ireland in 1985 and had some obligatory kind words.

Despite all the power and access to the pope that Magee enjoyed, questions clearly still lingered about him and what happened the night the first John Paul died.

The thirty-three-day Pope himself expected to die, and Magee revealed an extraordinarily mystical moment to journalist John Allen of the *National Catholic Reporter* in April 2005 when he flew back to Rome for the funeral of John Paul II.

The election of Cardinal Karol Wojtyla as pope in October 1978 was a sensation worldwide, a break with four and a half centuries of Italian popes. But Bishop Magee told Allen it came as no surprise to at least one man: John Paul II's immediate predecessor, John Paul I.

Allen wrote:

Though Magee worked for John Paul I only 33 days, he retains vivid memories of the experience—some of which come across as either mystical or spooky, depending on your point of view.

"Two nights before he died, he asked, 'Why did they select me?'" Magee recalled. "There was somebody much better than me. Paul VI had even indicated him as his successor."

Magee said he shrunk from asking whom he had in mind.

"He will come, for I am going," Magee recalled John Paul I as saying, at which point Magee said John Paul even called his successor "The Foreigner." Magee changed the subject. . . .

Another time, Magee said, John Paul I said that the "much better" choice, the man Paul VI had wanted as a successor, was sitting across from him during the conclave.

Later, when John Paul II appointed Magee as his master of ceremonies, Magee arrived at the office for a tour, and stopped before several cupboards marked "Conclave of 1978." He asked a sister what was inside, and she informed him that it was the office's records from the organization of the conclave. They were locked, the sister said, and the key was in a safe. Only Magee now had the authority to open them. He asked the sister to bring him the key.

Magee pulled out the records from the first conclave of 1978, the one that elected John Paul I, and found a large cardboard plaque with the seating chart from inside the conclave. Sure enough, he said, directly across from Cardinal Albino Luciani, later John Paul I, was Cardinal Karol Wojtyla, John Paul II.

"It is an extraordinary story," Magee said of his own account. Reflecting for a moment about John Paul I, he said: "Wasn't he a saintly man?"[18]

But in 1979, miraculously back at the top echelon of the Vatican, Magee was the key figure in plotting the first-ever papal visit to Ireland in September 1979.

His power with the pope was affirmed by a secret Irish diplomatic assessment in 1982. "He was one of two men the Pope would turn to for advice on Irish affairs. The other was the Nuncio Alibrandi," the diplomat wrote.[19] Indeed, Magee had shown that clout by privately intervening on behalf of the pope to try and stop an IRA hunger strike that resulted in the death of Bobby Sands and nine others in April and May of 1981. That mission failed, but there was no doubt he was speaking for the pope when he undertook it.

Magee was also close to the highly popular Cardinal Tómas Ó Fiaich, the Primate of All Ireland and Archbishop of Armagh, and, like him, a Northern Ireland man. Magee was always considered very likely to succeed him.

A visit to Ireland had been widely discussed almost as soon as John Paul II was seated on the throne of Peter, but Magee in particular was said to have pressed hardest of all. There were signs that the faith in the Catholic church was fading, that young people were starting to desert, that vocations were sharply down. It was a great opportunity to have a younger, more vigorous pope make a historic visit to Ireland and solidify the Catholic message.

Then there was Magee's own position. It could do no harm to be side by side with the pope on his historic visit to what might soon be Magee's very own fiefdom as Ireland's leading churchman. And with his Rome contacts, who knew where he would end up?

But Magee, once destined for the very top of the Irish church, would eventually flounder like the Church he served. He would not escape what was coming, but in September 1979, and incredibly, by the side of his third pope in succession, he was a very powerful man not least for the secrets he held close.

Without him at the Vatican, nothing like the pope's visit to Ireland would have happened. There had never been anything like it before. With one exception.

CHAPTER 5

Faith of Their Fathers—The Eucharistic Congress of 1932

"The men and women of long ago . . . from the high place in Heaven won by their heroic piety . . . must have looked down upon this glorious scene with serene happiness and benediction."

Dundalk Democrat editorial 1932

The closest equivalent to Pope John Paul's visit in 1979 was the 1932 Eucharistic Congress given to Ireland because it was the 1,500th anniversary of St. Patrick's coming to Ireland in 432. As a gauge of how religious the country had become, the Eucharistic Congress is a defining moment, the highest-ever point of Catholic Church influence in Ireland, at least until the visit of the popes.

Like with the two subsequent papal visits, the final public Mass of the Congress—the high point—was held in Phoenix Park with approximately one million present of the Irish population of 3.1 million.

The Mass was celebrated by Michael Joseph Curley, Archbishop of Baltimore. Count John McCormack, the world-famous Irish tenor, sang "Panis Angelicus" at the Mass. Following the Mass, four processions left the park to O'Connell Street, where approximately five hundred thousand people gathered on O'Connell Bridge for the concluding blessing given by the Papal Legate, Cardinal Lorenzo Lauri.

The event was a landmark in several ways. It brought a coming together of the population under the Vatican flag just a decade after a bloody civil war had ended. Irish leader Eamon de Valera had actually been excommunicated by the Church when he decided to take up arms against the first Free State government over the treaty the ill-fated Michael Collins had signed with the British.

Now that was forgotten as he met and chatted with senior Vatican and Irish bishops. He also appeared with the opposition leadership, which only a decade before had been intent on killing him and vice versa.

Second, the fledgling Irish Free State proved it could manage a massive public event even in the time of an international economic depression. Seven ocean liners were docked along the Liffey River to serve as floating hotels and meeting places. The half dozen rickety planes of the Irish Air Force even managed an overhead flyover in the flying formation of a cross.

Irish radio had just become a major part of people's lives. The 2RN government station, later RTÉ, covered the World Eucharistic Congress in Dublin in 1932 using the new high-powered transmitter installed at Athlone.

Listeners heard the voice of John McCormack singing at high mass. The event was also relayed by the BBC and several national stations in continental Europe. This was the largest event broadcast in the early years of Irish radio, making it a massive communal experience. Large crowds gathered at neighbors' houses all over Ireland and in public places to hear the divine word.

Last, it was a massive affirmation of the bond between church and people, one the British had tried for centuries to break. The Congress left indelible evidence that the faith of their fathers was just as strong in the new generation. Fifteen hundred years after Saint Patrick, his church was seemingly embedded forever in the lives of the Irish people he once served.

The *Dundalk Democrat* described the event:

Here men and women are proud to give evidence of their
Faith: proud of being sons and daughters of the dead and gone
Catholics who kept the flame alive in evil days of persecution
and spoliation. . . . The men and women of long ago . . . from
the high place in Heaven won by their heroic piety . . . must
have looked down upon this glorious scene with serene happiness and benediction.[20]

Protestant Ulster, recently separated from the Catholic Free State
by partition, felt very differently. Some Catholic members of Belfast
Corporation attended the Congress in their robes.

The Belfast Orange Lodge objected in the strongest terms. On
May 26, 1932, the Belfast County Grand Lodge passed the following resolution:

[A]s a Protestant Organisation we feel compelled to register
an emphatic protest at the action of the Belfast Corporation
in giving permission to Aldermen and Councillors to wear
their Robes at the forthcoming Eucharistic Congress in
Dublin and thus representing in an official capacity the Belfast
Corporation. We feel that the presence of these Aldermen
and Councillors robed . . . will be taken as an indication that
Protestant Belfast is weakening in its attitude to the idolatrous
practices and beliefs of Rome.[21]

Despite the rank opposition from the North, the Eucharistic Congress was an incredible success unmatched in fealty to the Catholic
Church until September 1979.

Looking back at the event eighty years later, the *Irish Times* was
not as enthused, to put it mildly:

At a top-down level, the Catholic Church at the time of the
Congress was already "rigid and authoritarian in its govern-
ance, conversionist in its attitude to Protestants, Marian in
its devotional emphasis and strongly focused on external religious practice rather than interior spirituality."[22]

CHAPTER 6

The Pope Cometh

If Pope John Paul II did not believe he was flying into the maw of a troubled country in September 1979, a deadly IRA operation on two fronts two weeks before he landed surely convinced him and led to speculation the trip might be canceled.

On August 26, 1979, a beautiful and sunny Irish day, a bomb exploded aboard the boat of Lord Louis Mountbatten, an uncle of Prince Philip, a mentor to Prince Charles, and a hugely popular member within the British Royal Family known within the royal circle as "Dickie."

The bomb had been placed aboard his fishing boat—the white-and-gray-painted, twenty-eight-footer *Shadow VI*—at Mullaghmore Pier in Leitrim just inside the Irish Republic and a dozen miles from the border.

The question—why such a prominent member of the royal family was fishing from a boat in the Irish Republic just a few miles away from Northern Ireland at the height of the Troubles—was widely asked after the killing. Mountbatten obviously felt safe and had Irish police protection.

The officer on duty that day was a twenty-five-year-old detective, Kevin Henry, who ushered Mountbatten and his party of six, including twin fourteen-year-old grandsons, Nicholas and Tim

Knatchbull, and the twins' maternal grandmother, Dowager Doreen Brabourne, onboard for their day of fishing and a picnic from Classiebawn Castle.

Henry's job was done for the day, but just as he was leaving the harbor, there was a large explosion, the ground shook, and an angry plume of black smoke and flame lifted toward the heavens. A fifty lb. bomb had exploded under the engine, placed there by the IRA during the night.

Mountbatten, one of his grandsons, and a local boy who was a helper for the boat trip were killed instantly. Dowager Brabourne died the next day from her injuries. The shock bombing was followed hours later by a further IRA bombing when eighteen British soldiers were killed in an ambush in Warrenpoint, County Down.

Tensions ran very high. Suddenly there were fears for the pope's safety that Protestant militants might try and take him out in an act of revenge. A trip to Northern Ireland with Mass at the cathedral in Armagh had to be scrapped, much to Monsignor Magee's chagrin. He would not get the pope to cross the border after all.

Instead, a very surprised, prosperous Irish farmer with massive land outside the town of Drogheda but in the Archdiocese of Armagh had his farm rented for the day by the Catholic Church. He was told a crowd of 40,000—the estimate was incorrect by 250,000.

A few weeks before the news became definite that the pope was coming, workmen in twenty-four-hour nonstop shifts built a 135-foot-tall cross in Phoenix Park, Europe's largest open space. It later turned out it was constructed without planning approval or any oversight of the planning authorities, but who was going to stop a giant cross for a great pope? "The pope is coming" hysteria spread throughout Ireland, creating a bedlam of frantic preparations including a moral crusade to sanctify the souls of the Irish prior to his arrival.

In an absurd moment befitting the comedians involved, *The Life of Brian*, a Monty Python film satire about a man mistaken for Jesus, was banned by censor Frank Hall, who uttered the incredible ruling was because it "made Christians and Jews look like awful gobshites." He was said to be especially upset by the scene when the Monty Python cast mistake "Blessed are the peacemakers" for "Blessed are the cheesemakers."

Even one of the movie's satirical songs, "Always Look on the Bright Side of Life," fell under the censor's pen. Ireland was going to be both good and holy for the papal visit.

When he arrived, fittingly on the Aer Lingus jet named St. Patrick, the pope strode off the plane, blessed the Irish people, and dropped to his knees to kiss the ground. Not since a young president named John F. Kennedy in the summer of 1963 had visited Ireland was there a similar momentous occasion when the nation flew its brightest colors.

The great and good of Ireland were waiting in serried ranks. It fell to the Irish President Paddy Hillery to escort His Holiness.

There had been rumors for years of a Hillery mistress, or maybe two or three.

As the *Irish Independent* reported, "These rumours went on for months in 1979, in the run-up to the Papal visit here. They were so persistent and pervasive that the then-*Taoiseach* Jack Lynch advised Mr. Hillery that he had to deal with the situation."[23]

This came to a head when the editors of the national newspapers and the head of news in RTÉ were summoned to the Aras, his official residence, where Hillery denied a story that had not been published anywhere, completely confusing the public at large who knew nothing about the inside gossip.

Either way, in order to escort the pope, Paddy Hillery would have to be without sin, and he insisted that the rumors were completely false and that he would not be resigning, thereby gaining absolution. The sensational story was international news.

The pope thus began his whirlwind journey around Ireland by shaking hands with a beleaguered president.

The reception for *il Papa* was incredible. Estimates of crowd figures were staggering. About 2.7 million people turned out to welcome the pontiff at six venues: Dublin, Drogheda, Offaly, Kildare Galway, Limerick, and Knock.

New York–based Irish journalist Cahir O'Doherty, who saw the pope in Mayo, remembers the countrywide hysteria: "It was as though The Beatles and Jesus had arrived together to play a concert," he said. "It was mass hysteria; it was unprecedented. It was morning in Ireland."[24]

Deirdre Falvey, now an *Irish Times* writer, was a schoolgirl at the time:

> I remember trekking through fields at night to our designated pen. The wait for hours in the dark and cold was long but it was exciting to be out and about in the middle of the night among thousands arriving in the dark. By the time Mass started we were tired but the infamous double-act (abusers Father Cleary and Bishop Eamon Casey) whipped up excitement. The man himself was on a distant platform, and between the echoey PA and the accent I barely heard what he said. Still, we roared and cheered and were thrilled: the hysteria and the crowds were like a rock concert.[25]

Nuala McCann from Northern Ireland wrote for the BBC years later what she remembered:

> Up at dawn and on our way to the wild fields of Galway to Ballybrit racecourse where thousands of young people had gathered to get a glimpse of this man. There, on the stage, Bishop Eamonn Casey and Father Michael Cleary whipped up the crowd. "Listen, listen. . . Is that a helicopter, I hear?" and we all cheered and roared and sang "By the Rivers of Babylon" jumping about in the icy field, wishing we had remembered to go to the toilet. Then, suddenly, he was among us. He told us in endearing English, heavy with a Polish accent, that he loved us. "Yo[u]ng people of Ireland, I lof you," he said—and we cheered wildly and tried to get within distance of the popemobile as he headed out among the crowds.[26]

Damian Corless, a papal steward for the day, remembers how high the stakes were: "Young Irish Catholics for a decade had been lapsing at a rate of knots, but generally not in favour of godlessness or open hostility to the Mother Church. Instead, many were shopping around for new beliefs and it was a boom time for maharishis, swamis, and a host of eastern and Christian offshoots . . ."[27]

When you take into consideration the population of the Republic was 3,368,217 in 1979, the numbers were incredible. More than one million people from all over Ireland and some cities in England attended the first-ever papal Mass in Ireland's Dublin's Phoenix Park.

Afterward, the pope traveled to that huge private farm outside Drogheda, where 300,000 people, many from Northern Ireland, had gathered. There, he made his most significant speech when he appealed to the men of violence: "On my knees I beg you to turn away from the path of violence and return to the ways of peace."

Listening was a Belfast Redemptorist priest based in West Belfast at the core of the Troubles. Father Alec Reid was prompted by the pope and his own sheer revulsion at the violence to begin an extraordinary peace mission that grew into the Irish peace process that ended the violence with the Good Friday Agreement in 1998.

Amazingly, three years later, Father Reid—on a much-needed break from his peace work—was in St. Peter's Square on May 13, 1981, when there was an assassination attempt on the pope's life that occurred just after the popemobile had passed him by.

Pope John Paul began the second day of his tour with a short visit to the ancient monastery at Clonmacnoise in County Offaly. Later that morning he celebrated a Youth Mass for 300,000 at the Racetrack in Galway. It was here that the pope uttered perhaps the most memorable line of his visit: "Young people of Ireland, I love you."

The Irish visit by Pope John Paul II was destined to dwarf the crowds for the Eucharistic Congress in 1932 and prove that the "Faith of our Fathers" was just as strong in the new generation.

In Galway, hundreds of thousands of young people chanted, "We love the Pope." As the *Irish Independent* reported, at one point "the swaying and ecstatic gathering broke into song with 'He's Got the Whole World in His Hands' symbolising their feelings of love of Christ's Vicar on earth."[28]

As *Independent* newspaper reporter Kim Bielenberg noted: "The song title was used as the banner headline across the front page of the *Irish Independent* on the following day, summing up perfectly the rapturous mood of the visit."[29]

It was the Irish Catholic Woodstock, presided over by two deviant clerics whose names would eventually become notorious. Bishop Casey and Father Cleary led the anthem calls and roused the young to fever pitch.

The *Irish Independent* report focused on the music festival atmosphere: "Woodstock, the Isle of Wight, and all the Ballisodares (an Irish festival) one could imagine could not give the right impression of volume and enthusiasm in Ballybrit yesterday."[30]

As Bielenberg points out, the Church was in its prime still in terms of its influence. "At the time, Church teaching was powerful enough to ensure that certain key doctrines dominated the political sphere. Seven years after the visit, traditionalists wielded their power by ensuring that attempts to introduce divorce were defeated in a referendum. In 1983, they also introduced the eighth amendment to the constitution, banning abortion. On those autumn days in 1979, the façade of the Church looked secure and stable, but inside the structure was already crumbling."[31]

The *Irish Independent*, using language that was incredibly devout, editorialized that: "The 59-year-old Polish Pontiff is coming to ensure that Ireland remains faithful . . ."[32]

In retrospect, Irish-American History Professor James Donnelly of the University of Wisconsin, Madison, said the red lights were flashing despite the adulation for the pope. "Apart from conferring certain limited short-term benefits, the papal visit did not in fact better equip the Catholic Church in Ireland to deal effectively with its challenges and problems."[33]

Such sober analysis may be history's verdict on the papal visit, but for those who were there it became almost hysterical at times, including for the VIPs. But it was not just the ordinary folk who became overexcited. A papal steward at the event, speaking anonymously, remembers amazing occurrences right after the Phoenix Park Mass:

> I had made my way back up to the altar when there was a sudden commotion nearby. I turned and was amazed to see Pope John Paul II himself, struggling to make his way through an admiring, enthusiastic group of cardinals, ambassadors, and various dignitaries.
>
> Suddenly I felt a hard clout on my shoulder. Surprised, I wheeled around indignantly to see who it was that had delivered such an uncalled-for whack. There, standing behind me, was Dublin Archbishop Dermot Ryan. Before I could utter a single word he shouted at me, "Get up there and help that man!"—that man being His Holiness the Pope. Without any further encouragement I ran up to where His Holiness was and linked arms with other volunteers.
>
> We surrounded the Pope, protecting him from the admiring mob of dignitaries. Together, we were able to escort John Paul off the altar into his rooms. The next time I saw him, he was on route to his helicopter, on his way out of the Phoenix Park and onwards in his pilgrimage to Ireland.[34]

The *Irish Times* reported:

> Dublin events alone required a mammoth amount of equipment, including various fittings, banners, piping, benches (about two thousand), tarps, tents, chairs, signage, plywood sheeting, stakes, tables, and about eight hundred umbrellas. The latter were specially ordered for visiting archbishops and bishops, only to go unopened as the nice weather made them an unnecessary expense.

When the crowds left, it all had to be dispersed somewhere. As the *Irish Times* explained, it was auctioned off by the Church in a series of bargain auctions held. The auction the *Irish Times* reporter attended on a freezing cold day the following winter was a sight to behold.

> A whole line of gentlemen was standing on a bench stamping their feet to keep the blood moving, when the bench collapsed and the man with the dozen umbrellas at £1.50 apiece, the man with the six slightly damaged communion trays, and the man with the roll of red carpet at £2 a yard, all crashed to the frozen mud floor.
>
> Des Kelly, who fitted the carpet, was there to buy it back in large quantities at £1 a yard—to sell it again . . . [and that] Tony Curran wanted carpets, too. "I'm going to make an overcoat with 'the pope walked on this' printed on the back."[35]

The country had gone certifiably crazy for the pope, and the immediate impact was full churches, deep expressions of devotion, and thousands of male children called John Paul. It was the high-water mark of 1,500 years of Catholicism.

CHAPTER 7

_____

Gays Abandoned

Criminalisation of homosexual behavior served "public
health and the institution of marriage."

Irish Supreme Court 1983

A round the time of the pope's visit, the men's public toilet just off
O'Connell Street in Dublin was the main meeting place for gay
men in Ireland. There were no private clubs or sleek hideaways, no
upscale bars with fine wine and good dining. A Dublin public toilet
identified as such by Geraldine Kennedy in the *Irish Times* sufficed
instead.

It was a dingy place where you would literally spend a penny to
enter the cubicle space. The walls were littered with phone numbers
with pleas to call if you wanted a good time. The smell of stale urine
was in the air.

The cops were well aware of the location and often trolled the
men's toilets looking for a quick arrest, as their headquarters was
just a few blocks away. Many a young policeman reached his arrest
quota by arresting some unfortunate man in search of company.

This was the island of Ireland pre- and post-John Paul as experienced by the LGBTQ community. The notion of gay marriage was
as likely as a meteor hitting Earth.

Tonie Walsh was a gay activist at the time, and years later he recounted in the *Irish Times* just what the atmosphere was like: "One night a panicked friend called. He had met a man and they went to a city center hotel together. Once there, the receptionist became suspicious because the two men were sharing a bedroom and called the police. They arrived and caught the two men together."[36]

It was 1986; gay sex would not be legalized for another seven years.

Senator David Norris, a gay man himself, Trinity College lecturer, and well-known public figure by dint of his seat in the Irish Senate, and his championship of all things Joyce and Wilde, was the lynchpin of the gay community for decades in Ireland. He waged a long and lonely fight for LGBTQ rights.

He remembers what it was like when gays were brought before a court:

> The court's attitude was one of derision and contempt. I remember on many occasions seeing people caught in those circumstances being subject to the most ignorant and personal questions by the judge. It was definitely viewed as a perversion and as an entertainment source for the ordinary decent criminals in court. These people were held up to ridicule. They were taken stage by stage through the sexual activities they engaged in and asked if they enjoyed it and all this kind of stuff.[37]

Cruising spots were few and far between (the Dublin mountains were popular) and were dark and dangerous at night. Several parks in Dublin were also frequented. A gay man of that era spoke anonymously to me about his experiences. "I hung out at the dog-racing track either in Harold's Cross or Shelbourne Park. Quite often I meet priests dressed in civilian wear."

Amid the roaring crowd, as the dogs chased the artificial hare, he said he secretly masturbated a well-known monsignor from down the country. The good father was done and gone before the dogs crossed the line.

On another occasion he remembers he had oral sex in the ladies' room with a well-known dog trainer. Very few women were dog-racing enthusiasts at the time, so the ladies' room was usually empty. However, on this occasion it wasn't, and a woman screeched, "Mother of God!" before running for her life as two men emerged from one cubicle.

There was history behind the homophobia. In 1930, Police Commissioner and Nazi supporter Eoin O'Duffy noted that homosexuality "is a form of depravity that is spreading with malign vigour."

O'Duffy would go on to head the Blueshirts, the fascist equivalent of what was happening in Italy and Germany with the Blackshirts and Brownshirts. O'Duffy sailed for Spain to fight for Franco with the enthusiastic blessing of the hierarchy. Masses were said almost every Sunday for Franco.

Over the decades, official Ireland did little to change or liberalize the law. Similar sentiments to O'Duffy's were often repeated. The very topic was avoided, and the prosecutions continued.

In 1979, the year of the pope's visit, there were a reported forty-four prosecutions for homosexual acts in the preceding three years. Historian Diarmaid Ferriter detailed many of the cases in his book *Occasions of Sin: Sex and Society in Modern Ireland.*

Ferriter relates: "In 1927, a Kildare businessman was convicted of 'attempting to procure an act of gross indecency' after a detective noticed him staring at him in a public toilet. They met again a week later and the gay man produced his penis. He got 12 months in jail and no doubt this led to his social and work life ruin."

There were likely hundreds of cases a year. Between 1962 and 1972, there were 455 convictions.

Strangest of all, as Ferriter relates, twenty men were arrested in the small town of Tullow, County Carlow: "Apparently two men were caught by the cops, and they named everyone they knew who was gay in order to avoid prosecution."

When arrested, the men were charged for being in breach of section 11 of the Criminal Law Amendment Act 1885. The 1885 law was passed as the British were suffering through another era of Victorian moral outrage. Sodomy had once been punishable by death, but now it merited a long prison term. Then the moralists in parliament asked what about touching, feeling, and fellatio by men on men: "An outrage, sir!" was the response from the government.

A bill against such perversions was called for and eventually passed.

The tenor of the Victorian times can be gauged from the *Yokel's Preceptor*, a contemporary magazine:

> The increase of these monsters in the shape of men, commonly designated margeries, poofs, etc., of late years, in the great Metropolis, renders it necessary for the safety of the public that they should be made known. . . . Will the reader credit it, but such is nevertheless the fact, that these monsters actually walk the street the same as the whores, looking out for a chance? Yes, the Quadrant, Fleet Street, Holborn, the Strand etc., are actually thronged with them![38]

Clause 11 mandated imprisonment "not exceeding two years," with or without hard labor, for any man found guilty of gross indecency with another male, whether "in public or in private."

However, no definition was given of what, exactly, constituted "gross indecency." "Gross indecency" was widely interpreted as any male homosexual behavior short of actual sodomy, which remained a more serious and separate crime.

One hundred years later, the same law that snared Oscar Wilde was still operating in Ireland despite the fact that the British, who originally advocated it, had since decriminalized such behavior.

While cops were arresting gay men, the business of women as lesbians was completely ignored as not possible.

The ethos of the Victorian times remained intact even when challenged. In 1983, David Norris lost his case to strike down the arcane law by a three-to-two decision by the Supreme Court, who noted in their judgment the "Christian and democratic nature of the Irish State" and argued that criminalization served "public health and the institution of marriage."

The fear of discovery in rural Ireland was frightening and very real. Cahir O'Doherty, a Donegal native and the Arts Editor of the *Irish Voice* newspaper in New York, is one of the best-known Irish journalists in America. A Yale graduate, he has vivid recollections of those dangerous times.

Growing up gay in Donegal in the 1980's, the question of being in real danger because I was gay wasn't academic for me.

Boys could choose girls and girls could choose boys, but if a boy chose another boy then he was wandering off the reservation, into an unmapped territory where wild things could happen.

Being queer in Ireland back then wasn't just a social faux pas, it wasn't like selecting the wrong serving spoon in a fancy restaurant. No, the social taboo around gay people in that decade was raw and life altering and it was underscored with the threat of social ostracism and fatal violence.

Overnight you could be un-familied, your name erased from the book of your community and nation. It was a kind of Shakespearean banishment but in the modern era. Your parents became afraid that the world would be a violent, hostile place for you, and in their panic and distress they often created a violent, hostile home life for you, too. If you didn't die of their well-intentioned but destructive ignorance, then you might have died of the irony.

When I cast my mind back to those times now I think of how much violence there was all around me, a kind of music that was mostly out of ear-shot for others but I could hear it echoing loudly in even the most humdrum social interactions: guards, soldiers, priests, GAA players, RUC, teachers, doctors, all the unquestioned and unquestionable agents of the state, all of them drawing red lines and uttering threats to unsanctioned interlopers like me, threats that ranged from the contemptuous to the homicidal.

Men don't understand the world they have created for others that I discovered. Men can't even see it. Back then it felt to me like I was living under an occupation, waiting for the loud knock on the door where some outraged neighbor, shining with self-regard, would finally inform my shocked relatives about what was being said about me all over town.

The cruelty of all this oppression was part of the point, I believe. The cruelty existed to send a chilling message to anyone who might have even contemplated standing beside me. At 16, at the very moment when I was most vulnerable, I was also charged with making the most consequential admission of my life.

Coming out has a "before" and "after," although from the vantage point of the 1980's the "after" part seemed unpromising and unpromised to me (let's remember that the TV news was full of images of AIDS and stories of family abandonment, you could still be arrested and imprisoned for being gay until 1993).

Back then there wasn't a story I could read anywhere that offered a hint of a happy ending. Back then I had to make it—and myself—up.[39]

As the *Irish Times* reported, slowly the tide turned:

By the early 1980s prosecutions of gay men began to drop off, partly thanks to Norris, who started assisting in the defense of arrested men.

[Norris said,] "I started going down to the court with Garrett Sheehan [a solicitor and now an Appeal Court judge] and he was simply wonderful. Up to then, the guards got away with it because anyone who was found in those circumstances

was deeply ashamed and would plead guilty and hope everything would go away. The *gardaí* just gave up. Because we had
been so successful in fighting these charges, they found it to be
useless to bring them."[40]

The prosecutions stopped, but the consequences of the century of
shame in which LGBTQ activity was considered somewhere in the
realm of child abuse and pedophilia would leave its mark. In 1993,
when the government finally repealed the relevant 19th Century
Acts, the damage had indeed been done.

Brian Sheehan of GLEN (Gay and Lesbian Equality Network)
told the *Irish Times*:

When HIV hit in the 1980s the State was very slow in
responding because LGBT people were still criminals. . . .
So at the time of the greatest health crisis for gay men the
response of the State was terrible because of the criminalisation of gay men. . . .

[The law was] a huge weapon, a cudgel.

It ensured lesbian and gay people never raised their head
and became visible. The consequences of that are still felt by
some people today who never got the chance to be who they
were. Among those was Declan Flynn, the closest Irish equivalent of a Harvey Milk, the San Francisco supervisor shot for
being gay by a former cop.[41]

CHAPTER 8

The Savage Killing of Declan Flynn

"One thing that has come to my mind is that there is no element of correction that is required. All of you come from good homes and experienced care and affection."

Judge Sean Gannon in 1982 refusing to jail teenagers
who beat a gay man to death

Declan Flynn was a thirty-year-old Dublin Airport employee who was attacked and murdered by a gang of youths, all in their teens, with one as young as fourteen, on the night of September 9, 1982.

Fairview Park in Dublin was a common meeting place for gay men like Flynn who lived nearby, and the park had been targeted by youth gangs from Dublin's tough North side. There had been several beating incidents the summer of 1992, but as the season changed to autumn, police showed little interest in pursuing the perpetrators.

Flynn had helped with a resource center for gay Irish in the City Center in what is now Temple Bar, but he was not widely known in the gay community. Flynn's family did not know his sexual orientation, and his father protested his son was not gay even after he was killed during the summer of 1982.

Earlier that night, Flynn had gone to a local pub and then walked home through Fairview Park. He was never seen alive again. His body was found with fatal injuries. At 1:48 a.m. the following morning, the local fire brigade was called to Fairview Park, where they found Flynn lying dead.

Cops originally declared he was the victim of a robbery, as he had no wallet or ID on him. The truth was a lot worse.

On Sunday, September 12, 1982, cops arrested five teens and charged them with Flynn's murder. The fourteen-year-old boy was first to be tried. He told how he was cycling through the park and came across the gang waiting to beat up a gay man.

One of the gangs told him, "Hide behind a tree; we are going to bash a queer." Another member served as the setup man, sitting on his own on a park bench with a "come on" look as Flynn walked by.

As Flynn sat down on the bench, the gang appeared from behind the trees. Flynn ran for his life but was tripped up. They beat him mercilessly with sticks. Flynn died from asphyxia, choking on his own blood.

As reported by Maggie O'Kane, "One of the lads thought it would be a good way of getting a few bob—robbing a few queers like. In the beginning it was just a chase; then they started to get sticks from the trees. A few of them had been queer bashing for six weeks before and had battered 20 steamers. Steamers, they called them. They used to grab them and if they hit back they would give it to them."[42]

Incredibly, despite the damning evidence, all five walked free after Justice Sean Gannon essentially gave them suspended sentences and did not order them jailed. In suspending the sentences of all, Justice Gannon said, "One thing that has come to my mind is that there is no element of correction that is required. All of you come from good homes and experienced care and affection."[43]

As for queer-bashing, he said he did not even know what it meant.

All hell broke loose after the verdict. Flynn's father said, "I had expected that justice would be done and be seen to be done."

The *Irish Times* reported one woman saying there was audible cheering in the area where the defendants lived.

There was a different political reaction with demands for an immediate inquiry and the judge to be removed. The sentence was widely compared with a twelve-month sentence passed on a man who had stolen a woman's purse with twenty Irish pounds in it. David Norris said, "It could be interpreted as a license to kill."

The killing created a massive shock and fear among the LGBTQ community. They understood for the first time ever they had to take their cause to the streets. On Saturday, March 19, 1983, about four hundred men, women, and children marched in the biggest protest ever against street violence against gays. Suddenly they were risen people.

CHAPTER 9

Women in Their Place

> The light of evening, Lissadell,
> Great windows open to the south,
> Two girls in silk kimonos, both
> Beautiful, one a gazelle.
>
> *William Butler Yeats*

Yeats dedicated his poem "In Memory of Eva Gore-Booth and Con Markievicz" to two remarkable women who blazed a trail through Irish history, Eva Gore-Booth, born in 1870, and her sister, Constance—later Countess Markievicz—born in 1868.

The historical accounts of the gay movement in Ireland usually omit women, yet they had a remarkable part to play in the 1916 Rising as just one example and as lifelong advocates for human rights as another example.

Mary McAuliffe, a lecturer in women's studies at University College Dublin, points out that Elizabeth O'Farrell, who was famously airbrushed out of the historic photograph of 1916 commander Patrick Pearse surrendering to a British Army officer (only her boots are visible), was gay and had carried the flag of surrender at great personal risk to the enemy lines.

McAuliffe told the *Dublin Inquirer* that Elizabeth O'Farrell and her fellow nurse Julia Grennan were a couple:

> These two rebels were based in the GPO on O'Connell Street during the Rising. They cared for the wounded, including James Connolly. After days of fighting, the rebels moved to Moore Street, where Pearse decided to surrender.
>
> "When Elizabeth was going to bring out the surrender flag, Julia Grennan talks about the fact that she was terrified and anxious watching her step out onto Moore Street, where there were bullets whizzing around," says McAuliffe.
>
> The two women are buried together in Glasnevin Cemetery, and their gravestone reads "Elizabeth O'Farrell . . . And her faithful comrade and lifelong friend Sheila [Julia] Grennan." [A very brave inscription for the love that could not speak its name.][44]

In all, McAuliffe says seventy-seven women fought in the Rising, a huge number.

Of course the most famous was Constance Gore-Booth, who married a somewhat dubious Polish count and became known as Countess Markievicz. Both Eva and Constance were born to privilege and wealth in Lissadell House in Sligo, where the family home was a stately mansion that Yeats loved to visit.

Their father was the 5th Baronet, the equivalent of bearing a knighthood. He was often absent on Arctic explorations, and his five children were mainly left to their own amusement. Eva and Constance, however, are said to have been heavily influenced by a near famine that struck in 1879, when they witnessed local tenants coming to beg for food at their doorstep.

Constance channeled her energy into revolution, becoming a hero of 1916 and the first female in the Irish parliament. She achieved legendary status as a revolutionary later in life.

Eva went a different path; she made her home in London and channeled her energies elsewhere—she was especially motivated to work for the underdogs. Esther Roper, her companion and lover, later remarked that Eva was "haunted by the suffering of the world and had a curious feeling of responsibility for its inequalities and injustices."

She focused on women's issues, especially the fight for universal suffrage and the right to vote. She was also a strong voice for sexual freedom and published a magazine that was scandalous, given the tenor of the times. It was called *Urania* and most likely derived from a word meaning "homosexual." It was published privately by Gore-Booth and featured progressive articles on topics like education mingled with photos of women dressed as men, and discussions on sex and gender.

The magazine went to her lesbian coterie with a circulation of about 250 copies. It was as revolutionary for its time as anything her sister achieved.

The 1916 Rising also featured other queer Irish women leaders. Dr. Kathleen Lynn was a member of the Irish Citizen Army, which fought in the 1916 Easter Rising. She was chief medical officer in the General Post Office, which was the location of most of the fighting during the 1916 Rising.

She was also a prominent figure in the suffragette movement. She described herself as "a Red Cross doctor and a belligerent" when she was arrested. She was imprisoned in Kilmainham Gaol with her comrades Countess Markievicz and Madeleine ffrench-Mullen, the latter also a lesbian who fought bravely for her country.

Historian May McAuliffe says the love letters passed between Lynn and ffrench-Mullen, who were both jailed for their roles in the Rising, demonstrated their love. "Then they spend their lives together," says McAuliffe. "They lived together."

There had been attempts to criminalize lesbianism and make it illegal, but polite post-prudish society never considered such acts were occurring. In 1921, British MPs attempted to add a clause to a new Criminal Law Amendment Bill being debated at the time, which would have made lesbianism into a criminal offense: "Any act of gross indecency between female persons shall be a misdemeanour and punishable in the same manner as any such act committed by male persons under section 11 of the Criminal Law Amendment Act 1885."

However, this was ultimately dropped out of concern that legislation would only draw attention to the "offence" and "encourage women to explore their sexuality." If you could imagine a gloomier place in the Western world than Ireland for gays and lesbians for the twentieth century, it would be very hard. The governing law dated from 1885, and it became known as the blackmailer's act, as gay people were especially vulnerable to being found out, as Oscar Wilde found out.

As for women, the idea of lesbian love was so outrageous that it was not felt necessary to have a law against it. The right to gay marriage for either sex was as alien a concept as green men on Mars. The issue of abortion was never even spoken about.

CHAPTER 10

The Case of the Woman Pregnant by Two Men Simultaneously

> "A network" of people in positions of influence "could do wonders quietly on passing the most restrictive laws without coming out openly as Knights of Columbanus."
> *Anti-abortion militant and Knights of Columbanus leader*
> *John O'Reilly*

Whatever the stigma about gays, the notion of abortion ever becoming legal even for women who were raped or whose lives were in danger would have struck the Irish of the time of the pope's visit as beyond all belief.

After all, the Abortion Act of 1861 legislated for penal servitude for life for any woman found guilty of attempting one. It was as heinous a crime as there was on the books. Indeed, the Eighth Amendment to the Irish Constitution passed by 67 percent to 33 percent in 1982 specified that the fetus had the same rights as the mother and dictated that no court should ever alter that right. Rape and incest were no excuse; neither was suicidal intent.

Emily O'Reilly's 1992 book, *Masterminds of the Right*, revealed that the 1983 referendum was planned and carried out by a secretive Knights of Columbanus group headed by a vocal anti-abortion activist John O'Reilly, who stated a "network" of people in positions of influence "could do wonders on passing the most restrictive abortion law quietly without coming out openly as knights."

University College Dublin historian Diarmaid Ferriter noted that the politicization of the issue had a disastrous effect. The minister for justice at the time, Michael Noonan, it appears, was more concerned for his own political reasons with what would be acceptable to the Pro-Life Amendment Campaign than with confronting the consequences of flawed wording.

The prolifers were composed, in many cases, of stalwart members of his own political party, Fine Gael, and he had far more to fear from them.

Thus the language was heavily weighed against the mother's rights, a blunt truth that was certainly borne out by subsequent events. There was relevant history in reproductive issues being dictated by the religious right. All forms of contraception had been outlawed in 1935 as the Church flexed its muscles and pious politicians bent the knee.

The Irish legal prohibitions did not stop Irish women terminating pregnancies, however. Ivana Bacik, professor of criminal law in Trinity College Dublin and a women's rights advocate, believes that up to 150,000 Irish women had terminations in Britain over the first forty years after abortion was legalized there in 1967. Many desperate to end their pregnancies resorted to backstreet abortion practitioners before the British law was passed.

By far the most famous abortionist was Irish-American Mamie Cadden. Mamie Cadden was born in Scranton, Pennsylvania, in 1891 but moved to Mayo at a young age. She qualified as a midwife and began opening maternity nursing homes. One of her sidelines was providing abortions. Soon, pregnant women who wanted to terminate found their way to "Nurse Cadden," and she became very well known.

She had a taste for the high life—drinking and carousing and driving a 1932 MG sports car. She cut quite the figure in dreary '30s Ireland. It all came to a halt in 1944, when she was convicted for killing a young woman, Helen O'Reilly, who died as a result of an abortion carried out on Cadden's kitchen table. Cadden had little sympathy for the mother of six whose husband had deserted her. Historian Diarmaid Ferriter notes:

> She labelled the women who sought her services "whores" and suggested in her statement to *gardaí* after O'Reilly's death that O'Reilly had "the mouth of a prostitute." O'Reilly was a 33-year-old mother of six whose husband had deserted her and who was forced to put her children in care in various convents. She had already tried and failed to induce a miscarriage through the use of abortifacient drugs.[45]

Cadden received a sentence of life in prison but was later declared insane and committed to an asylum, where she died in 1959. Ferriter believes Cadden was perfectly sane, but the idea of her being back on the streets was too much for authorities to contemplate.

Infanticide or resort to Nurse Cadden care. Such were the options desperate pregnant women had before the British law of 1967 legalizing abortion.

That British law utterly changed the landscape down to very recent times. According to the Irish authorities, 4,000 Irish women, including 128 legal minors, who gave Irish addresses went to England for abortions in the year 2012 alone.

Activists are quick to claim that there were many more—up to two thousand women a year who never came under the government radar mainly because they furnished British addresses. The government turned a blind eye to the sad litany of young women having abortions in Britain: not for the first time had England solved an Irish problem—women seeking abortions, just as it had provided work for thousands of unemployed Irish men and women forced to leave Ireland.

The pregnant and scared young women were often fleeing from rural Ireland due to rape and incest or sexual abuse that caused their pregnancy. To help them cope, just two years after the pope's visit, Irish activists in Britain began what was essentially an underground railroad for pregnant and desperate young women from Ireland.

Until the British route opened up, infanticide was a yearly reality for Irish women. Historian Dr. Elaine Farrell of Queens University, Belfast, estimates that 4,500 infanticide killings occurred between 1850 and 1900.

Babies were often thrown into rivers with rocks tied around their necks, others were suffocated. There was even a popular song—"Weela Wallia"—about a "woman in the wood" who had a three-month-old baby and "stuck a knife in the baby's head."

Infanticide numbers dropped very shortly after the British abortion act was passed.

But the tenor of the times post-Pope John Paul II's visit can be gauged by the extraordinary case of the Kerry babies in 1984. A dead baby with twenty-four stab wounds was found on a beach near the town of Cahirciveen, and police immediately suspected a local woman, Joanne Hayes, who had been pregnant but no longer appeared to be.

Hayes protested her innocence and stated that, yes, she had given birth to a baby boy, but the child had died of natural causes right after birth. She led police to a small grave on her parent's farm where a body was found. The dead child's blood type was the same as Joanne Hayes's and that of a local married man with whom she was having an affair. So, one baby was accounted for, but what about the baby on the beach?

Desperate for a conviction, the police created a scenario that was utterly confounding. They accused Hayes of being the mother of the beach baby, too, and suggested she had very likely gotten pregnant by two different men on the same night! The story was widely carried until the beach baby's blood type was found not to be a match for Hayes.

The fact is that the cock-and-bull story of the "extraordinary" pregnancy of Joanne Hayes, who allegedly conceived two babies by two different men and killed both of them, was widely believed. It was an indication of how deeply ingrained the bias against unmarried mothers and women generally was.

Joanne Hayes stood trial for the death of the beach baby—whose murder she had "confessed" to under police interrogation. The police theory was Hayes had become pregnant simultaneously by two different men through something called "heteropaternal superfecundation" and was the mother of both children, killing the one found on the beach.

However, the different blood types of the beach baby and Joanne caused somewhat of a problem for the prosecution, and the case was dismissed. The Hayes family alleged they had been beaten and threatened in custody, and Joanne Hayes withdrew her guilty plea and confession once the real facts became clear.

Leading feminist and *Irish Times* columnist Nell McCafferty wrote at the time, "The treatment of Joanne Hayes, who stood accused of no crime, was a model for Irish male attitudes to women."[46] Ireland was a place where the Church had a "moral monopoly."

In 2018, thirty-four years after the Kerry babies case, the Irish government apologized officially to Joanne Hayes.

But even the Hayes case was surpassed in 1992 by the incredible Miss X case, one of the most hotly discussed court cases in Irish history and a classic example of the outworking of the laws of a rigidly Catholic state and the unseen consequences of such laws.

CHAPTER 11

Miss X Case Delivers Ireland into Evil

"It seems to me, therefore, that having had regard to the rights of the mother in this case, the court's duty to protect the life of the unborn requires it to make (allow) the order sought." (The order was to prevent the suicidal, raped, and pregnant fourteen-year-old having an abortion in Britain.)

Justice Declan Costello

The 1991 Miss X case marks the moment the tide began to turn on the issue of legal abortion in Ireland. It was a case with so many bizarre yet frightening aspects; it is best explained by a timeline similar to those published in the *Irish Times* and *Journal. ie* at the time.

December 1991: A fourteen-year-old Dublin girl (Miss X) is raped by Sean O'Brien, forty-one, a neighbor and businessman who was friendly with the family. It transpired he had been abusing her for two years. Miss X tells her parents she is pregnant.

Court judgments subsequently call him an "evil and depraved" man.

January 27–30, 1992: The teenager tells her mother she is suicidal and deeply depressed, and her parents report the rape.

February 4, 1992: The family is deeply worried about the mental state of their daughter and decide she will be taken to London for an abortion. They ask the police if a sample of the fetus should be kept to help convict O'Brien.

The police forward the query to the attorney general, who asks a judge whether such evidence could be used in court.

February 6, 1992: The girl has traveled to London with her parents and is awaiting an abortion when the then–Attorney General Harry Whelehan obtains a ruling stopping her having it, and the family is forced to return home.

The injunction was based on Article 40.3.3 of the Constitution on the 1983 amendment that gave the unborn child's life equal footing to the right of the mother's life. The attorney general says he is upholding the constitution.

February 10–11, 1992: Justice Declan Costello hears the case over two days. The parents tell the court their daughter had threatened to throw herself down the stairs or under a train. A medical expert who examined her says there is definitely a risk of suicide.

February 17, 1992: Justice Costello rules against the girl, saying the right to life of the unborn child must be upheld. He orders she be stopped from leaving Ireland for nine months. He accepts the suicide risk but says it is insufficient reason to overrule the constitution. He states:

> I am quite satisfied that there is a real and imminent danger
> to the life of the unborn and that if the court does not step in
> to protect it by means of the injunction sought, its life will be
> terminated.

The evidence also establishes that if the court grants the injunction sought there is a risk that the defendant may take her own life. But the risk that the defendant may take her own life, if an order is made, is much less and of a different order of magnitude than the certainty that the life of the unborn will be terminated if the order is not made.

I am strengthened in this view by the knowledge that the young girl has the benefit of the love and care and support of devoted parents who will help her through the difficult months ahead. It seems to me, therefore, that having had regard to the rights of the mother in this case, the court's duty to protect the life of the unborn requires it to make the order sought.[47]

February 21, 1992: An appeal is made to the Supreme Court.

March 1992: The court overrules Costello's ruling by a majority of 4–1 and agrees the girl can have the abortion because of the risk of suicide. Ultimately the girl miscarries, but her ordeal made possible the first crack in the blanket abortion ban. As a result of the X case and the judgment in the Supreme Court appeal, the government put forward three possible amendments to the Constitution in a referendum.

Journal.ie reported that the minor remedies were passed, but there was no access to legal abortion. The freedom to travel outside the State for an abortion and the freedom to obtain or make available information on abortion services were passed.

There was a stunning aftermath. The child rapist O'Brien served four years but reoffended when he kidnapped and sexually assaulted another underage girl whom he picked up as a cab passenger. Fortunately, she memorized his badge number; otherwise, he quite likely would have escaped.

Miss X case was by no means the only time a deeply vulnerable young woman clashed with authorities over provisions in the 1983 law. After the X case, it is hard to imagine any worse scenario, but the 2014 Miss Y story came close.

Miss Y was a political refugee fleeing persecution when she landed in Ireland, pregnant as a result of a rape. "She claimed asylum," the draft report on her case states.

As Kitty Holland in the *Irish Times* reported, "Ms. Y became very distressed and stated she could not be pregnant, that she could not have a baby and that no one could know. . . . Ms. Y stated that she had been raped in her own country."[48]

At fourteen weeks, Ms. Y was given the crushing news: she would not be allowed to enter Britain because of her status: "Ms. Y appeared extremely upset at the prospect of not being able to travel."

Thursday, July 22, 2014: A physician who examined her found that Ms. Y has a strong death wish. She tells another doctor that "she did not wish to go ahead with her pregnancy and that she would rather be dead."

She was brought to a psychiatric hospital, and a consultant psychiatrist that evening wrote: "It is documented that Ms. Y's presenting symptoms were as follows: feeling very low, self-isolating, poor appetite, feels abandoned by everyone/no help given/feels deceived; wants to terminate pregnancy, has nightmares and flashbacks of rape; says pregnancy resulted from rape . . . determined to end her life rather than have baby; feels hopeless and helpless."

Wednesday, July 23: She was told it is too late for an abortion. She starts to cry "and stated that she was going to commit suicide and that she had a plan and . . . she then gave details of the plan." Psychiatrist 1 tells her she will need to see an obstetrician. "Ms. Y indicated that she was not going to give birth and that she was going to die.

"Ms. Y indicated she had been told 'all the time' that she would be helped and that time had passed and now it was too late. . . . Throughout the interview Ms. Y continued to state that the only way she could be helped was by carrying out a termination . . . and if this did not happen she would kill herself."

She refuses offers of help and "stated she would not stay in hospital and that she would go home to 'end it.'"

Ms. Y's conversation is "very fixed. . . . There was evidence of suicidal intent."

[As Holland reports,] Ms. Y is transferred to a maternity hospital. A scan establishes she is 24 weeks pregnant. . . . She is to have one-to-one nursing care and metal cutlery is "to be avoided" at meals.

She is seen by a consultant obstetrician who tells her the baby is viable. She tells of her "plan to kill herself if the pregnancy continued."

Thursday, July 24: Ms. Y goes on a hunger and thirst strike and refuses supper at 7:30 p.m. while refusing fluids, as well. She tells the staff she "just wanted to die."

Ms. Y is reviewed by consultant psychiatrist number 2: "Ms. Y described that she had thought of harming herself. . . . When asked if Ms. Y had made any previous attempts of self-harm Ms. Y indicated that she was planning to hang herself in the toilet beside her room [in her previous accommodation] but that she had been disturbed.

"Ms. Y 'presented as a significant risk of suicide which was directly related to her unsuccessful efforts to secure an abortion and . . . the ongoing pregnancy was a reminder of Ms. Y's traumatic experience.' It is their view 'that the baby should be delivered.'

A plan to deliver the baby early, on Monday, August 3rd, is made. Ms. Y is told. She agrees to eat and drink."

Tuesday, July 29: Ms. Y tells social worker "she would kill herself if the plan put in place the previous week did not proceed on Monday."

Wednesday, August 6: Caesarean section performed. Baby boy taken to neonatal unit and into care. Mother does not want to see, feel, or touch child.

Wednesday, August 13: Ms. Y is discharged. Baby is making good progress and remains in care of neonatal team.

The authorities had dodged and weaved around the abortion strictures in the case of Miss Y, but there could be no dodging around about the biggest case of all in 2012, which changed Ireland forever. One tragic woman, an Indian immigrant, Savita Halappanavar, provided a horrific example of the consequences of a muddled law that resulted in her death.[49]

CHAPTER 12

Here's to You, Mrs. Robinson

"A censorious approach was taken to the life of the senses, human existence was referred to as 'mourning and weeping in this valley of tears.'"

Professor Enda McDonagh

The treatment of unmarried mothers and defenseless children, the X case, the scot-free murder of a gay man, and the death of a woman in childbirth all showed how desperate the need for change in Irish law and in the Irish Constitution was.

Change is never conceded without a fight, so who would lead a New Ireland charge? One woman above all others created the momentum for profound change for women and gay rights in Ireland and in the process became one of the best-known female leaders in the world. Without her, there is real question as to whether Ireland would ever have emerged from its long nightmare for gay people, ordinary women, and marginalized groups all over Ireland. Incredibly, she had once almost committed herself to a nunnery.

In 2010, RTÉ Ireland's national television station asked millions of viewers to vote in a poll on the greatest Irish person of the twentieth century. The winner was Northern Ireland peacemaker and Nobel Peace Prize winner John Hume, second was War of

Independence hero Michael Collins, but third was the only woman in the top five: Mary Robinson, Ireland's first female president from 1990 to 1997 before becoming the UN High Commissioner for Refugees.

Born in County Mayo in 1943, the child of two medical doctors, Mary Robinson had a privileged position in Irish life from the start. Yet the obstacles she faced were typical ones for all Irish women at the time. The constitution even spelled it out that women belonged at home.

Sexuality, especially strange inventions like same-sex relationships, was essentially forbidden, especially for women. As for abortion, even for rape or incest, well, good luck. Professor of Moral Theology Enda McDonagh stated, "A censorious approach was taken to the life of the senses generally; human existence was referred to as 'mourning and weeping in this valley of tears'. . . . Sexual repression . . . was strongly associated . . . with religious dominance."[50]

There was a reason why the Church glorified the Virgin Mary above all others but Jesus. Her perfect purity with no dirty sexual overtones—she didn't even have sex to give birth to Jesus—was the preferred state for women.

Robinson was surrounded by such iconography growing up. She remembers in her autobiography, *Everybody Matters*, that:

> Religion played a central role in our family life. We attended Mass, in Latin, every Sunday. In the evenings we would kneel in our own set places in the drawing room . . . and say a decade of the Rosary. We said grace before and after every meal. Crucifixes hung in most of the rooms as well as pictures of the Sacred Heart and the Virgin Mary. During Lent, these would be covered with black cloth, and my parents would wear mourning clothes and fast . . .

She remembers her mother bringing flowers to the altar, her grandparents as daily communicants. She wrote: "With this sense of importance of the Church, the importance of prayer and faith. . . . Our relatively new constitution (enshrined in 1937) placed God and the Roman Catholic faith at its centre."

She noted that single mothers were "pariahs" who had their children taken from them. The sinning women were condemned to horrible lives as virtual slaves in Magdalene Laundries.

That air of oppressiveness affected her childhood deeply. In school, children learned everything by rote: math tables, poetry, the Ten Commandments, and even the entire catechism. Corporal punishment, slapping the back of the legs with a cane, was a commonplace occurrence. Even at home, her beloved father resorted to smacking his children's hands and sometimes their backsides when they stepped out of line.

But she also learned compassion and caring when she accompanied her father on his house calls. Aubrey Burke spent endless hours just chatting to the patients he visited. He was also delivering babies, and Mary learned firsthand how undervalued girls were. A usual question was "Is it a boy or a child?"

Her Aunt Ivy, a Sacred Heart nun in England, became a major influence in her life. Ivy "went foreign," as they used to say, serving in India and regaling the Robinson family with tales of her faraway exile, which fired Mary's imagination.

A vocation for the priesthood was considered a gift from God. A vocation to be a nun was further down the scale. However, it was the era of Pope John XXIII and the Second Vatican Council, and it appeared as if the Church had been reinvented for the modern era.

At the age of ten, Mary had been sent to an exclusive Sacred Heart-run boarding school called Mount Anvil in Dublin. Every morning the pupils, wearing white veils, were summoned to church. Robinson began to seriously consider the nunnery as she entered her senior year.

Much impressed with the rituals, Mary told her parents her desire was to be a nun, but they were somewhat gobsmacked upon hearing it. All the other girls in her class were full of marriage talk, which did not interest her at such a young age.

Resistance to her becoming a nun came from a surprising source—the Mother Provincial of her order, who advised her to wait for a year to think about it, which her parents heartily agreed with. Thus, the future president of Ireland went off to Paris to a finishing school.

Soon the attraction of convent life faded amid the gloss, glamour, and cultural diversity she encountered in Paris. When she returned, she had done a 360-degree turn, and she scandalized her parents by announcing she would no longer attend Mass or the sacraments.

> I cannot identify any moment of a break with the past, but I had embarked on a different journey. . . . The change in me was fundamental. . . . It is difficult to explain how isolated and helpless I felt in the face of my parents' utter opposition to this path.[51]

She stayed home in Mayo for a year, and her parents yearned for a change in attitude. But their young daughter was not for turning. The family lost a devout and unquestioning young woman; the nuns lost a wonderful recruit; but Ireland gained a formidable leader, central to the massive political, social, and cultural upheaval to come.

She was a woman, and Ireland of the 1970s and '80s was still an overwhelmingly male-dominated world. Her experiences working as a professional woman were common to many women at the time.

Ireland appointed only its second female members of Cabinet (1916 heroine Countess Markievicz was first) in 1979, when Maire Geoghan Quinn became a minister. Still nursing her baby son, the first thing she noticed was a complete lack of facilities for working mothers in government buildings.

Robinson was facing the same type of prejudice. After earning a first-class law degree from Trinity and attending Harvard, she was appointed a law professor at Trinity College. She might easily have become swallowed up in academia, but she desired a public forum and was elected as one of the three Trinity College senator nominees to the Irish upper house known as the Seanad in 1968 and immediately set about destroying the ancient regime from the inside in 1969.

There was no shortage of issues: family planning was forbidden, condoms and birth control pills were illegal, women could not serve on juries, women had to retire from teaching and other civil service positions when they married, and women were paid about half the rate men were for similar jobs.

Her outspokenness marked her early as a disruptive liberal voice. The Church honed in on her advocacy of family planning, not surprising given their obsession with female bodies. They became aware of this uppity woman early on when she proposed a family planning bill. The local bishop denounced her from the pulpit in her own home town of Ballina for advocating contraception. Her parents, who were present, left the Cathedral in deep anguish.

The young senator was summoned to an audience with the Irish Primate, Cardinal William Conway. She was hopeful of getting a fair hearing and explaining the need for family planning, but instead she experienced a terrible coldness toward her. She was clearly threatening the throatlatch hold the Church had on the people of Ireland.

Voters, many taken aback by her strident advocacy, rejected her in 1997 for a seat in the *Dáil*, the more powerful chamber in Irish politics. Her political career looked in ruins; anyone predicting she would become president of Ireland just thirteen years later would have had astronomical odds on the wager. But, unbeknown to most, the times they were a-changing—but old ways die hard in Ireland, and newest thinking in the Robinson era was viewed with great suspicion, especially from the mouths or typewriters of women.

CHAPTER 13

"No Sex in Ireland before Television"

"From the first persecutions till the present moment, you will find Jews engaged in practically every movement against Our Lord and his Church. A Jew as a Jew is utterly opposed to Jesus Christ and all that the Church means."

Archbishop Charles McQuaid in 1932 before he was named Dublin archbishop in 1940

The tenor of the times that Mary Robinson and Edna O'Brien, Ireland's most controversial author, grew up in was described as a "dreary Eden" by writer Seán Ó Faoláin.

Ó Faoláin and the small intellectual set felt the dead hand of the Church and state on every aspect of life but especially as it related to sex. That is apparent from the arrival of busty Hollywood movie star Jayne Mansfield into Ireland in 1967 to perform a cabaret act at the Mount Brandon Hotel in Tralee.

Mansfield was a major Hollywood sex symbol during the 1950s and early 1960s. She was also talented enough to win a Golden Globe on Broadway. Her films, however, would be labeled soft porn today, as in *The Girl Can't Help It* (1956) and *Too Hot to Handle* (1960). She was the first major Hollywood actress to be featured in a nude scene in the film *Promises! Promises!* (1963).

A brassy buxom blonde, she was married and divorced three times and had five children. Mansfield's lovers, allegedly, included Robert and John F. Kennedy.

Quite how this dazzling vision of Hollywood appeared in remotest Kerry while her career was still flourishing has never been explained, but the poor woman was immediately named a harlot and worse. As the *Irish Independent* reported, on Sunday morning, April 23, 1967, a statement was read at all masses in Killarney:

> Our attention has been drawn to an entertainment in Tralee tonight. The bishop requests you do not attend.
>
> [Monsignor Lane, who was the Dean of Kerry and parish priest of Tralee, also made a statement of his own:]
>
> A woman is brought here to give a show for which she is being paid £1,000. This woman boasts that her New York critics said of her "she sold sex better than any performer in the world." I appeal to the men and women, to the boys and girls of Tralee, to dissociate themselves from this attempt to besmirch the name of our town for the sake of filthy gain. I ask the people to ignore the presence of this woman and her associates. They are attempting something that is contrary to the moral teaching of our faith, that is against our traditions and against the ordinary decencies of life, something that is against everything we hold dear.[52]

Paddy White, the manager of the Mount Brandon Hotel, quickly issued a statement: "Owing to the controversy caused by the visit of Jayne Mansfield, the management of the Mount Brandon Hotel has decided to cancel her appearance."[53] He later said this had been issued by mistake and the band would not be able to make the cabaret. This was a lie, as the band were all locals who bore the name the Kerry Blues Band.

After she departed the sacred shores, the Tralee Vocational Education Committee formally protested over the visit. Jack Healy, a local teacher, denounced the program. "To my mind, the sketch was suggestive and immoral [RTÉ, the national TV station, had avidly covered the arrival of Ms. Mansfield and interviewed her] and should not have been presented on our national television service," Healy said.[54]

Only Rev F. J. McMorran, the local Presbyterian minister, dissented from the demand for an apology. Tragically, Mansfield died in a car accident a few months later back in the US.

Ironically, a week or so later, to make amends, the hotel signed up a show that would help bring forgiveness. Up stepped Father Michael Cleary, the singing priest, the monster who made his seventeen-year-old housekeeper pregnant twice (she had been committed to a mental hospital after her father abused her) and disavowed all knowledge of another priest raping her. He helped to restore Tralee's sacred status.

The Mansfield saga hogged the headlines for weeks. Such were the passions around the issues of sexuality in Ireland at the time when the Church reigned supreme. It was a backward era where all was hidden behind a facade of decency and holiness. There was also an obsession with appearing purer and more conformist than the Godless British, the source of so much pain and anger.

Ireland was effectively a theocracy, and there was little opposition for fear of a belt of the crozier from some angry bishop. There was also, in some quarters, a great dislike of outsiders, the inevitable consequence of a deeply insular culture. The Jews were an obvious target given the temper of the times.

There had been a pogrom led by a Catholic priest in Limerick in 1904 against the local Jewish community. In the more recent era, a virulent dislike of Jews was evident in some high circles in Ireland, none more than from Charlie Bewley, Irish ambassador to Berlin in the key period leading up to World War II.

As noted in *Irish Central*:

Bewley made "no attempt at hiding his virulent anti-Semitic and pro-Nazi outlook," saying, "[W]here they exist in any quantity, the Jews are regarded as an alien body."

He blocked any efforts to have Ireland take in Jewish refugees. He told the Irish government that he was unaware of any cases of "deliberate cruelty" towards Jews by Hitler's government or any episode that "could even be remotely compared with the atrocities" of the Communists in Spain or Russia, the English in Palestine or the Black and Tans.

Bewley justified Kristallnacht saying Hitler had little choice but to teach Jews a lesson. Speaking of Jews, he said[,] "[W]hen the interests of the country of their birth come into conflict with their own personal or racial interests, [they] invariably sacrifice the interests of their birth to Jewish interests.

"It is thus claimed that during the War [WWI] German Jews in the vast majority acted against the interests of Germany, and that, as soon as England had definitely espoused the cause of Zionism, they worked for Germany's defeat in the War."

German anti-Semitism was "comprehensible," he wrote when it was found that "the Jew had not only succeeded in avoiding military service but also in enriching himself during the agony of the country."[55]

Archbishop John McQuaid, the most powerful clerical figure in Ireland for three decades, would have no qualms with Bewley, and he laid out his position on Jews early and often.

"From the first persecutions till the present moment, you will find Jews engaged in practically every movement against Our Lord and his Church. A Jew as a Jew is utterly opposed to Jesus Christ and all that the Church means."[56]

Oliver J. Flanagan, Minister of Defence in 1966–67, was a controversial politician widely known for raw anti-Semitism, which proved no obstacle to higher office. When he was elected to the *Dáil* in 1943, his first speech infamously promised to "rout the Jews out of this country."

He clearly held Nazi sympathies. In another speech, he remarked: "There is one thing that Germany did, and that was to rout the Jews out of their country. Until we rout the Jews out of this country it does not matter a hair's breadth what orders you make. Where the bees are there is the honey, and where the Jews are there is the money."[57]

In fairness, his son Charlie Flanagan is widely known as a moderate progressive politician who shares none of his father's rabid convictions. Perhaps Oliver J's most infamous quote is "There was no sex in Ireland before television," which has gone down in the history books.

Books and films were frequently banned often for the most asinine reasons. The most infamous banning was of the classic *Casablanca* in 1942. Considered by many experts as among the best films ever made, the officially neutral Ireland saw only Allied propaganda and felt sorry for the poor Nazis and how they were portrayed. It was banned on March 19, 1942, for infringing on the Emergency Powers Order (EPO) preserving wartime neutrality, by portraying Vichy France and Nazi Germany in a "sinister light."

It was later passed with cuts on June 15, 1945, after the EPO was lifted—this time the cuts were to the dialogue between Rick (Humphrey Bogart) and Ilsa (Ingrid Bergman) referring to their love affair. It seemed even talking about affairs was forbidden.

Amazingly, even in 1974 the people of Ireland had to be saved from *Casablanca*. The censor passed it with one cut on July 16, 1974. RTÉ asked about showing the film on TV—it still required a dialogue cut to Ilsa expressing her love for Rick.

Needless to say, the film of Joyce's *Ulysses* was banned in 1967 mainly because of the Molly Bloom soliloquy, which was deemed too pornographic for the tender ears of Irish filmgoers. Perhaps the most bizarre banning was WWF Wrestling, which the censor in 2001 said showed "gladiatorial bloodlust" and baying crowd.

CHAPTER 14

Edna O'Brien, Rebel Heart of the Sexual Rebellion

There was one other dissident female voice in Ireland in addition to Mary Robinson whose depiction of the sad morality plays that dominated life there was as true as it was unwelcome.

Edna O'Brien was born in Clare in 1930, the youngest child of a strict, religious family.

She trained as a pharmacist but wanted to be a writer instead. She married another writer, the much older Carlo Gebler, and they escaped to London. She worked as a reader for the Hutchinson Publishing house and wanted to write a novel—*The Country Girls*—about the trials, travails, and sexual encounters of three friends. It was written with a fifty-dollar advance and published in 1960.

It was open, frank, and superbly written and spoke honestly about female sexuality. It was as if the Church and Irish society were being exposed in all its paralysis and fake morality. The book blurb alone set Puritan minds racing:

Caithleen "Cait/Kate" Brady and Bridget "Baba" Brennan are two young Irish country girls who have spent childhood together. As they leave the safety of convent school in search of life and love in the big city, they struggle to maintain somewhat tumultuous relationship.

Single girls cavorting in the big city! A frisson of sex-tinged reality writing from a hellacious woman had invaded Holy Catholic Ireland!

The Church and the respectables went insane—a woman no less writing about sex and longing and love and dreams. Such ideas were considered amoral.

As O'Brien recalled in an interview in the *Guardian* newspaper:

> The novel, published in 1960, caused a bit of consternation. People were outraged. The few copies purchased in Limerick were burnt after the rosary, one evening in the parish grounds, at the request of the priest. I received anonymous letters, all malicious. Then it was banned; nameless gentlemen who sat in some office in Dublin added it to that robust list of novels which were banned in Ireland at that time. . . . In the big world the reactions were a little chauvinist. Frank O'Connor, in the New York Times, concluded that I had appalling taste in men, and LP Hartley, on English television, dismissed it, deeming Baba and Kate a pair of nymphomaniacs.[58]

The denouncement by Justice Minister Charles Haughey was especially rich. He stated, "The book was filth and should not be allowed inside any decent home and that it was taking away from women's dignity."

Haughey was a serial womanizer, whose mistress had her own column in a leading Irish newspaper where she constantly hinted at their relationship.

Archbishop McQuaid, who prided himself on having intelligence on the foibles of leading politicians, ignored such obvious hypocrisy and praised Haughey's comments as a family man who "like so many decent Catholic men with families was just beaten by the outlook and descriptions."

The Irish censorship board slapped a ban on *The Country Girls* upon its publication. The Irish response to the book and its two subsequent follow-ups and O'Brien's undaunted stand in defense of the book are considered key moments in women finding their voices in Ireland. According to Irish novelist Anne Enright, "O'Brien is the great and the only survivor of forces that silenced and destroyed who knows how many other Irish women writers."

As James Kelly wrote in IrishCentral.com:

> . . . This visceral reaction to O'Brien's writing was typical of the regressive, deeply conservative Ireland of the day.
>
> Over the next five decades, O'Brien would continue to challenge the commonly held assumptions on what women should write about. The topics of her work regularly deal with the relationship between the sexes from a female perspective, how women are changed by their relationships with men and how they can retain their personhood in a male-dominated world.[59]

According to Scottish novelist Andrew O'Hagan, her place in Irish literature is ensured: "She changed the nature of Irish fiction; she brought the woman's experience and sex and internal lives of those people on to the page, and she did it with style, and she made those concerns international."[60]

Where did O'Brien's brave insight come from? In an interview she did with the *Paris Review* in 1984, she described Tuamgraney, the hometown of her youth, as "enclosed, fervid, and bigoted."

From 1941 to 1946 she was educated by the Sisters of Mercy— a circumstance that contributed to a "suffocating" childhood: ". . . I rebelled against the coercive and stifling religion into which I was born and bred. It was very frightening and all pervasive. I'm glad it has gone."[61]

In 1986, she talked to Susan O'Grady Fox in *Irish America* magazine about growing up in Taumgraney, County Clare, and her early influences:

My life in Ireland as a young girl was quite lonely and was devoid of anything literary. There were no books at all in my house. My mother was most mistrustful of the written word.

But for some reason I always had this total vocation to writing. I loved writing compositions. I would actually ask the other girls to let me write theirs.

Our house was about a mile from the village, and it's kind of pathetic, but on the way home from school I was so excited about doing these essays that I used to sit down on the road, or on a wall, and start writing.

The Traveling Players were the other big excitement in those days. They came about twice a year and put on melodramas, always melodramas: "East Lane," "Murder in the Old Red Barn," and those sorts of plays. I thought they were the most truly vivid, wonderful people I had ever seen.

I dreamed of going away with them, so I wrote a little play called "Dracula's Daughter" in which the girl went to Dracula to see if she could go away with him. When I think of it in retrospect, obviously it was complete romantic masochism.

So these were the sort of excitements of my youth. . . .

. . . I had a sense of sin and a sense of guilt just drummed into me by people who had had it drummed into them. I'm not blaming them as much as saying, just tough luck.

Religion was vitally important. Holy pictures hanging in the kitchen and every night the rosary said. I remember the kneeling down, it was a tiled floor and it was very cold, there was just one fire and just one lamp—no electricity—and there were mice. They used to come out of the shoe closet. We'd be kneeling, praying and my mother would jump up screaming because of the mice.

Then we went to Mass, of course, Holy Communion and Confession. The religious life wasn't as in other countries where people pray and wear medals and all that—it was, so to speak, part of one's fears, and feelings and fantasies and everything about sexual desires were all smothered over.

I remember once seeing a couple who had been courting for five or ten years. They never met except on Sunday in the afternoon, they would go for a walk—she was quite fat, this woman, she had a kind of bustle—and I remember once hearing the man, he sort of touched her on the back and said, "You have a big backside." I thought it was the most sinful thing I had ever heard. I did not think it was crude though. I thought it was sinful. That's how regressive it was.

The women—I can remember them all very clearly in my mind. I can go up the street of the village I lived in and think of them all swathed in clothes and knitted stockings. I think that's where I must have conceived some love of glamour, because there was no glamour at all. Glamour was a ticket to "you know what," to sin. So that formed part of my character and part of my fear.

I think that a lot of people who leave Ireland, and indeed many who stay there, have that [love-hate] syndrome. Love-hate seems to apply more to Ireland than to any other country. It's amazing because it does haunt you. You do want to go back and at the same time, when you go back, you realize that you feel constrained and constricted.[62]

In a different interview with *Irish America* magazine, this time with editor-in-chief, Patricia Hardy, O'Brien talks about writing and her mother:

. . . [T]he irony is that friends say my mother made me a writer, and I don't dispute it. Yet it was something that caused her a lot of suffering and shame, because with the first book, *The Country Girls*, everybody was in an uproar in County Clare, and indeed in the country at large.

There was the banning and the scalding exchange of letters between Archbishop McQuaid and Charlie Haughey who was Minister of Culture at that time, saying the book shouldn't be let in the hands of any decent family. It was daft, daft [laughs].[63]

Even *dafter* and more passing strange was the fact that in 2007, a plaque extolling Edna O'Brien was unveiled near the entrance to her old home, Drewsboro, Tuamgraney, in County Clare. It was an honor well deserved, said the parish priest. Older attendees might have remembered when his predecessor burned her book or the post-mistress telling her father she deserved to be "kicked naked through the town."

That act alone of the priest attending the event in honor of a one-time "fallen woman" showed how incredible change was happening. But why? What forces had been unleashed by the Furies that would change Ireland forever? The answer lay in the profound changes that would alter the Church forever, causing it to lose its temporal power. The Church, founded by St. Patrick in the fifth century, would never be the same.

Yet Patrick was the ultimate peaceful revolutionary, converting an entire island to his religion apparently without violence. But his vision of his church was very different to what became the modern Irish Catholic reality. His Celtic pastoral and outward-looking spiritual church would eventually become didactic, inward-looking, Rome-directed, and sex-obsessed Jansenist-dominated.

That journey to Jansenism would define Ireland for centuries but would all come crashing down in a spectacular perfect storm fifteen centuries after Patrick preached the word.

SECTION TWO

CHAPTER 15

Come Walk among Us, Patrick

"I arise today with a mighty strength."

St. Patrick's Breastplate poem

Shortly after escaping slavery in Ireland, where he had been brought as a captive at age sixteen, St. Patrick describes in his "Confessions" how an unearthly vision came to him.

> There, in a vision of the night, I saw a man whose name was Victoricus coming as if from Ireland with innumerable letters, and he gave me one of them, and I read the beginning of the letter: "The Voice of the Irish"; and as I was reading the beginning of the letter I seemed at that moment to hear the voice of those who were beside the forst of Focult . . . and they were crying as if with one voice: "We beg you, holy youth, that you shall come and shall walk again among us." And I was stung intensely in my heart so that I could read no more, and thus I awoke . . .[64]

He was deeply reluctant to return to where he had been a captive after being snatched from his Welsh home by Irish pirates and sold to a farmer in Northern Ireland whom he worked for as a slave for six years.

Still doubting the vision, Patrick says he was visited again the following night. "And another night—God knows . . . most words which I heard I could not understand, except at the end of the speech it was represented thus: 'He who gave his life for you, he it is who speaks within you.' And thus I awoke, joyful."[65]

Armed with those visions, Patrick, likely in his midtwenties and despite the harsh objections of his family—we know his father was Calpurnius, a tax collector in Roman Britain—began studying for the priesthood in order to return to the country where he had been held in bondage.

Ireland had been inhabited since the Stone Age about 6,000 BC, and what "religion existed was a form of sun worship." Newgrange in County Meath, with its famous sun chamber is the greatest example.

About 600 BC came the arrival of the Celts. They spoke a separate language related to the Irish language of today. They were a warlike race, aided by superior weapons, and were greatly feared as a fighting force. They sacked Rome in 390 BC. The Greeks painted them as chariot soldiers and were afraid of their size and ferocity.

The Celts themselves created separate kingdoms in Ireland and often fought. Among the most famous warrior was High King Niall of the Nine Hostages, that number of hostages dictating how many fiefdoms he reigned over.

A team of geneticists at Trinity College Dublin led by Professor Dan Bradley discovered that as many as three million people worldwide may be descendants of the Irish warlord, who was the Irish "High King" at Tara, the ancient center of Ireland from AD 379 to AD 405. He and Alexander the Great are widely considered two of the most fecund men who ever lived.

Professor Bradley stated, "In many countries, powerful men historically have more children, and it's not that hard to believe that it happened in Ireland, too. We estimate there are maybe two to three million descendants in the modern age, [of Niall of the Nine Hostages] with a concentration in Ireland, obviously."[66]

The Celts had a vibrant culture. Poets and harpers and other musicians attended the king's court. Hostages, whose lives had been handed over as pledges of fealty by lesser kings, often provided amusement at banquets. Brehon laws ruled, covering every aspect of life and adjudicated by judges known as Brehons.

This was the Ireland that Patrick entered in AD 432 on his proselytizing mission. Up until Patrick's time, nothing was written other than in *ogham*, a "cumbersome system of representing letters by short lines."

According to the late Cardinal Tómas Ó Fiaich (pronounced "O Fee"), a leading early Christian historian, St. Patrick was the author of the first known documents to be written in Ireland. Ó Fiaich describes Patrick's Latin (remember, he was a Roman Britain) as "rugged and abrupt," but its impact was incredible.

As Ó Fiaich notes, Patrick's writings provide us with our only contemporary narrative of the conversion of Ireland to Christianity. There is dispute over how many converts there were to Christianity already in Ireland. Palladius, an emissary from Rome, had been in Ireland before Patrick and baptized significant numbers.

Patrick did not openly fight the pagan beliefs he encountered, rather he co-opted them, and major pagan festivals became Christian Holy Days, too. He baptized thousands, ordained clerics everywhere, and swept through the land like a veritable hurricane.

He knew the pagan Druids feared him. It is recorded that they even aimed a curse and prophecy at him:

> Across the sea will come . . .
> crazed in the head,
> his cloak with hole for the head,
> his stick bent in the head.
> He will chant impieties
> from a table in front of his house;
> all his people will answer:
> "so be it, so be it."[67]

He befriended many in the wealthy class, and many of the women followed him to become nuns and brides of Christ.

He writes:

> . . . There was a blessed Irish woman of noble birth, a most beautiful adult whom I baptised. She came to us a few days later for this reason. She told us that she had received word from a messenger of God, who advised her that she should become a virgin of Christ, and that she should come close to God. Thanks be to God, six days later, enthusiastically and well, she took on the life that all virgins of God do. Their fathers don't like this, of course. These women suffer persecution and false accusations from their parents, and yet their number grows! We do not know the number of our people who were born there. In addition, there are the widows and the celibates. Of all these, those held in slavery work hardest—they bear even terror and threats, but the Lord gives grace to so many of the women who serve him. Even when it is forbidden, they bravely follow his example.[68]

Patrick had two goals: to convert the pagans and to set up church structures throughout the land. To do so without modern communications, roads, rail, telecommunications, and so on was an incredible feat, but Patrick never weakened.

He used the blueprint of the Church structure in his native Britain with bishops controlling dioceses. In addition, however, he set up Monastic settlements staffed by monks whose great goal was to spread the word of Jesus all over the known world.

Given how political the Church would become in later centuries, it is jarring to see the original spirit was one that was ascetic, contemplative, and soft-spoken in its proselytizing. There are no reports of pogroms or deaths as a result of the takeover by Christianity of the pagan land.

Far from being bellicose, the monks, in essence, retired from the world, fasted, devoted themselves to God, and composed prayer.

It was the golden age of Irish Christianity. Saint Colum Cille in Derry, Saint Kevin in Wicklow, Saint Brendan in Clonfert, to name but a few, spread the gospel, preserved manuscripts, and lived the aesthetic life. The monks soon spread the new gospel all over Europe, founding over 150 monasteries where they studied the sacred scriptures, copying important manuscripts, none more so than the Book of Kells, the unfinished eight-century masterpiece barely saved from destruction from rampaging Vikings who landed on the Scottish island of Iona and attacked the monastery there. The book is now Ireland's most valuable manuscript ensconced in Trinity College Dublin. According to Arthur Kingsley Porter, Yale professor, the success of the Celtic Church was a success of major political and religious magnitude.

The French writer Charles De Montalembert said, "It cannot be sufficiently repeated that Ireland was then regarded by all Christian Europe as the principal center of knowledge."

Cardinal Tómas Ó Fiaich stated, "The achievement, culturally as well as religiously, borders on the incredible."

What occurred over those centuries created an unbreakable bond between the Irish Celtic Church and its devotees, inspired by the pastoral message of Patrick, his monks, and holy men who had spread the gospel throughout the world.

The bonds would be tested in full by the foreign invaders massing on their shoreline in 1169 lured to Ireland by a chieftain who would go down as one of Ireland's greatest traitors.

CHAPTER 16

A Bitter Lover Invites the English In

"Here's a health to the Protestant Minister
And his church without meaning or faith
For the foundation stones of his temple are
The bollocks of Henry the Eight."

Irish poet Brendan Behan

Religiously colonized in the fifth century by Patrick, the Irish faced a very different colonization battle when the Anglo-Normans turned their attention to the smaller island to the West. As noted historian FX Martin stated, "No other event (the Anglo-Norman invasion) except the preaching of the gospel by Saint Patrick and his companions has so changed the destinies of Ireland."

But before the Normans came the Viking raiders in their longboats. They established several settlements in Ireland, disturbing the old order.

The Norsemen met their match when the fabled Brian Boru, high king of Ireland, defeated them in a pitched battle in 1014 at Clontarf outside Dublin. Brian is said to have died at battle's end giving thanks to the Lord and praying in his tent when he was assassinated.

With the Vikings defeated, the Irish went back to their minor and major kingdoms, secure, they believed, in the knowledge their island would not be invaded again.

Celtic Catholicism and identity were about to face a far greater enemy, however, than the Vikings, the impact of which echoes down to the present day. Unlike most wars that follow a well-defined battle plan created over several years, the Anglo-Norman invasion began abruptly over a wife's affair and a star-crossed couple who eloped.

Dermot MacMurrough, King of Leinster, and Tiernan O'Rourke, King of Breffni, nowadays known as Cavan, were bitter enemies. The reason was plain to be seen. O'Rourke's wife, Dervorgilla, had either been abducted or eloped with MacMurrough in 1165.

The ancient Irish historian Geoffrey Keating says Dervorgilla sent a secret message to MacMurrough urging him to seize her husband, who, it was said, was old and unappealing to her.

Keating notes:

> As to [Dermot] when this message reached him he went quickly to meet the lady, accompanied by a detachment of mounted men, and when they reached where she was, he ordered her to be placed on horseback behind a rider and upon this the woman wept and screamed in pretence as if [Dermot] were carrying her off by force; and bringing her with him in this manner, he returned to Leinster.[69]

Neither was a spring chicken. He was forty-four, she was forty, and the elopement only lasted a year; but O'Rourke, who never resumed the marriage, was hell-bent on revenge. The struggle for supremacy and the title of High King was raging in the years 1156–1166 among several kings.

Dermot was one of those seeking the high kingship, but O'Rourke joined up with Rory O'Connor, king of Connacht, and destroyed MacMurrough's army. Dermot—who barely made it away safely to Bristol in England—was consumed with thoughts of revenge and raising a new army from Britain's Norman rulers.

He went to France seeking aid from Henry II, ruler of much of Europe including Britain. Henry lived mostly on the continent. In 1166, Dermot MacMurrough reached him and urged him to make Ireland part of his conquered lands.

Dermot was described by a contemporary Gerald of Wales as "A brave and warlike man . . . he preferred to be feared by all rather than loved. [In Ireland] 'all men's hands were against him, and he was hostile to all men.'"

Dermot made his offer to Henry:

> . . . Your liege-man I shall become
> Henceforth all the days of my life
> On condition you be my helper
> You I shall acknowledge as sire and lord.[70]

Henry obliged and wrote an open letter to his subjects, urging them to join Dermot. There was little enthusiasm. However: Ireland was terra incognita controlled by warlike Celts. There be dragons.

Dermot found one warrior, Richard Fitzgilbert De Clare, known as Strongbow, a Norman leader in Wales. Strongbow agreed to send an army but demanded the beautiful Aoife, Dermot's daughter, in marriage and the right of succession to Dermot. Dermot fatefully agreed.

Dermot went ahead with an advance party and succeeded in winning back his kingdom. He sent a message to Strongbow that all of Ireland was for the taking. In the summer of 1170 at a rocky headland in Wexford named Baginbun, the Normans landed. The local Irish attacked but were defeated. A rhyme ran: "At the creek of Baginbun Ireland was lost and won."

The earthen ramparts the Normans dug at Baginbun are there to this day.

Shortly after, Waterford was won, and Strongbow claimed his prize—the beautiful Aoife. Gerard of Wales described the ruler as having reddish hair and freckles. . . . He was a generous and easy-going man. What he could not accomplish by deed he did by the persuasiveness of his words. When he took up position in the midst of battle he stood firm as an immovable standard, round which his men could group.[71]

Dublin fell to the invaders on September 21, 1170. In October 1171, Henry II came to view his new kingdom. The Normans, the Irish, the Norsemen all paid homage to him. The old Ireland was dead.

By the year 1250, the Normans had conquered three quarters of Ireland, and by 1300, English and Welsh settlers had taken possession of the arable land. The era of the Gaelic kingdoms was over, but the Irish would never give up their dream of recapturing their land.

That fight would also be about keeping the religion Patrick had so ingrained in them. Church and people were interwoven as one, and the wars after the Reformation would seek vainly to break them apart.

The "indomitable Irishry," as W. B. Yeats called them, and their clergy would never yield to the alien religion of Protestantism, which, as writer Brendan Behan savagely noted, did not exactly have august beginnings:

> Here's a health to the Protestant Minister
> And his church without meaning or faith
> For the foundation stones of his temple are
> The bollocks of Henry the Eighth

It would be something far more insidious and centuries away that would break the deep covenant between them.

Chapter 17

King Henry VIII Is Upset with His Irish

On June 11, 1509, newly crowned King Henry VIII and his betrothed, Catherine of Aragon, were married at Greenwich Palace in London. He was the second Tudor king. She was the daughter of the king and queen of Spain.

As a cementing of a powerful alliance, this marriage made enormous sense, despite the fact that Catherine had been married at fifteen to Henry's older brother, Arthur, the Prince of Wales, who died of a deadly virus known as "sweating sickness" in 1502.

The betrothal question asked by the Archbishop of Canterbury William Warham was weighed with historical importance. This was to be a marriage of two kingdoms, England and Spain, and approved by the pope:

> Most illustrious Prince, is it your will to fulfil the treaty of marriage concluded by your father, the late King of England, and the parents of the Princess of Wales, the King and Queen of Spain; and, as the Pope has dispensed with this marriage, to take the Princess who is here present for your lawful wife?"
>
> The King answered: I will.
>
> Most illustrious Princess, &c. (*mutatis mutandis*).
>
> The Princess answered: I will.[72]

The first wedding of King Henry VIII (just turning eighteen) to Catherine of Aragon, widow of his brother and five years his senior, had massive importance for Ireland. Despite the ethnic strife between the Irish and English, there was only one church, that of Rome, which was worshipped in both countries. The edicts of the pope had massive impact throughout Europe. That would soon change.

Pope Julius II (who had fathered a child when a cardinal) had approved the marriage to Catherine even though there were questions about the wife's right to marry her dead husband's brother.

But when Catherine failed to deliver a male heir who survived, Henry began a plot to marry again to Anne Boleyn. He knew the pope would refuse him the Catholic rites, so, because he was desperate to produce a male heir, the new Reformation Church started by Martin Luther in 1517 suited his circumstances beautifully.

In 1541, Henry VIII acquired a new title, King of Ireland. He was the first foreign king to acquire and use the title, and it boded ill for the Irish.

The reign of the Tudors meant everything would change for Ireland. The Tudors claimed the throne of England after the Battle of Bosworth Field on August 22, 1485. Henry's father, King Henry VII, led an invasion from France to place the House of Lancaster on the throne, though he had dubious Lancaster connections.

He defeated Richard III, of the House of York, at Bosworth Field near Leicester in the climactic event of the War of the Roses. Though the Tudors would only reign for 118 years, their impact on Ireland was profound.

In the centuries after Ireland was conquered in 1172, the Anglo-Norman influence diminished greatly as the old order reestablished itself. At one point the British only controlled what became known as "the Pale," an area that included Dublin city and "twenty miles in compass" around the Capital. (A pale was a sharp stick driven into the ground to depict a boundary.)

Beyond the Pale lay the Gaelic Irish and also the Anglo Irish, who like the Norse and the Norman invaders had mainly become, in the famous phrase, "more Irish than the Irish themselves." The old

Gaelic order was resurgent; the Gaelic kings ran their fiefdoms and deeply resented the usurpers of power in Dublin.

A short-lived rebellion against Henry VII led by Kildare chieftain "Silken Thomas" Fitzgerald, whose family backed the pope after Henry had imprisoned his father, bore no fruit. Henry, as king, forced matters to a head and sent in the army to wipe them out.

When aid from Catholic Europe never arrived, Fitzgerald's uprising petered out, and he and his five uncles were executed by the British. The Irish air was full of mutiny after the savage wipeout of a deeply respected family.

Henry's worst nightmare was invaders from Catholic Europe using Ireland as a backdoor to attack England. It was a time of empire building, and the Catholic powers of Europe were deeply suspicious of Henry and his embrace of the Reformation, which conveniently allowed him to ignore the pope's excommunication edict for leaving his first wife and marrying a second. (He, of course, continued right on to have five more wives.)

Henry realized he had to somehow contain the Irish, in order to nullify the backdoor invasion threat. The Gaelic lords had a political and cultural life of their own that their ancestors had lived for centuries. They were also ferocious warriors who opposed the alien invaders with all their might, and their links with Catholic France and Spain were extensive. They were the enemy within the king's realm.

Henry proved adept at undermining the old ways, not by war but by flattery and munificence, in his own words "good and discreet persuasions." Many of the top chieftains came to Britain at his invitation, were wined and dined and given wonderful-sounding new British titles such as earls and lords. They gave up their lands but had them automatically restored while held under their new British titles.

Somewhat surprisingly, many of the most important chieftains agreed to give up the old Gaelic ways, learn English, and dress like the lords and ladies of Henry's court. Henry's plan was what was called "one class only"—leaders and followers, loyal to the king, not the different allegiances the tribal Irish held. Henry succeeded brilliantly in bringing down much of the old Gaelic world.

But Henry failed utterly in one other aspect: imposing the Reformation and Protestantism on Ireland. Henry had used the Reformation to rid himself of Rome and the pope's hostile edicts on his marriage.

In a speech to parliament in May 1532, as recorded in the annals, he signaled the pope's writ would no longer run in his realm:

> Well-beloved subjects! We thought that the clergy of our realm had been our subjects wholly, but now, we have well perceived that they be but half our subjects; yea, and scarce our subjects, for all the prelates, at their consecration, take an oath to the Pope clean contrary to the oath they make to us, so that they seem to be his subjects and not ours.

By 1534, Henry had banished the pope from Britain and established himself as "Supreme Head on Earth of the Church of England." All the religious monasteries were forced shut and the friars and monks scattered. It was Henry's church now.

He resolved to add the ranks of his Irish subjects to his new church and dismiss Catholicism forever from the Emerald Isle. In 1536, the rubber stamp parliament in Ireland passed an Act that made Henry "the only and supreme head of the whole Church of Ireland." His new church established, Henry was expecting the same obeisance in Ireland that he had received from his British subjects. After all, he had easily outmaneuvered many of the Gaelic lords and brought them to heel.

The loyalty to Catholicism, however, ran far deeper than in Britain. The Celtic church and its priests were admired, loved, and respected. They were immediately to the forefront, warning the Irish chieftains to keep the faith of their fathers. They went so far as to preach open revolution. The pope drafted in Jesuits from the continent to Ireland. Irish colleges for the priesthood all over Europe sent their recruits back to ensure Ireland kept the one true faith.

Rebellion against the Reformation was everywhere. In 1539 it was written that priests ". . . do preach daily that every man ought, for the salvation of his soul, [to] fight and make war against our sovereign lord, the king's majesty and if any of them die . . . his soul . . . shall go to heaven as the souls of [Saints] Peter, Paul, and others, which suffered death and martyrdom for God's sake."[73]

Henry, in vain, tried to make Ireland Protestant by legislation, but the new religion was an alien way of worshipping for the Irish. They knew well Henry's true reason for embracing the new faith had more to do with sex than sanctity. As time passed, it became clear the established religion would be embraced only by invaders and settlers. The Irish were not for turning.

Despite that, Henry's successors continued their efforts to conquer the Irish and force-feed them the new established religion. Elizabeth the First, 1558 to 1603, the last of the Tudors, became the most insistent and bloody-minded about the effort. She was at war with Spain for three years from 1585 to 1588 and greatly feared a Spanish attack and a contemporaneous uprising by the Irish.

She and her advisors hit on the idea of plantations of loyal Protestant English being given huge tracts of land to oust the local chieftains. The plantation of Munster, a noticeably rebellious area, was the first major effort with mixed results.

However, it was in Ulster that the plantation would have a massive impact on Ireland at the time, and its effects can be seen right down to the present day. The Ulster chieftains, Hugh O'Neill and Hugh O'Donnell, had remained outside English control.

Hugh O'Neill, in particular, was a beloved chieftain and devout Catholic as well as a mighty warrior. He ensured along with other Northern chieftains that English writ never run in Ulster. He defeated an English expeditionary force handily in 1598 at the Battle of Yellow Ford in Armagh.

He was also an ally of Philip, the king of Spain, thereby reawakening England's worst nightmare of the Spanish using Ireland as a backdoor to invade Britain. The Ulster chieftains eventually succeeded in convincing Philip that victory in Ireland aided by the chieftains and the priests was the way to also conquer England.

That recurrent English nightmare came through finally with the landing of a Spanish force at Kinsale in County Cork and the capture of the town by six thousand troops. Alas, due to storms at sea, they had landed at almost the farthest geographical point from O'Neill and his men in Ulster, where they had been fighting what in modern terms would be called a nine-year guerilla war against English troops sent by Elizabeth Tudor to end the rebellious Irish impunity once and for all.

O'Neill and his men were left with no option but to force-march 250 miles in freezing winter conditions to meet the Spanish army who, by this time, was surrounded by Lord Mountjoy and English forces. The ensuing battle of Kinsale was one of the most important in Ireland's long history. Superior cavalry and the astute generalship of Mountjoy won the day for the English.

Defeated and on the run, the leaders of Gaelic Ireland barely made it back to Ulster, but their resistance had collapsed, and the chieftains departed Ireland in 1607 in what is now termed "the Flight of the Earls."

Their departure left Ulster conquered, and the 1609 Plantation of Ulster, which drove the Catholics off the best land and replaced them with soldiers and lowland Scottish believers in the Reformation, completely changed the ethnic makeup of the province. Unlike earlier plantations, the 1609 plantation of Ulster would stick and become a bastion of the British presence in Ireland down to this very day.

The impact on the Irish of this sudden Protestant onslaught was perhaps predictable. As more parts of Ireland fell to the armies of England, they clung tighter to the faith of their fathers in spite of "dungeon fire and sword."

That faith would be sorely tested and not found wanting during the dark decades of the seventeenth century. It would bring pain and suffering in the name of converting the wild Irish, most notably by the murderous deeds of Oliver Cromwell, who butchered nine thousand men, women, and children in the town of Drogheda alone.

Despite all the horrific repression, the Irish chieftains rose again and backed the Catholic James I on the throne, and it was to the Irish he turned when the Protestant King William set about deposing him. At the Battle of the Boyne in 1690, Seamus a Cacha ("James the Shit," as the Irish called him) turned and fled before King Billy's forces. Once again, the Irish leaders were sent into exile, and the Treaty of Limerick ended their resistance.

The British then decided the Irish were incorrigible and would remain chained to their despised religion. Fresh measures would need to be taken to end the bond once and for all between the Irish and Catholicism.

CHAPTER 18

The Priest Hunters

Despite their best efforts, the English kings and queens were unable to pacify the Irish. The Penal Laws were introduced in 1695 and in subsequent years. Their aim was to finally break the link between the Catholic church and the native Irish.

Among the laws:

- Any person who apprehended a "Popish Bishop, Priest, or Jesuite" who was then prosecuted for "saying Mass or exercising any other Part of the Office or Function of a Popish Bishop or Priest within these Realms" was to receive £20 reward
- Exclusion of Catholics from public offices
- Ban on intermarriage with Protestants
- Catholics barred from holding firearms or serving in the armed forces
- Bar from membership in either the Parliament of Ireland or the Parliament of England
- Disenfranchising Act 1728, exclusion from voting
- Exclusion from the legal profession and the judiciary
- On a death by a Catholic, his heirs could benefit by conversion to the Church of Ireland

- Popery Act—Catholic inheritances of land were to be equally divided between all the owner's sons with the exception that if the eldest son and heir converted to Protestantism, he would become the one and only tenant of estate
- Ban on Catholics buying land under a lease of more than thirty-one years
- Prohibition on Catholics owning a horse valued five pounds or more
- Ban on Catholic education: "'No person of the popish religion shall publicly or in private houses teach school, or instruct youth in learning within this realm' upon pain of twenty pounds fine and three months in prison for every such offence."
- Any and all rewards not paid by the crown for alerting authorities of offences to be levied upon the Catholic populace within parish and county

This draconian legislation was an all-out attempt to drive a wedge between the Church and the faithful. It also created one new class of employment—priest hunters. With bounties as high as one hundred pounds, a fortune by today's standards, there was no shortage of bounty hunters, ready to find and betray any bishop or priest who was trying to keep the faith alive.

In Kinsale, on January 31, 1716, one George Hooper of Cork City was petitioning the court for payment for capturing not just a priest, but a schoolteacher, too: "Sheweth that your petitioner apprehended one Corneilius Madden a Popish priest and also Daniel Sulivan a Popish schoolmaster who were tried and convicted and ordered to be transported."

In his excellent book *The Priest Hunters*, Colin Murphy notes that many priest hunters were drawn from within the Catholic ranks, some from the landed gentry, and also from ex-soldiers who had claimed land in Ireland.

By far the most infamous priest hunter was Sean Na Sagart (John the priest), an Irish Catholic whose real name was John Mullowney and who was raised in an orphanage in Mayo. He was briefly a rapparee, that is, a member of rural bands of guerrilla fighters, Irish peasants who struck back against repression with raids on landlords' livestock and occasional ambushes on troops.

Mullowney was caught and sentenced to be hanged for his activities. The local Crown official Sir George Bingham then made him an offer—he would save his life if he became a priest hunter. He promised him twenty pounds for every priest he caught. Mullowney took to the task with relish. He is said to have killed his first priest in 1713 in a place called Pulnathanken on the Mayo coastline, which contained a large sea cave where secret masses were said.

One Sunday during Mass, the lookout shouted that the priest hunters were coming, and the devotees scattered. Father Terence Higgins remained behind, desperately hiding the chalice and church vestments. Then he ran toward a small boat, which would allow him to escape. Sean Na Sagart hunted him down and killed him.

On another occasion the priest hunter, feigning illness, visited a woman suspected of harboring priests and explained he was deathly ill and wanted to confess on his deathbed. He clambered into her bed and began moaning loudly. The woman hesitated but eventually went for the priest, Father Kilger, who she knew was hiding nearby. Kilger came to give the last rites, but as he bent over the "dying" man, he was brutally knifed to death by Mullowney.

But Mullowney's own end was near. After the death of the priest, he knew another priest would officiate in disguise at Father Kilger's funeral; Mullowney recognized him as one of the pallbearers, and the priest fled. Mullowney caught up with him after a frantic chase, but the priest and a fellow mourner drew knives and killed Sean Na Sagart in a desperate fight.

To this day, Sean Na Sagart is often mentioned as a bogeyman by some Mayo people. The fact he was one of their own hurt very deeply, and there is still a chill in the air when he is mentioned.

Among the most infamous priest hunters was Edward Tyrell, who began his career as a priest hunter around 1710 soon after the penal laws. Tyrell had a ferocious reputation for hunting down priests, so much so that he took to women's clothing to disguise himself.

"I have left Dublin the 4th ins.t in women's apparel," he wrote to a London politician because he feared for his life. He traveled to the Irish college in Louvain, where Irish priests were being secretly trained, and reported the college had been sending "Popish bishops into Ireland to foment rebellion." Many of those priests were caught and transported when they returned to Ireland.

Here is a typical authorities' note of a Tyrell operation: "Gentlemen Edward Tyrrell hath given an Examination on Oath that one Thomas Feaghny who is reputed to be a Parish Bishop . . . now lodges at the house of Mr. Felix Coughlan and Tyrell undertakes to have him apprehend there if he may have sufficient assistance."[74]

Tyrell had also pinpointed a group of Dominican friars in a house nearby. In this instance the bishop was caught, but the friars escaped.

Men like Tyrell roamed at will throughout Ireland seeking the hated papist priests or schoolteachers. Yet the more the repression, the tighter the people seemed to cling. All over Ireland today are Mass rocks, locations where secret masses were said. The Catholic teachers taught outdoors or in secret hiding places known as hedge schools. Despite the best efforts of the Crown, the Penal Laws never succeeded.

The penal laws also led to one of the greatest poems in the Irish language, written by Eileen Dubh O Conaill. It is called the "Lament for Art O'Leary," who was her husband, an aristocratic Irishman who fought in the continental wars and returned to Ireland.

He fell afoul of the Penal Laws when a Protestant High Sheriff demanded his fine horse, which he had brought from the continent. He refused and was marked as an outlaw, eventually being shot to death by the landowner's hired killers in 1773. Eileen's poem in his honor is considered one of the finest in the Irish language. The first verse as translated by Eleanor Hull reads:

My closest and dearest!
From the day I saw you
From the top of the market-house,
My eyes gave heed to you,
My heart gave affection to you,
I fled from my friends with you,
Far from my home with you,
No lasting sorrow this to me.

CHAPTER 19

O'Connell Frees the Catholics

In 1798, the litmus paper was lit in Ireland for an entirely new political revolution that did not involve games of thrones between kings, but commoners and men of no property removing the royal regents.

The American and French Revolutions and the Enlightenment had proved that the divine right of kings could be overcome by the common man if properly led. In 1798, the French Revolution and writers such as Thomas Paine radicalized and inspired a group of Irish Catholics, Protestants, and dissenters to seek to replicate the success of that uprising. Thus, Irish Republicanism was born.

Theobald Wolfe Tone, a Dublin Presbyterian, saw himself as Ireland's George Washington with his stated intent:

> To subvert the tyranny of our execrable government, to break the connection with England, the never-failing source of all our political evils, and to assert the independence of my country—these were my objects. To unite the whole people of Ireland, to abolish the memory of past dissensions, and to substitute the common name of Irishman, in place of the denominations of Protestant, Catholic and Dissenter—these were my means.[75]

He led the United Irelander uprising of 1798, which was a complete failure. The British had spies it seemed in every United Irelander secret gathering, and Tone was captured after his ship from France was forced to surrender on Lough Swilly. A landing of French troops in Mayo briefly raised hopes, but they were soon dampened down when the French, after an early victory, ran afoul of a British detachment at the Battle of Ballinamuck.

An earlier attempt in 1796 of enlisting the help from Catholic France never bore fruit, as ships, with Wolfe Tone on board one, were turned back by fierce storms in Bantry Bay in Cork. They were almost close enough to "toss a biscuit" ashore, Tone wrote, but the fierce storms drove them back.

The main action in 1798 took place in Wexford, where Father John Murphy, a local priest, led an ill-prepared peasant army to surprise victories until losing the battle of Vinegar Hill. He was subsequently hanged. Murphy was an exception, as the priests shunned the Rising, refusing to give confession to rebels.

The Catholic hierarchy had a strong interest in undermining the revolutionary free thinking from the US and Europe that was taking root abroad. It clearly threatened their hegemony.

The 1798 uprising was a glorious but abject failure, leaving the British more in control than ever. To hammer home the victory, they permanently prorogued the Irish parliament and created an Act of Union in 1800 inextricably linking the two countries with all decisions on Ireland made in Britain. It would have a tragic aftermath during the Irish famine, where there was no sympathy from London for the Irish peasants starving in their millions.

In 1801, after the Act of Union, it seemed Ireland and its people were once again crushed under heel. But then came Daniel O'Connell, the Liberator, the Uncrowned King, the Emancipator whose name is forever immortalized in Dublin's main thoroughfare and who is considered by many historians as the greatest Irishman of all times. He was a lifelong pacifist and presented a very different challenge to the Crown than Wolfe Tone.

He was that rare exception, from a wealthy Catholic family in Kerry. The O'Connells of Cahirciveen had been Munster chieftains since the fourteenth century. English rule never fully dominated in Kerry, where hostile terrain, soaring mountains, and deep dense woods kept the Sassenach from ever gaining total control. As a result, smuggling and other skullduggery went on at a large scale. Given such realities, the fate that befell many aristocratic Catholics never befell the O'Connells.

Daniel O'Connell was born in 1775 into the chieftain O'Connell family and was essentially raised by his childless uncle, Maurice "Hunting Cap" O'Connell. Maurice lived in Derrynane House, a massive Georgian farmhouse, now a national museum.

O'Connell, like many wealthy Catholic sons, was sent to France for further education. He witnessed the aftermath of the French Revolution and indeed was threatened and suspected of being a Jesuit priest. He acquired his love of pacifism from the experience.

He became a hugely successful lawyer, even though as a Catholic he was forbidden to ever become a judge or take silk. Along the way he killed a man in a duel, gained a fierce ladies' man reputation, acquired a wig (he was quite vain), and had ten kids himself by his wife, who was also his cousin. Not always a practicing Catholic, he became deeply devout later in life. He saw his struggle as both spiritual and nationalistic. His aims were to remove the Act of Union, restore Ireland's parliament, and end the Penal Laws once and forever by "Catholic Emancipation," the cause he first espoused.

He wanted to enter politics and knew he could not be elected as a Catholic to the British Parliament. He also knew that Catholics could never serve in high positions of power and that Catholics still had to disavow the pope and transubstantiation if they wished to progress. He made Emancipation his first priority and founded the Catholic Association in 1823 and organized monster rallies throughout Ireland to that end.

He was astute, brilliant on his feet, and always well prepared. He left little to chance. Here he is, for example, writing to a colleague before one of his speeches in 1836:

If there be any [public] procession [beforehand], the principal managers, three or four, should meet me in an open carriage with four horses. I would have my own and go into *that* carriage when I meet the people. This is the most *approved* mode of conducting the *imperator triumphans* of a popular procession, with four horses a force is obtained just sufficient to get through the crowd. . . . At the close of the procession, I would address the people from any *well-arranged* public vantage ground. Look to the strength and solidity of any erection used for that purpose either old or new. Let me speak *with* the wind. You will smile at these minuteness matters, but I know the value of attention to details.[76]

The Catholic Association collected a penny a month from the Irish peasantry nationwide, and soon this grew so big nationwide that the British overlords feared a war would break out.

O'Connell decided to force the issue by standing for election to the British Parliament in 1828 from County Clare. The peasants had the vote but were always instructed by the landlord for whom to vote. This time, however, the clergy stepped up. They knew Catholic Emancipation depended on O'Connell being elected. The only question was whether the tenants would disobey the landlords.

On election day it became obvious O'Connell would win. Ignoring landlords and following the priests, the small freeholders came in their thousands to vote for O'Connell.

Here is how a contemporary journalist covered the event on Tuesday morning at eight o'clock:

Between 300 and 400 of [John] Vandeleur [Clare landlord] freeholders are now passing up the street to the courthouse, preceded by colours, every man with a green leaf in his hand and amidst the loudest cheering from the townspeople. They are western men from Kilrush, and brought in by their clergy to vote for O'Connell. Along the road the general cry of these men are "Here's Kilrush, high for O'Connell, high for our priest." O'Leary the priest of Kilrush is with them and the town is full of catholic clergy.[77]

At 11:00 a.m., the reporter wrote that O'Connell had arrived and was chaired to the courthouse and at the door implored the people to be true to their religion and to vote for O'Connell.

The Liberator won in a landslide but was not allowed to take his seat. The issue of Catholic Emancipation had reached boiling point, and The Duke of Wellington, the British prime minister at the time, feared all-out war. Reluctantly, he acceded to emancipation for all Catholics in Britain and Ireland.

Thus, on April 28, 1829, all present in the House of Lords were aware of the historic nature of the occasion. The Duke of Norfolk, Lord Clifford, and Lord Dormer were together at the front table of the chamber, waiting anxiously. As the Clerk entered, a silence fell, as the nature of the historic oath the Clerk was about to administer became apparent. Finally, the Clerk began, "I do sincerely promise and swear, that I will be faithful and bear true allegiance to His Majesty King George the Fourth . . ." The three men solemnly repeated the Clerk's words, fully aware of this incredible and momentous occasion. They finished the oath with "So help me God!" and were congratulated by their peers. For the first time in 148 years, Roman Catholics held seats in Parliament, thanks to O'Connell, who also took his seat.

For the Catholic Church and their people, it was the crowning glory, the inseparable bond between them tightening even harder. Nothing, it seemed, would come between them. The Liberator became known as the "Uncrowned King."

Repeal of the Act of Union was next and the restoration of the Irish parliament. Home Rule no longer seemed like a mirage. Just as the future for Catholics brightened, however, a dreadful darkness came their way.

CHAPTER 20

Sex and the Famine

"All the Irish Protestants whom I saw speak of the Catholics with extraordinary hatred and scorn. The latter, they say, are savages, and fanatics led into all sorts of disorders by their priests."

Alexis de Tocqueville, 1835

Out of the west it came, across the Atlantic, carried on a ship from somewhere in the Americas. It was a fungus called *Phytophthora infestans*, which spreads through the air and develops when the weather conditions are damp. Ireland had a wet summer that year of 1845 and proved a perfect host for the fungus known to destroy potato crops and leave them as black rotting pulp. The course of Irish history was about to change as the Irish version of the Holocaust began.

Daniel O'Connell was never able to replicate the success of the Catholic Emancipation drive with his Repeal Campaign.

Though he continued to hold Mass rallies—one at Tara was said to have approached one million—British governments remained un-yielding. They had Ireland under their parliamentary control: the Protestant wealthy class was content, and the electoral arithmetic in parliament never created O'Connell's ideal scenario where either the Whigs or the Tories would need Irish party votes to gain power.

At the end, a prison term for a trumped-up conspiracy charge damaged his health. A young radical insurgency called the Young Irelanders was coming to the fore, but the full weight of the Famine crushed his people's spirits. He died a broken man in 1847 as famine raged.

He was told by William Makepeace Thackeray (1811–1863), "You have done more for your nation than any man since Washington ever did." William Gladstone (1809–1898) described him as "the greatest popular leader the world has ever seen." Honoré de Balzac (1799–1850) wrote that "Napoleon and O'Connell were the only great men of the 19th Century."

But he could not help his people now.

O'Connell's old friend Frederick Douglass, who befriended the liberator after O'Connell had condemned slavery, visited Ireland and was shocked by what he saw.

> I had heard much of the misery and wretchedness of the Irish people . . . but I must confess, my experience has convinced me that the half has not been told. . . . Here you have an Irish hut or cabin, such as millions of the people of Ireland live in, in much the same degradation as the American slaves. . . . I see much here to remind me of my former condition, and I confess I should be ashamed to lift up my voice against American slavery, but that I know the cause of humanity is one the world over. He who really and truly feels for the American slave, cannot steel his heart to the woes of others.
>
> *Frederick Douglass, August 1845*

As the millions died and the millions fled, the Malthusian concept of clearing the land until it was profitable took hold among the landlord class, whose lack of caring about their starving renters was callous in the extreme:

Rotten potatoes and sea-weed, or even grass, properly mixed, afforded a very wholesome and nutritious food. All knew that Irishmen could live upon anything and there was plenty of grass in the field though the potato crop should fail.

The Duke of Cambridge, January 1846

As a result of the Irish Holocaust, the Church and consequently the people began to change.

As historian David Millar of Carnegie Mellon University noted, postfamine the "one million dead and one million fled" completely changed the ratio of priests to parishioners.

The decimation of the famine years was followed by "widespread postponement of marriage among a peasantry determined to eschew its pre-famine practice of recklessly sub-dividing land holdings to accommodate married sons and daughters."

Before the famine, with the Catholic population at over six million, the Church did not have enough priests to keep up with the population explosion. In 1840, there were only 2,150 priests to minister to 6,500,000 Catholics on the island. By 1900, however, there were about 3,700 priests for 3,300,000 Catholics after the catastrophic decline in population due to the famine. In addition, both the Church and its people were never the same after the famine. One man had a profound influence on that.

The old Celtic church, far less judgmental, rigid, or top-down, was about to be swept away by an oncoming tide.

CHAPTER 21

He Who Must Be Obeyed

An all-powerful cleric, Cardinal Paul Cullen, twenty years a Vatican insider and head of the Irish college in Rome, was appointed as Archbishop of Armagh and subsequently as a cardinal in the Dublin archdiocese.

He arrived into a stricken and broken land and molded it into his and Rome's preferred vision, a bastion of orthodoxy, Rome-centered politically powerful, narrow and conservative, and obsessed with denying sexuality.

His vision of the Catholic Church has been adhered to almost down to the present day. His near-thirty-year reign is matched only in influence by his twentieth-century successor, Archbishop John McQuaid, who lasted longer.

As Charles Morris, the leading American Church historian, has noted:

[T]he extent to which the modern Irish Church—which, because of the extraordinary influence of Irish clergy in this country, is in many respects the American Church as well— was the invention of a small group of strong-willed Victorian clerics, led by Dublin's Cardinal Paul Cullen. Pre-Cullen, Irish Catholicism was "one of the most ragtag national churches in Europe; post-Cullen, it was one of the most unified, rigorous, enthusiastic and militant branches of Catholicism in the world.[78]

Its vision saw the Church leaders as potentates infallible in their beliefs and authority. They who must be obeyed.

As Morris writes:

At the same time, it was one of the most hierarchical and clericalist, with priests and bishops who were invested with nearly-unchallengeable authority, and who became accustomed to extraordinary deference from civil authorities. And on sexual matters, it was a far more puritanical Catholicism than, say, the Mediterranean or Latin American varieties, or for that matter than the Gaelic Catholicism it had superseded.[79]

To combat the Celtic church and its rituals, most of which were joyful celebrations dating back to pagan times, Cullen introduced a "devotional revolution." Historian David Miller pointed out that new devotional exercises such as the rosary, perpetual adoration, vespers, devotion to the Sacred Heart, and retreats, and the use of such devotional aids as scapulars, missals, and holy pictures, were introduced.

There is no question prior to Cullen and Jansenism that the peasant Irish, especially in rural areas, were a ribald lot. Historian Morris described eighteenth-century Ireland:

The Irish village enforced powerful sanctions against premarital sex and illegitimacy, even compared with other European peasant cultures, and the chastity of Irish maidens was the wonder, or frustration, of travelers. But at the same time, rural Ireland was a highly sexual society, with sexual tensions resolved by very early marriages. Nudity or semi nudity were not uncommon, and visitors were surprised to see Irish men and women bathing within sight of one another.

Gaelic songs and folk dances were notoriously bawdy, while games at the weeklong wakes, like "Mock Marriage," were full of sly double entendres. Cross-road dancing—nightlong outdoor gatherings of several villages for sexually charged dancing, raucous drinking, and usually a rousing fight—was the despair of reforming clergy. The legendary prudery of Irish Catholicism, once again, is a post-Cullen phenomenon.[80]

Jansenism, an extreme form of doctrine about man's unworthiness as a result of original sin, was propagated by generations of priests at Cullen's behest. Saint Augustine's theories on the purity of the mind and disgust of the body became the deeply ingrained ethos of Irish Catholicism.

The consequences of the famine for the old Celtic ways were recognized by, among others, Sir William Wilde (father of Oscar Wilde). In 1849, he wrote:

The old forms and customs, too, are becoming obliterated; the festivals are unobserved, and the rustic festivities neglected or forgotten; the bowling, the cakes and the prinkums (the peasants' balls and routes), do not often take place. . . . The faction-fights, the hurlings, and the mains of cocks that used to be fought at Shrovetide and Easter, these twenty years, and the mummers and May-boys left off when we were a gossoon no bigger than a pitcher. It was only, however, within those three years that . . . [they] ceased.[81]

Rural Ireland's version of Saturnalia was not uncommon, as many shocked, uptight protestant clergy found.

Here is the account of a Protestant clergyman, around 1815, on a holy well near Malin Head in Donegal:

The patron days of the place are, Saint John's eve, [the Church's version of Midsummer Eve] and the assumption of the Virgin, [which may have been a substitution for Lughnas] and they are celebrated there by the most disgusting drunkenness and debauchery, under pretence of paying adoration to saint Moriallagh, the patron of the well. This saint is not acknowledged in the calendar; and the clergy of the Church of Rome have, very properly, forbidden the offensive orgies by which he is worshipped: it is, however, to be regretted, that his votaries have not attended to the salutary advice of their pastors on this subject.[82]

One of the most ribald poems that would have done justice to any of Rabelais's is "*Cuirt an Mhean Oiche,*" or the "Midnight Court," written as *gaeilge* (in the Irish language) by the Clare schoolteacher aptly named Brian Merriman. It was first published in 1850, forty-five years after his death.

This was a one-thousand-word celebration of women's sexuality amid their complaints about too many men waiting to marry until they are too old or just as useless to women as if they joined the priesthood. Part of the final session is the female judge Aoibhean accepting the young women's complaint and passing judgment on the useless men.

The English translation reads thus:

He who reaches twenty-one without a mate
Shall be dragged off by the hair of his head
And tied to a tree there among the dead
His coat to be taken and he be made to strip
And the daylights beaten out of him with a whip.
Two: Those of the men who are old and sick
Who shamelessly failed to use their prick
And wasted the best years of their youth
Without giving pleasure however minute
With women willing, they could have had a spree
But hung round like Mad Sweeney in the tree
The design of their torture to you I entrust,
You women of dashed and disappointed lust;

Use female ingenuity to plan the details
Of a hell of fire and a rack of nails
Put your heads together and stay the course
I'll give you the power to put it in force
You are free to punish the old men at will
In their case, I don't care if you torture or kill.

The original Irish version was never banned, but when Cork writer Frank O'Connor published an English version in 1945, it was immediately banned.

The famine sounded the end of the good times and the wild Irish ways. A deep sepulchral gloom lay over Ireland, its fields like stirred-up battlefields with every acre dug up in search of any food for solace. Guilt lay heavy with the battered survivors as to how they had offended their God and brought such a monstrous calamity down on them.

Into this space swooped the Church, no longer Celtic and contemplative as in the monks' time of saints and scholars, but arrogant and sure that the evil done had to be repaired.

Soon the orthodoxy was a narrow guilt-ridden authoritarian doctrine that became the fundamental Catholic doctrine for Ireland, and some would say the US, for the next 175 years.

The original author was Dutch-born Cornelius Jansen who died in 1638, but his doctrine of salvation through punishment took hold, especially in France. Because Ireland had no seminaries until 1800, the major influence came from priests who were educated at Irish colleges throughout Europe where Jansenism doctrine often reigned.

They brought the doctrine back to Ireland and found in Cardinal Cullen a willing partner to help hammer home the doctrine of original sin caused by sexual depravity and the need to cleanse the body and mind of all impious thoughts and acts.

Jansenism was Catholic Calvinism, and the Irish, stunned by the Famine and their heavy load of guilt for somehow causing it, embraced their Jansenist priests.

The Jesuits strongly opposed its doctrines, as did two popes, but it became the dogma of the Irish church.

Its insistence on human depravity associated with the body ensured that a culture of shame and shaming would take hold. Women's sexuality was an extreme threat, which is why the virginity of Mary and Marian devotion were so central. Irish Catholic Jansenism, with its superior attitude and all-knowing demeanor, contained the seeds of its own destruction because of the need to defend the institution at all cost and to demonize and dismiss any critique, rather than allow dialogue.

In the aftermath of the famine, it became all-powerful, with Cardinal Cullen and local priests also taking over many of its political functions. The creation of the Catholic Tenant League, overseen by priests, fought for rent relief. The local bishop often functioned as a political boss anointing candidates who agreed with the tenets of the Church. Cullen had no time for physical force advocates, either. In 1867, when the Irish Fenian Movement organized a rebellion against the British, he enlisted the support of Pope Pius IX, who personally excommunicated all members, both in America and Ireland.

Cullen despised the Fenians and revolutionary groups generally. He had a willing acolyte in the Bishop of Kerry, John Moriarty, who stated that the Fenian leaders were "criminals, swindlers and God's heaviest curse." He also declared, "When we look down into the fathomless depth of this infamy of the heads of the Fenian conspiracy, we must acknowledge that eternity is not long enough, nor hell hot enough to punish such miscreants."[83]

However, their biggest intervention by far came when O'Connell's true successor, Charles Stewart Parnell, a Protestant from Wicklow, was on the verge of achieving Home Rule for Ireland. Parnell had been "scandalously" living with Kitty O'Shea, a married woman of ten years with three children by her, before her estranged first husband, egged on by the British, divorced her. Cullen had departed the Earth by then, but when it came to a choice of Home Rule or Rome Rule, the Romans always won out. Sex outside marriage, shacking up with a divorcée, what was Ireland's desire for Home Rule but a puny issue compared to the sex-addled behavior of a Protestant.

On November 30, 1890, when O'Shea's husband divorced her, Thomas W. Croke, the Archbishop of Cashel, sent a telegram calling for Parnell to stand down.

"In God's name let him retire quietly and with good grace from the leadership." On the same day, twenty-six priests in Cork called on Parnell to step down, and the Bishop of Cork, Thomas Alphonsus O'Callaghan, stated, "In consequence of recent proceedings, I have lost all confidence in him."

As historian T. Ryle Dwyer pointed out, four Irish Catholic archbishops—Michael Logue of Armagh, William Walsh of Dublin, Thomas Croke of Cashel, and John McEvilly of Tuam—condemned Parnell as unfit to lead the IPP.

"We cannot regard Mr. Parnell in any other light than as a man convicted of one of the greatest offences known to religion and society," proclaimed the archbishops. Their views were formally endorsed by nineteen bishops.[84]

So successful was the takedown of Parnell, who was not even a Catholic, that a former Parnellite MP, Patrick O'Brien, remarked the priests had "done more to defeat Home Rule than all the bluster and drumming of the Ulster Orangemen."

As the twentieth century dawned, the Church seemed omnipotent. It was not a merciful church, but one consumed by pain and punishment, especially when it came to sexual miscreants.

In James Joyce's *Portrait of the Artist*, disputes about Parnell erupt during the Dedalus family's Christmas dinner.

Joyce was fascinated by Parnell, and his short story "Ivy Day in the Committee Room" is all about the legacy of the Home Rule leader.

Mr. Hynes delivers a maudlin poem about Parnell and how the Church brought him down:

Shame on the coward, caitiff hands
That smote their Lord or with a kiss

Betrayed him to the rabble-rout
Of fawning priests—no friends of his.

The Fenians and Parnell had been vanquished, after they dared to cross swords not just with the British, but with the clergy, too. But as a new century dawned, a new and more dangerous foe to the established order would appear—the men and women of Easter 1916.

CHAPTER 22

The Rising and the Church

Dublin, Easter Monday 1916, 11:00 a.m.: Around 1,250 members of the Irish Volunteers and Irish Citizen Army, including two hundred women from *Cumann na mBan* (translates as the Women's Association), assembled across Dublin.

About 150 rebels, under James Connolly and Patrick Pearse, two signatories to the Proclamation of the Irish Republic, marched up Dublin's main thoroughfare, O'Connell Street, as far as the Imperial Hotel. Connolly gave a sudden command to wheel left and charge the General Post Office. The Easter Rising had begun, and nothing would ever be the same again after eight hundred years of continuous British rule.

Patrick Pearse, a thirty-seven-year-old schoolteacher and writer, as president of the new Republic, stepped outside the GPO and read the historic proclamation that begins with the iconic "Irishmen and Irishwomen." For the first time in any revolutionary proclamation up to that point in history, women were included.

A small crowd gathered, some cheered, some were hostile but silent. This rising was not popular at first, as many families had members fighting in the Great War and this tumult looked like treachery. Stephen McKenna, an eyewitness, noted about Pearse,

"For once his magnetism had left him; the response was chilling; a few thin, perfunctory cheers, no direct hostility just then, but no enthusiasm whatever."

Within the first hour of the rebellion, rebels stormed and occupied several of the capital city's most important political and economic buildings: Jacob's factory, the Four Courts, Stephen's Green, the South Dublin Union (now St. James's Hospital), Jameson Distillery, the Mendicity Institute, Boland's Mills and Bakery, plus 25 Northumberland Road and Clanwilliam House.

The British poured in reinforcements, and after six days with Dublin burning and in ruins, the Rising was over, but in the words of Yeats, "All changed, changed utterly."

The Vatican blundered badly with its first statement, as historian Oliver J. Rafferty S. J. of Boston College noted:

> The Secretary of State at the Vatican, Cardinal Pietro Gasparri, sent a telegram on 30 April to the Archbishop of Armagh, Cardinal Michael Logue, asking the Irish hierarchy to cooperate with the authorities in reestablishing law and order and not to inhibit the task of the government in subduing the rebels. . . . The first telegram was leaked to the . . . British and Irish newspapers. In some Irish Catholic circles, it generated hostility and resentment.[85]

Seven bishops bowed to the instruction from Rome and rushed to condemn the rising. The Bishop of Ross said it was a "senseless, meaningless debauchery of blood." The Bishop of Ardagh called it a "mad and sinful adventure." The Bishop of Kerry declared the leaders "evil-minded men." The Bishop of Kildare stated it was "a mad insurrection."

However, the majority waited to see which way the wind was blowing, and as the executions commenced, the public and hierarchy's mood switched. They realized they had badly misread the mood of the country and misunderstood the intense wave of nationalism that was sparked by the Rising. Bishop O'Dwyer of Limerick, previously anti-Republican, was dismayed by the mass executions and did a volte-face.

After the Easter Rising, General John Maxwell, the effective ruler of Ireland after martial law was declared, continued to order executions, despite desperate pleas for mercy from families and some clergy. He wrote to Bishop O'Dwyer on May 6, demanding that "he restrain two priests in his diocese," whom the general regarded as a "dangerous menace." He accused them of involvement in subversive activities and threatened to arrest them. The *Irish Times* reported that in his letter of reply (which he had published), the bishop defended his priests and rejected Maxwell's appeal for help "in the furtherance of your work as a military dictator of Ireland. Even if action of that kind was not outside my province, the events of the past few weeks would make it impossible for me to have any part in proceedings which I regard as wantonly cruel and oppressive."[86]

O'Dwyer became an overnight hero. It could have been too little too late, but the hierarchy was fortunate with the sequence of events that happened.

How did the Church miss the shifting paradigm? Arrogance at the very top, the belief that the citizenry was docile and would never go against the Church teaching that violent revolution was wrong. After all, the Fenians had been excommunicated for defying this rule, and it was thought that this new generation would never risk such a punishment.

Nobody thought that this era would subsequently be called "the Celtic Revival," because Irish language revivalists like Douglas Hyde (later to become Ireland's first president) and great literary figures like the poet Yeats and the playwright J. M. Synge joined revolutionaries like Pearse and Connolly in transforming culture and beliefs. They were further strengthened by a new and powerful force, the newly minted Irish Diaspora.

Back in 1892, Irish nationalist and Australian politician Sir Charles Gavan Dufy wrote presciently that the younger generation of Irish were "beginning" to reassert and examine their Celtic roots:

> A group of young men, among the most generous and disin-terested in our annals, are busy digging up the buried relics of our history, to enlighten the present by a knowledge of the past, setting up on their pedestals anew the overthrown statues of Irish worthies, assailing wrongs which under long impunity had become unquestioned and even venerable, and warming as with strong wine the heart of the people, by songs of valour and hope; and happily not standing isolated in their pious work, but encouraged and sustained by just such an army of students and sympathizers as I see here to-day.[87]

He was part of a new phenomenon the Church was dimly aware of—the newly formed Irish Diaspora. The famine, mass deporta-tions, and postfamine migrants had meant that the Irish footprint had now spread across the globe. The Diaspora members' outlook was militant and radical (not surprisingly, given their origins in the wake of the famine or the British attempt at genocide as many con-sidered it). They embraced the rising, and many were wary of the hierarchy for their excommunications of Fenians, even those living in the US, and the too-cozy arrangement that existed between the Church and the British overlords.

In New York, leaders like John Devoy, an old Fenian warrior, controlled vast funds and loyalty and constantly plotted the next revolution. He was a powerful presence in Ireland though exiled in America. Like many of the 1916 leaders, he was also no admirer of the Catholic hierarchy—in 1865 he had been denounced from the pulpit of Our Lady and St. David's Catholic Church in Naas, County Kildare.

There were many who wound the clock for the Easter 1916 Ris-ing, but the man who made it strike was Kildare native Devoy. Like many of the 1916 women and men, he was not cowed by Mother

Church. This was the big worry and fear for the clerics. What if their writ stopped running?

There was not a single Irish event of resistance to British rule that Devoy was not aware of throughout his long life (he lived to age eighty-six).

He was a chief funder of the Easter Rising, and one of the first people informed by the Irish Republican Brotherhood of the proposed date of the 1916 Uprising. In his biography *Irish Rebel* by author Terry Golway, Devoy vividly recalled meeting an emissary from Ireland in a New York restaurant and realizing with mounting excitement as he deciphered the coded message that the Rising was to go ahead. His was a very important voice, likely the person who inspired the words in the Easter proclamation that acknowledged "our exiled children in America."

Devoy's issues with the Church were reflected by many in the Rising. The challenge to the Church was considerable. The Irish Parliamentary Party, partly nationalist post-Parnell, was lockstep with the Church. Its leader, John Redmond, had urged the Irish to fight for the British in the First World War, "urging young Irish to join up and 'account yourselves as men, not only in Ireland itself, but wherever the firing line extends.'" The hierarchy likewise urged young men to fight for Catholic Belgium.

The leaders of the Easter Rising were a different breed. As Devoy, several had felt the backlash of the Church and had little affection for the hierarchy. Of the leaders of the 1916 revolution, James Connolly, commander of the Irish Citizen Army and a leading figure in the labor movement as well, was the fiercest critic of the Catholic hierarchy and a dangerous opponent to them. He summarized his views in a pamphlet titled "Revolution and the Church":

In all the examples covered by this brief and very incomplete retrospective glance into history the instincts of the reformers and revolutionists have been right, the political theories of the Vatican and the clergy unquestionably wrong. The verdict of history as unquestionably endorses the former as it condemns the latter. And intelligent Catholics everywhere accept that verdict. Insofar as true religion has triumphed in the hearts of men it has triumphed in spite of, not because of, the political activities of the priesthood. That political activity in the past, like the clerical opposition to Socialism at present, was and is an attempt to serve God and Mammon—an attempt to combine the service of Him who in His Humbleness rode upon an ass, with the service of those who rode roughshod over the hearts and souls and hopes of suffering humanity.[88]

Thomas Clarke, the oldest man to sign the proclamation and the guiding light behind the Irish Republican Brotherhood, the largest unit in the Rising, died without Catholic church rites after he ejected a priest from his death cell for asking him to apologize for the Rising.

Another one of the seven leaders of the Rising had strong views on the Church, even though earlier he had seriously contemplated entering a seminary. Thomas MacDonagh, a schoolteacher, was far too radical for the church's liking.

Historian Shane Kenna noted: "MacDonagh was involved in several political crusades including labour politics, women's suffrage, and cultural nationalism. In 1908, he was hired as deputy principal in Patrick Pearse's revolutionary educational project 'Scoil Éanna.'"[89]

Pearse, the leader of the Rising, was a religious nationalist who cast much of the struggle in a quasi-religious context. However, his social thinking was radical and was becoming even more so under Connolly's influence. The bishops would have been wary of him, too.

Indeed, all seven men who signed the proclamation were far more radical in social outlook. They were heavily influenced by freethinkers of the French and American revolutions as well as by the flaming rhetoric of Wolfe Tone, which had upset the Church back in 1798.

The seed for the 1916 rising was sown in 1913 at a Tone commemoration at which Pearse spoke and stated bluntly, "We pledge ourselves to follow in the steps of Tone, never to rest either by day or night until his work be accomplished, deeming it the proudest of all privileges to fight for freedom, to fight not in despondency but in great joy hoping for the victory in our day."[90]

Most of the sixteen leaders executed after the Rising shared suspicions about the role of the hierarchy. One young man, Michael Collins, too junior in the ranks to be executed, would some time later advocate killing an anti-Republican bishop and wrote a scathing paper about the hierarchy, suggesting maybe they should be "exterminated."

Collins, once a fierce opponent of the Church, was outraged by its decree of excommunications and condemnations of Republicans. However, once he commenced his love affair with the devout Kitty Kiernan, his tenor changed completely, and he ended up a daily Mass-goer and communicant.

One wonders if he had survived the Irish Civil War, would he have been as much a supplicant to the Church as his great rival Eamon de Valera became?

American-born, Eamon de Valera was an orthodox knee-bending, ring-kissing, devout Mass-goer, and hierarchy supporter. He was the person who stood out as the highest level leader not executed after the rising was over, most likely spared from execution by his American birth.

It is tempting to wonder what kind of Ireland it would have become if Connolly had been spared. There were sixteen potential leaders shot before de Valera. Gerry Adams, the modern-day leader who revived Sinn Féin, thinks it would all have turned out differently. In an interview with the author he stated:

> . . . [A] very important point is when the British came in and actually executed the 1916 leaders. It wasn't just a knee-jerk sort of imperial reaction. It was quite ruthless and it removed— and I think it was quite deliberate—the main thinkers and writers of the period.
>
> It removed the republican cohort, the revolutionary leadership that had succeeded, against all the odds, in organizing the rising and in making the Proclamation.

. . . This particular group of men and women who actually pushed the issue and the 16 that were killed were the real leaders.[91]

Maire Comerford of *Cumann na mBan,* the women's revolutionary group, has written that it was little wonder that there was a counterrevolution because—and she was talking about de Valera—those who ended up coming into power weren't of the same caliber in leadership ability as demonstrated by the heroic men of the 1916 Rising, who subsequently signed the proclamation.

Adams stated:

I stand in amazement of them. They were just enormous. I heard James Connolly described them as the golden generation, you know, and they really were. They were just so idealistic and brave.

Well, Connolly and Pearse stand out but the two states that evolved in Ireland (Northern Ireland and the Republic of Ireland) had very different ideals from those of the 1916 leaders because of the counter-revolution.

There were two very mean-spirited, really nasty little conservative states set up. When you think of all the authors that were banned . . . it had become a very intolerant country.

No wonder so many people left . . .

So for me, that was the counter-revolution personified in that type of state. Understandably, the focus was on the Orange State, but what was happening in the south was absolutely horrific too. If you read . . . the Peadar O'Donnells and the Seán Ó Faoláins and the Frank O'Connors you get some sense of what was really going on, and then we didn't even know about the Magdalenes, etc. [It could have been different] after 1916, but the leaders like Connolly and Pearse were gone.[92]

It was now de Valera Ireland, but the man who once expressed the wish he had been a cardinal rather than a politician was certain the politics and policies of an independent Ireland would be approved by the men in cassocks. More, they would help write the most restrictive laws in the Western World as it concerned women, sex, and family issues.

CHAPTER 23

The Unholy Alliance, de Valera
and McQuaid

"... A land whose countryside would be bright with cozy
homesteads, whose fields and villages would be joyous with
the sounds of industry, with the romping of sturdy children."
Part of de Valera's vision for Ireland

The man who would dominate Irish life for over a half century
was not even Irish.

Eamon de Valera was the son of Kate Coll, an Irish immigrant
who moved to New York in 1879, and Juan Vivion de Valera, a
Cuban/Spanish exile—or was he?

All his life, de Valera was haunted by the mystery of his father
and of his real identity. His vulnerability on this issue made him an
easy target for derogatory names such as the "Irish Dago."

There is little question that his status, as perhaps the offspring
of an unmarried mother, worried him and may well have created his
overwhelming desire to cement his leadership in the Irish state by
embracing the one institution that could grant him immediate legiti-
macy, Mother Church.

The official story as told by de Valera's mother seems sure and
certain. Catherine (Kate) Coll emigrated from Limerick to the United

States in 1879. She met a handsome Spaniard, Vivion de Valera, a former sculptor turned music teacher after an eye injury curtailed his sculpting ability. They were married in 1881, and the following year their son, Edward, was born.

Kate stated that Vivion, because of ill health, traveled west, where he died in Denver, Colorado. Kate was then forced to work full-time and sent her son back to Limerick to be raised by his grandmother.

Except, as respected de Valera biographer David McCullough notes, "To believe Kate Coll's story is to believe that no record survives of her marriage; that all written evidence of her husband's existence was lost; and that no credible Spanish connection would emerge after her son became world famous . . ."[93]

The counterstory is that Kate Coll became pregnant by an employer or a married man and in the hysterical atmosphere of the times concocted the handsome Latino. The truth, it seems, will never be known.

Not that de Valera did not try seeking it out. Throughout his life he tried innumerable times and ways to identify the father he never knew. He even instructed the Irish ambassador to Spain to seek out de Valera's relatives.

But no proof would ever be found, as McCullough notes, despite the efforts of de Valera and his legion of helpers, and of future biographers and genealogists. "Neither would any proof be found of the supposed death of his father, Vivion de Valera, in Denver, or perhaps New Mexico, unless it was in Minnesota."

Then McCullough delivers the final sting. "Indeed, there is little evidence that Vivion ever existed."

Historian and author Tim Pat Coogan, who wrote *Long Fellow, Long Shadow*, a major biography of de Valera, admits to not knowing if de Valera's father actually existed. "In de Valera's childhood, and afterwards," Coogan wrote, "illegitimacy carried a stigma in Roman Catholic Ireland. If he knew or suspected that there was a doubt about his parents' marriage the knowledge must have been a burden to him."[94]

Kate Coll remarried and had two children by her husband Charles Wheelwright, one of whom, a young girl, died. Yet she never sent for her firstborn. Coogan wonders why Kate did not try to repatriate young Edward, as he was known as then back to the USA:

> But no call came to Bruree [where young Edward was living with his family in County Limerick] to bring the two half-brothers under the one roof. As to why this should have been we can only speculate. . . . Yet a typically Irish mother would have gone through fire and water to have her son with her. It is possible that her husband did not want someone else's child.[95]

Rejected by his mother, unable to locate his father, de Valera must have felt the deepest insecurities as a result.

A modern psychiatrist might argue that the absence of a father and the spurning by a mother may have driven him totally into the open arms of a surrogate mother—in this case Mother Church—and explained his lifelong awe of those stern church leaders. Craving certainty, he certainly got it from longtime friend Archbishop John McQuade.

A math teacher in Blackrock College and avowed Republican, de Valera was not in the top tier of the Easter 1916 leadership.

His bravery in 1916 was unquestioned at the time, and his status reached hero pitch after the execution of the leaders, and he was the highest ranking leader left.

He became leader of the provisional Irish government, toured America for a year, where massive crowds awaited him, filling Fenway Park in Boston, for instance, to overflow and forcing thousands to stand outside. Everywhere he went women and men reached out to just touch him—he was the embodiment of the dream for every Irish emigrant who longed for a free Ireland.

However, he split Irish America, as he would later split Ireland, into a civil war by insisting on his primacy in all things. This led to a fierce division with Irish America's most prominent leader, the old Fenian, John Devoy, who became so disenchanted with de Valera that he sided with Michael Collins in the ensuing civil war.

The legend of de Valera carried far and wide. He was next in line to be executed in 1916, but on May 12 the order had come down for the killings to be stopped, right after Connolly had died, strapped to a chair. What if Connolly had survived and de Valera died? Ireland would have turned out to be a completely different country.

But de Valera survived. This, then, was the man who would rule Ireland as both a prime minister and a president for the best part of forty years.

Why was his vision so narrow, his religious beliefs so conservative, his fealty to the Church so strong? So devout was he that one of his biographers, Thomas O'Neill, stated, "[H]is absorption in the life and teaching of Jesus might qualify him as an amateur Christologist."[96]

After all, he had mixed with revolutionaries and was fully aware of the fact he was excommunicated (though he denied this) after resorting to violence during the Irish Civil War.

He was educated by Holy Ghost Fathers at Blackrock College in Dublin, an order known for its world outlook, a powerful missionary message, and concern for the poor. Liberal Catholicism perhaps should have been his lot, but he went to the other extreme.

His most famous speech, "On Language and the Irish Nation," gives powerful clues to his beliefs.

Leading historian Diarmaid Ferriter called it "the most famous broadcast by any Irish politician of the twentieth century."

He made it on RTÉ Radio, the national broadcasting station, on St. Patrick's Day 1943. It is a call for isolationism in a time of war, a call for a return to simple country values, and a call for devotion to the Church. The speech has not aged well: the cry for a return to the Arcadian days of devout happy maidens and happy and hardworking men, a country where the people were "living the life that God desires that men should live," seems quaint and pietistic today, but de Valera was deadly serious.

It is useful to remember that he was speaking to a country where 500,000 out of 3.5 million would be forced to take the emigrant boat or plane between 1945 and 1960. Yet he persisted with his mythological vision of a perfect land:

> The ideal Ireland that we would have, the Ireland that we dreamed of, would be the home of a person who valued material wealth only as a basis for right living, of a person who, satisfied with frugal comfort, devoted their leisure to the things of the spirit—a land whose countryside would be bright with cozy homesteads, whose fields and villages would be joyous with the sounds of industry, with the romping of sturdy children, the contest of athletic youths and the laughter of happy maidens, whose firesides would be forums for the wisdom of serene old age. The home, in short, of a person living the life that God desires that men should live. With the tidings that make such an Ireland possible, St. Patrick came to our ancestors fifteen hundred years ago promising happiness here no less than happiness hereafter.
>
> It was the pursuit of such an Ireland that later made our country worthy to be called the island of saints and scholars. It was the idea of such an Ireland—happy, vigorous, spiritual— that fired the imagination of our poets; that made successive generations of patriotic men give their lives to win religious and political liberty; and that will urge men in our own and future generations to die, if need be, so that these liberties may be preserved.[97]

An island of Saints and Scholars where maidens danced and all were "happy, vigorous, spiritual" suited the Catholic Church overlords, too, worried as they were by this abrupt 1916 revolution just when they had the Irish political leadership literally on their knees.

Now it was time for the counterrevolution, and they moved fast.

They ensured they were on the right horse with 10 percent of the members to the first Sinn Féin convention after the Rising in April

1917 being priests. Father Michael Flanagan was elected vice president of the party; two other men of the cloth were on the executive.

The death of Thomas Ashe on hunger strike in September 1917 accentuated the church's influence. He had fought in 1916, had been released but reoffended with fiery speeches prophesying a new war. Jailed for a year, he went on hunger strike.

Ashe's death after forcible feeding infuriated the Irish nation. As *Century Ireland* put it:

> Diminished by hunger strike, the damage to his system was exacerbated by forcible feeding by the prison authorities.
>
> The deceased had been taken by cab to the hospital at 3 p.m. yesterday and was attended to by the hospital staff, alongside the Sisters of Mercy and the hospital chaplain, Rev. T. J. Murray, who administered the last rites to Ashe before his death.[98]

One hundred and fifty priests walked solemnly behind the hearse. "Bishop Fogarty of Killaloe front and centre and Dublin Archbishop Dr. William Walsh following on in a motor car."

They even countenanced the volley over his grave and Michael Collins defiantly proclaiming, "Nothing additional remains to be said. That volley which we have just heard is the only speech which it is proper to make above the grave of a dead Fenian."

It was a far cry just a year later from the guns of 1916 and the condemnation. The ecclesiastical tide had turned, not a moment too soon. If it had been Connolly who survived, Ireland would have become a much different place.

Without the leavening effect of the first-line leaders of the Rising and their nonsectarian outlook, the Church was taking power, and a conservative, sectarian Catholic outlook quickly dominated.

Consider the comment by the *Catholic Bulletin* newspaper to the granting of the Nobel Prize in Literature in 1924 to that well-known Protestant poet, William Butler Yeats: "It is common knowledge that the line of recipients of the Nobel Prize shows that a reputation for paganism in thought and word is a very considerable advantage in the sordid annual race for money . . ."

Such was the prevailing zeitgeist among the ruling Catholic class. With de Valera at the helm, the political and clerical became melded as almost one eventually embodied in the persons of de Valera and Dublin's all-powerful Archbishop John Charles McQuaid, a worthy successor to Cardinal Cullen.

Even when de Valera and his party were out of power, the new incumbents such as John A. Costello were every bit as obsequious as Dev, if not more so, and were ring-kissing and knee-bending and going rigid with excitement every time a prince of the church appeared.

De Valera survived the fraught years after 1916. As leader of the provisional government, he refuted the treaty of 1921, negotiated by Michael Collins and others, thus creating a civil war that ended in tragedy for Collins, who was killed at the age of thirty-one, and eventual triumph for de Valera. When his new party, Fianna Fáil, took power in 1932 he finally had the control he craved.

Tall, austere, and mostly grim-faced, de Valera lacked many social skills, which has led to speculation in the modern era that he had Asperger's Syndrome. He was an unlikely leader.

But he would, in all, be *taoiseach* of Ireland for a total of twenty-one years and president of Ireland for fourteen before finally retiring, as the oldest head of state in the world, at age ninety.

He would make Ireland in his own image. This was a man who once claimed all he had to do to know what the people of Ireland wanted was to "look into his own heart."

But there was one more man whose influence would arguably be as indelible as de Valera's: the Archbishop of Dublin, John Charles McQuaid. His biographer, John Cooney, subtitled his work "Ruler of Catholic Ireland."

It was McQuaid's church that the forces of modern Ireland encountered when the ultimate collision happened. For over thirty years, from his archbishop's palace in Drumcondra, he would dominate every political discussion and fiercely resent any modernist trend. Everywhere he looked, it seemed he found genuflection and acquiescence.

Unlike in "Song for Simeon," where the Temple elder, Simeon, sought God's blessing to depart in peace, once all had changed, McQuaid preferred to stand and fight fearlessly unto his death for the retention of the old ways and for influencing the new zeitgeist.

CHAPTER 24

Devil Women—How the Church Wrote the Irish Constitution

Article 45.4.2 The State shall endeavour to ensure that the inadequate strength of women and the tender age of children shall not be abused, and that women or children shall not be forced by economic necessity to enter avocations unsuited to their sex, age or strength.

From the 1937 Irish Constitution

In the Name of the Most Holy Trinity and of our Lord Jesus Christ, the Universal King, we the people of Ireland, so full of gratitude to God, who has so mercifully preserved us from innumerable dangers in the past; hereby, as a united independent Christian Nation, establish this Sovereign Society of the Irish people . . . and so in accordance with the principles laid down, we freely and deliberately to the glory of God and honour of Ireland, sanction this constitution and decree and enact as follows.[99]

The preamble to the Irish Constitution reads like a devout prayer, and in many ways it was one. It was the vision of two men joined together in Orthodox Catholicity of the most severe form. It trapped

Ireland in a hidebound, narrow, and insular vision, which only finally let go in the new century.

There was no doubt that the affairs of the new state were utterly entwined with the Church.

The *Irish Catholic* newspaper had reason to celebrate: "Irish Catholics will rejoice in the fact that the fundamental principles of the new Bunreacht [Constitution] are in close accord with Catholic social teaching."

As for McQuaid, biographer John Cooney wrote, "McQuaid could proclaim 'Catholic Ireland, I am Catholic Ireland,' the Irish equivalent of Louis XIV's alleged statement *L'état, c'est moi.*"

McQuaid, son of a doctor and a mother who died of post-childbirth complications when he was only a week old, was born in Cavan in 1895. He did not find out until his teen years that his stepmother was not his biological mother. In that respect, he and de Valera had unusual relationships with their mothers. De Valera never knew his own mother either, as she sent him back to Ireland from the US as a child.

McQuaid was a fire-and-brimstone cleric who was convinced Satan was at work in Ireland. He said so in his first major homily on Passion Sunday 1932 at a Mass in his home county of Cavan:

"It is in truth a favourite device of Satan to weaken reverence for the authority of those who command in the name of Christ . . ."

The local *Anglo Celt* newspaper reported him as saying, "The conspiracy was led by Jews, Freemasons, Protestants, and Communists."

Jews were especially malevolent: "A Jew, as a Jew, is utterly opposed to Jesus Christ and all the Church means."

Jews, he noted, "deliberately revolted against Our Divine Lord. Have chosen Satan as their head."

Next up for banishment were the revolutionaries. The French Revolution was excoriated.

The Declaration of the Rights of Man (written by French revolutionaries with the aid of Thomas Jefferson) is the political creed that explains the modern world. Modern parliaments and laws are instruments for putting its theories into effect.

He continued: "Modern newspapers and cinemas are the direct outcome of 'this virulent document' which 'after the manner of Satan sets man in the place of God.'"

His Cavan homily was his tabula rasa, his empty vessel into which he poured his lifelong convictions.

He was grossly anti-Semitic: "Modern movies such as 'Ben Hur,' 'King of Kings,' and 'The Ten Commandments' were showcases to show Christ as only a great man (not divine) and a member of the Jewish race!"

He addressed how to stem the flow of modern malevolence flooding the world. He excoriated anything that did not put God at the center.

He demanded the Church control the schools in the independent Ireland. They successfully did so by ensuring that the local parish priest had the final word in all issues for primary schools and that every school in Ireland would have religious instruction at the center of the school day.

McQuaid also set out to refute the modern notion that the Church should stay out of politics: "Priests must interfere in politics by Divine Right, to guide the faithful."

That final point became McQuaid's modus operandi. For fifty years, in lockstep with de Valera, McQuaid would control politics in daily life in Ireland to an incredible degree. It was an astounding reality that plunged Ireland into the realm of a reactionary state, determined to root itself in the premodernist past, rather than look to the future.

A clause in the 1937 Constitution, which recognized the special position of the Catholic Church in Ireland, was McQuaid's shining achievement. He was president of Blackrock College by then, three years away from being named Archbishop of Dublin, and he forged a resolute friendship with the former Blackrock pupil and teacher Eamon de Valera.

Apart from ensuring a special position for his Church in the Constitution, the controversial article in the constitution on "women knowing their place at home" was also McQuaid's, according to biographer John Cooney. He had long detested women's efforts to gain power and felt women were weak and belonged at home.

The framers even set up a clause covering the "inadequate strength of women." For de Valera, who showed little concern for women's issues, and the outright misogynistic McQuaid, it was a triumphant moment.

The relevant language ran:

Article 41.2.1: In particular, the State recognises that by her life within the home, woman gives to the State a support without which the common good cannot be achieved.

Article 41.2.2: The State shall, therefore, endeavour to ensure that mothers shall not be obliged by economic necessity to engage in labour to the neglect of their duties in the home. Article 45.4.1: The State pledges itself to safeguard with especial care the economic interests of the weaker sections of the community, and, where necessary, to contribute to the support of the infirm, the widow, the orphan, and the aged.

Article 45.4.2: The State shall endeavour to ensure that the inadequate strength of women and the tender age of children shall not be abused, and that women or children shall not be forced by economic necessity to enter avocations unsuited to their sex, age or strength

Article 42: 5 states the state shall endeavor to ensure that mothers shall not be obliged to engage in labor to the neglect of their duties within the home.

The Constitution, at McQuaid's urging, included a ban on divorce and abortion and would have included a ban on contraception devices, if a law had not already been passed in 1935.

McQuaid liked to intimidate women and soon made clear the depths he was prepared to sink to.

His ability to snuff out any mention or thoughts of their sexuality reached their zenith (or nadir) in March 1944 when the Irish bishops came together at Easter to express disapproval of the sale of Tampax, a new sanitary item. McQuaid personally brought his complaints to the deputy minister for health and laid bare his fears that young girls could be stimulated by inserting the tampons, which would lead them to display their passions. Incredible to say, but the government agreed, and Tampax was banned for a time!

McQuaid had also led a crusade, before he became archbishop, as president of Blackrock College to deny young women the right to play sports.

In 1934, the *Irish Times* received a scalding letter titled "Women in Athletics Protest from Blackrock College."

McQuaid was appalled, yes appalled, that women's athletics was taking place at the same time and places as men's events.

McQuaid quoted the pope to back up his assertion that the Christian modesty of girls must be in a special way safeguarded, for it is "surely unbecoming that they should flaunt and display themselves before the eyes of all." Most newspapers endorsed his view.

De Valera and the other Irish party leaders were completely on board with McQuaid's ferocious Jansenism. There was not a single voice in opposition, it seemed.

But there was a flickering ember when a brave, undaunted group of women remembered the role women played in the Easter 1916 Rising, when *Cumann na mBan*, essentially the female IRA, fought bravely, side by side, with their fellow revolutionaries. They cast their minds back to the Easter Proclamation, unique in the world, because it included women as equals in its very opening line with its call to "Irish men and Irish women."

But the erosion of women's rights since the Rising was clear. In 1927, they were essentially thrown off juries. In 1935, importation of any form of contraception was banned.

In an article titled "A 'Sinister and Retrogressive' Proposal: Irish Women's Opposition to the 1937 Draft Constitution," author Maria Luddy wrote that a brave statement from *Cumann na mBan* noted that:

> This constitution does not satisfy the aspirations of the Irish people. If the Proclamation of Easter Week meant anything, it meant the end of capitalism and the introduction of equal rights and opportunities for all. Our charter of freedom was laid down in the proclamation of Easter week. Only the establishment of a republic in accordance with that proclamation will satisfy our aspirations.[100]

Luddy writes that on publication of the draft constitution, many women were deeply concerned:

> On 1 July the Joint Committee of Women's Societies and Social Workers wrote to de Valera concerning "women's constitutional and economic condition." . . .
> It took the Joint Committee from July 1936 to 29 January 1937 to arrange a delegation to meet with de Valera on this issue of representation. A departmental memo, summing up his response to the meeting, noted:
> The president pointed out that any inadequacy in the representation of women in the legislature and public bodies was attributable to the state of public opinion. It would be difficult to do anything to give women a larger role in public life, while public opinion remains as it is.[101]

A prominent female columnist in the *Irish Independent*, Gertrude Gaffney, made quite a fuss when she attacked de Valera's constitution draft:

The "death knell of the working woman is sounded in this new constitution," she wrote. "Mr. de Valera has always been a reactionary where women are concerned. He dislikes and distrusts us as a sex and his aim ever since he came into office has been to put us into what he considers is our place and keep us there." Under the proposed constitution, Gaffney argued, "we are no longer citizens entitled to enjoy equal rights under a democratic constitution, but laws are to be enacted which will take into consideration our 'differences of capacity, physical and moral, and of social function."[102]

De Valera made clear he could care less. McQuaid warned him about "Godless feminism" and assured him women were being treated exactly as they should be. In addition, de Valera's very own newspaper, *the Irish Press*, slammed Gaffney and told her to stick to her knitting and let her betters decide.

De Valera cared far more for Church approval. In the ultimate act of submission, he even had the Irish Constitution draft sent to the pope himself for his benediction. De Valera did so, in part because McQuaid was pushing too strongly, even in de Valera's opinion, on forcing a Catholic, not an Irish, Constitution through.

His thinking was if the pope agreed with the draft, then McQuaid would, too. The pope refused to give his imprimatur, but the Constitution was voted through with McQuaid's fingerprints all over it. On December 29, 1937, the Constitution was approved. Ireland was officially the most ferociously Catholic state on Earth.

CHAPTER 25

Archbishop of Dublin, Ruler of Ireland

Under the 1937 Constitution, church would become state and state would become church. When the position of Archbishop of Dublin became vacant, de Valera mounted a full-scale lobbying effort aimed at the pope to ensure McQuaid, an outside contender at the beginning, would get the job.

The position had always gone to a diocesan cleric, and Dublin natives were preferred.

Undaunted, de Valera believed that because McQuaid had been so helpful to him in passing the constitution, he could butt into church affairs and try everything to get McQuaid selected.

There was even a code name for McQuaid, "Father X," which was used in the Vatican back channels, where most of the ground was laid.

Pope Pius XII was importuned by his own secretary of state, Cardinal Giovanni Montini, later Pope Paul VI, to appoint McQuaid.

On November 11, 1940, McQuaid was officially named archbishop. Now he was the most powerful cleric of the modern era in Ireland, the most influential since Cardinal Cullen, who had Romanized the Celtic church back in the postfamine era.

He moved quickly to consolidate that power.

John Charles McQuaid had spies everywhere. From his palace in Drumcondra, in North Dublin, he oversaw an FBI scale operation featuring clerical underlings and lay followers prepared to snoop everywhere looking for sin, sloth, and sex. They found plenty of it.

Historian Donal Ó Drisceoil notes:

> McQuaid's "eyes and ears"—his web of often well-placed informants and flunkies across all sectors of society—were on constant alert for any hints of deviance from, or challenges to, the conservative norms, defined and underpinned by church and state. Any green shoot of liberalism or free thought, especially Protestant ideals, alien notions such as women's rights, and of course the ultimate bogeyman—communism [were shot down, Ó Drisceoil says]. Members of the Catholic Action Network also performed less "ideological" functions, such as providing the archbishop with inside information from government departments and Dublin corporation's planning offices, which allowed him to buy land on behalf of the diocese for the building of schools and churches in the capital's expanding suburbs at bargain prices—a scam that would gladden the hearts of the heathen developers of a later era . . .[103]

Not surprisingly, McQuaid deeply admired J. Edgar Hoover, head of the FBI, the ultimate spy master.

Hoover heard, from a friendly monsignor, of McQuaid's admiration and forwarded him a copy of his book *Masters of Deceit*, thanking him for his "highly valued support."

Both men had much in common, a certainty of their righteousness, closeted and unknowable personal lives, obsessions with sex, and a determination to root out enemies, real and imagined.

Meanwhile, McQuaid's "volunteers" were discovering iniquity everywhere. As biographer John Cooney relates, one of the most popular programs on national radio was "Hospitals' Requests," where relatives phoned in requests for hospital-bound patients.

On one occasion, a Cole Porter number, "Always True to You," was played. "But I'm always true to you/Darling in my fashion./I'm always true to you in my way."

When the program was over, the presenter, Tom Cox, was summoned to the director general's office.

"His Grace is concerned at the morality of that song," the astonished Cox was told. "[It] advocates the proposition that a limited form of fidelity is somewhat acceptable."

Needless to say, the song was struck from the playlist.

McQuaid also used a magnifying glass to spot what he called a "visible mons veneris" shape in a drawing for a ladies' underwear advertisement in the *Irish Press*.

McQuaid also got to see every banned book and photo magazine and all in the spirit of educating himself. His trolls visited every bookshop and newsstand seeking filth. When a risqué play somehow got staged, he organized his Stormtroopers from the Catholic Action Organization to loudly and sometimes violently picket it.

On one occasion, Orson Welles fell victim to another McQuaid front group called "Catholic Cinema and Theater Patron's Association." He was due to play in a Gaiety Theater production.

Calling Welles a communist, they marched carrying placards outside the venue. One read "Dublin Rejects Communist Front Star." Police had to intervene when a riot threatened and cries of "Burn It Down" were heard.

On another occasion, Danny Kaye, the American actor and comedian, was also picketed for having communist sympathies. J. Edgar would have been proud of his archbishop friend. Opponents of McQuaid called it "Holy Hooliganism," but McQuaid didn't care. Playwright Arthur Miller was another big name who was accused of communist sympathies when he showed up in Dublin with a film version of *Death of a Salesman*.

In 1957, *The Rose Tattoo*, a Tennessee Williams play, was banned because of mention of a contraceptive.

A stage production of *Ulysses* was banned, as well as a Sean O'Casey play, *The Drums of Father Ned*, after which Samuel

Beckett withdrew his work in protest, but to no avail. Brian Moore, a Northern Ireland writer, found his brilliant novel *The Lonely Passion of Judith Hearne* on the banned list.

J. P. Donleavy's *The Gingerman*, starring Richard Harris, also came a cropper when one of McQuaid's underlings showed up at the Gaiety Theater and closed it down.

Likewise, any legislation with any possible impact on the Church, such as questions of adoption and education, was dutifully sent to McQuaid to adjudge.

He also took some parliamentary bills that had nothing to do with him such as extending pub opening hours to be within his remit. However, this was one of the few occasions he was defeated when extended hours were allowed. That defeat was at the hands of a 1916 fighter, Sean Lemass, a rising star, who was less afraid to challenge "the God" in Drumcondra.

In the main, however, it was one-way traffic. One of the few dissidents in the country, author Seán Ó Faoileán, wrote that it was a case of: "A parliament in Maynooth [home of the HQ of the Catholic Church] and a Parliament in Dublin [called the *Dáil*]. The *Dáil* proposes, Maynoth disposes."

McQuaid disliked Protestants and sought to avoid any ecumenical occasions. He spent his lifetime trying to ban Catholics from attending Protestant Trinity College, Dublin, and, incredibly, succeeded until the 1960s. He summarized his views in his 1947 Easter Pastoral letter, as reported in the *Irish Times*:

> Parents, the Archbishop says, had a most serious duty to secure a fully Catholic upbringing for their children in all that concerned the instruction of their minds, the training of their wills to virtue, their bodily welfare, and the preparation of their life as citizens. In the education of Catholics, every branch of human training was subject to the guidance of the Church, and those schools alone which the Church approved were capable of providing a fully Catholic education. Therefore, the Church forbade parents to send a child

to any non-Catholic school, whether primary or secondary, or continuation or university.

"Deliberately to disobey this law is a mortal sin," added His Grace, "and they who persist in disobedience are unworthy to receive the Sacraments."[104]

Apart from Protestants, McQuaid—as could be expected—reserved his greatest hatred for unmarried mothers and their children.

Victorian prudery and savage Irish indignation, that a girl could get pregnant outside marriage, was at the root of the most shameful banishings of all.

Thousands were condemned to a life of slavery in the infamous Magdalene laundries, treated like dirt and forced in many cases to give up their children for illegal adoption. Many were sexually abused by the very priests who committed them to life in these prisons.

As for young boys and girls who were born out of wedlock, many were sent to industrial schools and orphanages, and hundreds, perhaps thousands, were sexually abused by priests, nuns, and Christian brothers.

While McQuaid and others gladly did the dirty deed of condemning hundreds of thousands of Irish women to penal servitude for life for having sex outside marriage, the leaders of the civic state knew exactly what was happening and did nothing.

Indeed, they acquiesced in tearing babies away and profiting from their sale.

The traffic of unmarried mothers' babies to America began around 1947, according to McQuaid biographer John Cooney. By 1951, three hundred babies a year were being sold to wealthy Americans, mostly from Magdalene homes.

The women who bore those babies were described by the Catholic Welfare Bureau as "fallen women" and "grave sinners."

McQuaid insisted that the prospective American parents sign an affidavit, pledging to raise the child Catholic. Given that assurance, he allowed the trafficking to go on and demanded the state have no role in the church's business. Thousands of mothers would lose their children in the most brutal manner possible, having them snatched away by nuns and sold to the highest bidder.

It was the terrible conditions and harsh realities of these homes that stoked Father Flanagan of Boys Town on his Irish visit. He was horrified with what he saw. As earlier noted, he called Ireland's penal institutions "a disgrace to the nation" and later said, "I do not believe that a child can be reformed by lock and key and bars, or that fear can ever develop a child's character."[105]

McQuaid dismissed Flanagan, as did the Irish government. If he had been listened to, the Armageddon might never have happened to the Church, but McQuaid was listening only to himself. Like de Valera, he felt all that he needed to do was look in his own heart.

As for his own sexual proclivities, his reputation as a severe but saintly and chaste celibate would be put under severe scrutiny when the Murphy Report on sexual abuse by clergy in the Dublin Archdiocese was published in 2009. His reputation would also suffer irreparable damage when the extent of his cover-up for pedophile priests would become clear.

John Cooney, his biographer, writing before the Church inquiries, notes that Mrs. Mercy Simms, wife of the Protestant Archbishop George Simms, who worked with McQuaid on opening a school for travelers' children, spoke out on him. She stated McQuaid had an unhealthy attraction toward boys and very frequently sought to have them around him.

Cooney writes in his standout biography *John Charles McQuaid, Ruler of All Ireland* that he lectured to boys all the time about masturbation. McQuaid asked his confessor, Father Fenelly, to allow him to pursue "dirty books," sent to him by his acolytes in order to judge them. He must have enjoyed reading them as he re-upped his order many times.

But at the zenith of his power in the late 1950s, McQuaid suddenly began to feel the ground shift beneath him. Ironically, it was a new pope, John XXIII, who would ultimately hasten his downfall.

CHAPTER 26:

The Doctor Who Defied McQuaid

"Doctors trained in [Protestant] institutions in which we have no confidence may be appointed as medical officers . . . and may give gynecological care not in accordance with Catholic principles."

Archbishop John Charles McQuaid

It was the clash that in retrospect changed Ireland. The first major revolt against the hegemony of McQuaid's church. McQuaid appeared to have won the battle, but in the long term it worked out much worse for him.

An idealistic young doctor, Noël Browne, who had entered politics successfully was named minister for health at age thirty-one. In that position he quickly aimed a reputation for reform and efforts to staunch the then-deadly disease of tuberculosis, which had decimated his own family.

He also pointed out that birth fatalities in poorer areas were ten times higher than among the wealthy, and he set about creating a statewide free healthcare system for all. As a beginning, he proposed making healthcare free for mothers and children up to the age of sixteen.

He proposed the bill in July 1950 but found strong opposition from the powerful medical lobby who called it socialist medicine and, more important, McQuaid—who feared the state was about to take over the Catholic hospital system, which ran almost every major medical institution.

In July 1950, McQuaid summoned Browne to his palace and read him the riot act. He especially objected to the fact that doctors trained in non-Catholic hospitals would be ministering to Catholics.

As usual, the gynecological aspect exercised him most. In the name of all that was sacred, Protestants examining Catholic women's breasts and vaginas would just not do: "Doctors trained in institutions in which we have no confidence may be appointed as medical officers . . . and may give gynecological care not in accordance with Catholic principles."[106]

He was especially worried about Catholic girls in regard to "sex relations, chastity, and marriage." Non-Catholic doctors should never have the right to tell Catholic girls how they should behave in regard to this sphere of conduct at once so delicate and sacred.

McQuaid and his doctors feared birth control and abortion would somehow be allowed under the proposed new system.

Browne refused to back down, but the Church had rigged the game when it came to the government. The *Taoiseach* John Costello was even more of a McQuaid lap dog than de Valera ever was. On the day he presented the bill to his colleagues in Cabinet, Browne realized every single Cabinet member had the McQuaid statement in front of them. It was signed by all the Irish bishops but was clearly McQuaid's work.

He knew he had lost all political support and was forced to resign.

It was not a complete victory for McQuaid, however. Browne had been very popular, and his Mother and Child initiative was well received among ordinary voters who had to pay for every doctor visit.

Journalist Seán Mac Réamoinn told John Cooney ordinary people spoken to on the street in Galway at the time were downright angry at McQuaid and his involvement in the issue.

McQuaid would win the short-term battle, but his subsequent exposure as the puppeteer behind the opposition to the scheme played badly for him.

But the utter capitulation of the Cabinet meant, too, that McQuaid had every subsequent government over a barrel. If the Cabinet had stood with Browne, the arrogance of the Church might have been tempered and have forced them to handle the future crises with more humility. But like a certain American president, McQuaid would never get tired of winning.

Amazingly, it took an unlikely organization to stand up to McQuaid. The Irish soccer federation had set up a friendly game with Yugoslavia for Dublin in October 1955. McQuaid set out to stop it because of the persecution of a Yugoslavian cardinal, but he had picked the wrong opponent in Joe Wickham, secretary of the Football Association of Ireland. Wickham ignored all of McQuaid's threats, and the game went on with a massive twenty-one thousand people showing up. For his bravery, Wickham got denounced from the altar as Judas in his home church and, even worse, "a Protestant Catholic" by Father O'Sullivan.

Like the mother and child scheme, however, McQuaid came badly out of the dispute in the long run. Browne never ceased his criticisms of McQuaid and was widely seen as a heroic figure on the left.

Browne would only finally leave public life in 1990, when he failed to win the Labour Party nomination for Irish president. He was shortlisted in the Top Ten of the greatest Irish people ever in 2010. It was his narrative of a fiercely dominant church controlling craven politicians and ending the Mother and Child scheme for sectarian reasons that prevailed.

McQuaid would not live to see the triumph of Browne's version of the history of the Mother and Child scheme, but he was very much around when the next Exocet was launched at him.

CHAPTER 27

New Pope, New Era

Archbishop McQuaid told his diocesans on returning from Vatican II, "No change will worry the tranquility of your Christian lives."

The council, which took place between 1962 and 1965, reached a very different conclusion, as McQuaid would only realize subsequently.

After the election of John XXIII as pope, McQuaid had every reason to believe he would signal no change. McQuaid knew Angelo Roncalli since he had befriended him during a stay in Paris in 1950, when Roncalli was the Papal Nuncio.

However, once Pope John embarked on a revolutionary course calling the Vatican Council and insisting the Church come down from its high altar and become more with the people in a pastoral role, McQuaid was utterly surprised. In addition, Roncalli wanted closer links with other religions.

For a dictatorial figure like McQuaid, the man of the people initiative was abhorrent, and linking up ecumenically with the Protestant faith was against every fiber of his being.

He kept to the old ways as profound change swept through the Church and word went back to Rome that McQuaid was becoming a dissident.

The death of Pope John and the emergence of Pope Paul VI seemed a welcome development for McQuaid.

After all, he had been friendly with Cardinal Giovanni Montini and had spearheaded a massive fundraising campaign for the Vatican with Montini when a communist government in Italy loomed in 1948. Montini had also been a figure who carried much weight when recommending McQuaid, as Archbishop of Dublin in 1940.

McQuaid was initially delighted when Paul VI backed away from many of his predecessors' reforms. His 1968 *Humanae Vitae* encyclical banning contraceptive use by Catholics was heartily cheered by McQuaid, who immediately called a major press conference to hail the glad news.

He had recently learned to his horror that doctors in Dublin's first family planning clinic were ordering the contraceptive pill for medical reasons.

But the rush of euphoria soon faded. McQuaid was seventy-five, in fine health, and expecting to be allowed to carry on for a number of more years despite having reached retirement age.

However, he had reckoned without a powerful Vatican figure, Archbishop Giovanni Benelli, with whom McQuaid had clashed many years before when Benelli was in the Papal Nunciature office in Dublin. Their dispute about the relatively obscure meaning of some aspects of canon law had turned bitter.

All those years later, Benelli, now at the right hand of the pope and a moderate who disliked McQuaid's hardline, had his revenge.

On December 27, 1971, a pale and nervous Papal Nuncio Gaetano Alibrandi arrived at the archbishop's residence in Killiney to impart the news: McQuaid was out. Worse, his successor was an archenemy, the liberal university professor Reverend Dermot Ryan.

Stunned and mortified and in failing health, McQuaid lasted less than a year. He died on April 7, 1972, after thirty-one years as Archbishop of Dublin. No one had influenced the role of the Catholic Church in Ireland more.

In 2011, a postscript to McQuaid's thirty-one-year period as archbishop came to light when the *New York Times* reported the following:

> DUBLIN — The former Archbishop of Dublin, John Charles McQuaid, widely regarded as the most powerful Catholic prelate in modern Irish history, stands accused of serial child sexual abuse, The Irish Times newspaper said Thursday.
>
> Two specific complaints and a separate unspecified "concern" against an unidentified cleric were reported to the Murphy Commission, a state-sponsored investigation into the handling of clerical sexual abuse of children in the Dublin archdiocese. The newspaper reported that Archbishop McQuaid, who retired in 1972 and died a year later, was the unidentified cleric. . . . The newspaper is adamant that the allegations of abuse contained within it refer to the archbishop. One allegation is regarding abuse of a 12-year-old boy in 1961.
>
> . . . Patsy McGarry, the newspaper's religious affairs correspondent, said in an interview. The archdiocese "found a letter 'which showed that there was an awareness among a number of people in the archdiocese that there had been a concern expressed about this cleric in 1999,' the report states. The 'cleric' is Archbishop McQuaid."
>
> The main body of the Murphy report was highly critical of Archbishop McQuaid's attitude toward abuse, accusing him of showing "no concern for the welfare of children."
>
> [It concluded that] "[t]he Dublin Archdiocese's preoccupations in dealing with cases of child sexual abuse, at least until the mid-1990s, were the maintenance of secrecy, the avoidance of scandal, the protection of the reputation of the Church, and the preservation of its assets. . . . All other considerations, including the welfare of children and justice for victims, were subordinated to these priorities. The archdiocese did not implement its own canon law rules and did its best to avoid any application of the law of the State."[107]

The 720-page report said that it has "no doubt that clerical child sexual abuse was covered up" from January 1975 to May 2004:

> As charted by the Murphy commission, the complaints of parents and their children were ignored and other families placed in immediate danger as prelates from John Charles McQuaid onwards suppressed scandals and took refuge in canon law to protect offenders at the expense of children. Complainants alleged that most uninvolved priests turned a blind eye to their allegations. (*Irish Times,* November 27, 2009)

McQuaid took the heaviest criticism for the Father Edmondus case, one that was presented to him way back in 1960. It was a particularly horrible perversion, sexually assaulting sick children.

Edmondus abused young children between the ages of eight and eleven at Our Lady's Hospital for Sick Children in Crumlin in the late 1950s and early 1960s.

He had subsequently been caught posing little girls in sexual positions and taking photographs of them. McQuaid accepted the ludicrous explanation that Edmondus had grown up with all brothers (which was untrue) and was just curious about female genitalia. Nothing was done, and Edmonds went on to rape and abuse young girls for decades. One of the young girls he raped was Maria Collins, who became a powerful voice in later years for priest victims, chosen to meet the pope to explain the Irish situation to him.

Many of the worst offenders in the sexual abuse scandals were priests placed in their role by McQuaid. The Murphy Report named the figure as high as seventeen.

There is no doubt that the festering evil of child sex abuse first became prominent during McQuaid's rule in Dublin. Always lightning quick to attack an agency or person who transgressed his laughable concept of decency such as women using tampons, McQuaid showed another side altogether when it came to abuse by his fellow priests and the accusations against them. He quite simply turned a blind eye. In light of what has come out since about his own behavior, that should not be surprising.

He was in many ways the totem pole around whom the reactionary church in Ireland for thirty years gathered. When that pole began to topple, the extraordinary close Semper Fidelis relationship between Irish people and their church began to fall, too.

The times they were changing all over Ireland just as McQuaid was forced into retirement.

After decades in a soundproof chamber, women's voices were about to be heard, and forcefully. In addition, a massive change brought about by European Union membership and a daring new multinational industry policy would prove truly transformative.

CHAPTER 28

The Winds of Change Blow

"It was like a light switch was turned on, it felt like we went from black and white to color."
Officer Paul Mangan describing JFK's impact on Ireland

The winds of change fluttered gently at first in Ireland but increased in velocity to gale force in the generation after McQuaid.

On February 26, 1971, with McQuaid still in his pomp, Trinity Senator and human rights lawyer Mary Robinson informed the Senate, the Irish Upper House, she had drafted a bill to legalize contraception. She appeared on Ireland's top TV program, *The Late Late Show*, to announce her intentions to the flabbergasted nation. She said she was acting on behalf of a new group known as the Women's Liberation Movement.

On March 30, 1971, it was Robinson who again informed the nation she was introducing a bill to repeal the "Censorship of Publications" Acts from 1929, 1935, and 1946.

McQuaid gathered himself for one last blast of moral fury. If such legislation were passed, he boomed, it would remain "a curse upon our country." He said that access to contraceptives would prove an occasion of sin because of the enticement of bodily satisfaction.

The following week, the unthinkable happened. The Women's Liberation Movement mounted a picket outside McQuaid's residence with a banner accusing him of being a dictator. Robinson's bills were quickly voted down, but the die was cast, and the sea change had begun. Ideas long thought impossible were suddenly being discussed in the mainstream.

A far less docile press was also starting to ask questions that no amount of pomp and circumstance on the part of Irish leaders could dismiss, and McQuaid was gone.

Before he went, however, there was another event that surely left him apoplectic. On Saturday, May 22, 1971, forty-seven members of the Irish Women's Liberation Movement Group boarded a train in Dublin for Belfast in order to buy contraceptives in Northern Ireland and bring them back to the Republic where they were banned.

Contraception in the Republic of Ireland had been banned since 1935. In Northern Ireland, a doctor's prescription was needed to buy the pill. Instead, the women bought condoms and spermicide jelly and bought aspirins, trusting that Irish customs officers would never know the difference between aspirin and the pill.

Their adventure was followed by TV crews from Ireland, England, Japan, and the United States. The bishops might have suffered a collective coronary at the sight of the women arriving back in Dublin victoriously. This action was a landmark moment in the Irish Women's Movement.

In truth, just a few short years later, Ireland was mirroring what had occurred in Britain during the Swinging '60s. The music revolution created by the Beatles and the Rolling Stones, the widespread use of recreational drugs, the popularity of the miniskirt and Mary Quant inspired revealing fashion items, the cool Britannia of Carnaby Street and Abbey Road, and the birth of the hippies and "peace and love" slogans were a stunning contrast to the 1950s.

Ireland, meanwhile, showed some signs of waking from its silent reverie. Near riots, led by young girls, occurred in Dublin that day in November 1963 when the Beatles played two concerts.

That same year, John F. Kennedy's visit had an enormous impact on the Irish psyche with the realization that despite famine and poverty, one of their own had become the most important person in the world. "It was like a light switch was turned on; it felt like we went from black and white to color." These were the words of Sergeant Paul Mangan, an Irish police bodyguard for Kennedy, who saw the vast cheering crowds that greeted him as harbingers of a new era.

This great awakening was spreading. Alongside the Beatles and modern pop, a great revival began in Irish traditional music, which had long languished because of its association with the poor and backward.

A lone creator and musical genius, Seán Ó Riada, who would die prematurely at age forty from alcoholism, kicked off the Irish traditional music revival by scoring a hit film called *Mise Eire* (I am Ireland) with the traditional music of old. Its huge success brought him a prime-time slot on Irish radio called "Our Musical Heritage."

Between 1960 and 1969, Ó Riada formed "*Ceoltoiri Chualann*," a miniorchestra comprised of the finest traditional musicians in the country. Paddy Moloney, later of The Chieftains, was among its members.

A newly empowered young generation embraced the Ó Riada vision, and traditional music enjoyed a spectacular revival.

The same was true of Irish folk songs, as what was old suddenly became "new" and popular. Ballads, long shunned, came back into prominence. The people were beginning to reclaim a culture only dimly visible in the Celtic Twilight.

The ballad revival was mostly due to the Clancy Brothers and Tommy Makem, an Aran sweater–attired group, who sang the old songs with gusto and unquenchable spirit. They became famous in America after appearing on *The Ed Sullivan Show*, and they were notable too for the number of rebel songs they sang, such as "Four Green Fields," written by Tommy Makem, "Boolavogue," and "The Croppy Boy." These songs revived a genre that had seemingly been lost.

A more authentic Irish identity was struggling to emerge, associating broad culture with joy and insight and not with suspicion and censorship.

This was true in theater, too.

At the National Theater, "the Abbey," much of the fare into the 1950s was a version of the comely maidens dancing at the cross-roads, beloved by de Valera.

"A favorite amusement of the Dublin literati has been to reveal the poverty of the company's repertoire," wrote critic Robert Hogan.

Playwright Paul Vincent Carroll wrote, "The Abbey has degenerated, more or less, into an undistinguished repertory of sorts."

The era of John Millington Synge and Sean O' Casey, both revolutionary figures in their own right, was well and truly over, and there was a complete loss of nerve, in the censorship era, to try anything different.

An odd exception to the rule was gay couple Micheál Mac Liammóir and Hilton Edwards, who respectively acted in and produced modern plays in the "Gate Theater."

They were the only gay couple recognized as such in Ireland at the time.

The academic Éibhear Walshe of University College Cork notes, "Mac Liammóir and his partner Edwards survived, and even flourished, as Ireland's only visible gay couple." Walshe goes on to say, "When Mac Liammóir died in 1978, the President of Ireland and the *Taoiseach* attended his funeral."[108] Even Archbishop McQuaid was tolerant of them. Somehow, they glided past all the resentment and homophobia, which were rampant at the time.

In the 1960s, with de Valera coming to the end of his active career as a politician, the "Abbey Theater" and other theaters finally opened their doors to new and exciting drama. Amazing and talented playwrights such as Brendan Behan (who made his debut in the 1950s), Brian Friel, John B. Keane, and Hugh Leonard made their way through those doors.

Music, culture, and the arts gradually began to breathe, and even in politics a stunning sea change was about to occur. It was as if a magic potion had been quaffed and change were ushered in.

In politics, it came down to a truly visionary politician who flared across the political landscape before fading far too prematurely. His name was Donogh O'Malley.

CHAPTER 29

A Visionary Speaks

"We will be measured by what we did for the children of our time."

Irish Education Minister Donogh O'Malley
announcing free education

On September 10, 1966, in the Royal Marine Hotel, Dun Laoghaire close to Dublin Bay, a powerful ripple that became a wave swept away Ireland's antiquated educational system, unchanged since independence.

Donogh O'Malley, forty-five, tall, and strikingly good-looking, the recently minted minister of education in a Fianna Fáil government, took to the podium at a National Union of Journalists Conference.

His speech would reverberate for the ages, a foundational ideal without which modern Ireland could never have developed as it did.

O'Malley made his speech unknown to his Cabinet colleagues, who would certainly have been in an uproar over it. Debate rages to this day whether *Taoiseach* Sean Lemass knew it was coming.

The educational system was a farce. At the time, about a third of children who finished primary school were dropping out of education at age fourteen, unable to pay the fees for secondary school. Though these fees were not large, the reality of large families was that there were often too many kids, all of whom could not be paid for. Young girls in large families usually lost out.

O'Malley pointed out that the departure rate meant that one-third of the workforce could only perform unskilled labor. Ireland, he stated, was utterly unprepared for the world of tomorrow.

At fifteen years of age, less than 50 percent were still in full-time education, while by sixteen, only 36 percent were still at school. A tiny number from the elite could afford university education. As a result, Ireland had the equivalent of a Third World workforce.

O'Malley, an engineer and architect by profession, drew up the blueprint to change education forever. He did so single-handedly, aware that his political career was on the line. O'Malley sensationally called the education system "a dark stain on the national conscience."

His proposal was crystal clear. Education would be free to everyone in primary and secondary level, and bus transportation would be provided so that every child would be able to go to school even from remote rural areas. "We will be measured by what we did for the children of our time," he stated.

University education would also be heavily subsidized. If the student reached a certain achievement level in high school, the college/university would also be virtually free. He closed with a prophetic statement that Ireland needs to be "catering for the new age of technology." Those words could be his epitaph.

His Cabinet colleagues were aghast at the boldness of the move, but it proved so popular with the public, they were unable to go back. O'Malley went on to launch several technological institutes, thus creating the groundwork for the Celtic Tiger to emerge. He looked destined for the top in Irish politics but suffered a heart attack and died in 1968. Thirty thousand people came to his funeral. The Free Education Act was implemented in 1967; the leap in educational standards followed immediately.

Put plainly, it enabled the country to join the European Economic Community in 1973 and the Celtic Tiger to happen a generation later.

Much the same began to happen on the economic side with another visionary leading the way.

Kenneth Whitaker, a career civil servant, despaired of what was happening. He inveigled the then-*Taoiseach* Sean Lemass to try a daring new strategy to lure industrial companies into Ireland.

The truth was that Ireland was a dirt-poor country almost totally reliant on Britain for exports. It had only an agricultural economy because most industries were destroyed by tariffs and by a population that voted with its feet.

An economic war with Britain, over the refusal to turn over land rents owed to British landlords, had ended predictably with Ireland much worse off. Tariffs went up on both sides, but with Ireland 90 percent dependent on Britain for its exports, the country was seriously hurt.

In the aftermath, between 1945 and 1960, 500,000 emigrated from a country of only 3.5 million; de Valera's Ireland was stripped clean of its greatest asset, its young people. Plays like Brian Friel's *Philadelphia Here I Come* and John B. Keane's *Many Young Men of Twenty Say Goodbye* attest to this fact.

When the First Programme of Economic Expansion (1958) was introduced, its author, Secretary of Finance Dr. Ken Whitaker, noted: "The common talk amongst parents in the towns, as in rural Ireland, is of their children having to emigrate as soon as their education is complete in order to be sure of a reasonable livelihood."[109]

He was determined to change that thinking

The old ways held sway. Large families on small farms meant everyone but the firstborn son had to leave to find work elsewhere. That meant countless numbers had no option but to take the boat to Holyhead in Wales and then a train to London or a boat or plane ride to America.

In an interview with me, the *New York Times* columnist Maureen Dowd remembers the stories her father told her about having to leave. Though his refers to an earlier era, the circumstances hardly changed for decades after: "My dad left Ireland for a couple of reasons. He was the second youngest of sixteen and there was no way he was going to get any of the land belonging to his father. He was also playing around with the IRA and neighbors told him that his name was on a list."[110]

Michael Dowd, from Clare, was the son of a poor farmer in a poor country, the second child in the family named Michael after the first died. He was booked on the Titanic in 1912, but his mother cried all night, and he couldn't leave her.

His older brother and his favorite sister had gone to the US, so he wrote, and they told him to come and stay with them. He went to stay with his sister in Boston before coming to stay with his brother in DC. He joined the Army, which gave him his citizenship, and he never left DC.

He grew up in beautiful countryside in Clare, but "you can't eat the scenery," as the locals said.

Many of the best and brightest like Michael left, never to return, and the Irish Diaspora, built during and after the famine, swelled to record numbers again in the '40s, '50s, and '60s.

The country was an economic wreck saved by men like O'Malley and Whitaker.

Whitaker championed free trade over the policy of protectionism, which had proved a disaster.

He found a willing ear in Sean Lemass, the *taoiseach* who had taken over from de Valera and who immediately put Ireland on a free trade path, culminating in the Anglo Irish Free Trade bill in 1965.

Whitaker also seized on a particular government agency, the Irish Development Agency, to seek out multinationals and offer them very attractive terms to come to Ireland.

It was revolutionary thinking and incredibly successful. In 2014, the *Irish Times* noted, "Today, Ireland is host to 1,033 multinational corporations. They directly employ 152,785 and account for 70 percent or €122.5bn of exports."[111]

When protectionism—which had been in place since 1932—failed, Whitaker and Lemass in turn developed the IDA as the new spearhead for international development and realized this was the only way to develop the economy.

It began as a trickle. Pfizer came to Ireland in 1969. Coca-Cola and GE were also among the first to invest, brought in by the attractive tax rates. The IDA began targeting specific areas, pharmaceuticals, technology, medical devices, financial companies.

Fueled by the European Union, the economy would go from basket case to the envy of Europe over the coming decades.

As the *Irish Times* pointed out, "What started as a trickle soon became a flood" with the arrival of "Microsoft (1985), Intel (1989), Motorola (1989), Dell (1990), HP (1995), IBM (1996), Oracle (1996), Xerox (1998), and Cisco (2007).

(Citi, 1996; Deutsche Bank, 1991; HSBC, 2000), funds and investment management (State Street, 1996), payments (MasterCard, 2009; PayPal, 2003), and more.

Google (2003), Yahoo (2003), eBay (2004), Amazon (2005), Facebook (2008), Twitter (2011), LinkedIn (2010), Electronic Arts (2010), and Zynga (2010)."

The combined impact was incredible and only possible because of the well-educated Irish workforce. It was as far from the small potatoes economy of the previous decades as was possible.

Another powerful modernizing player had also entered the arena. On January 1, 1973, Ireland became part of what was then known as the European Economic Community, later the European Union.

Joining the European community has meant a $55 billion boost for the Irish economy, much of it creating new infrastructure with modern highways, updated railway and transportation system, extra airline terminals, and new airports, as well as massive investment in medical research, agriculture, and industry.

Most important, the Irish got to share in the single market, the largest in the world with five hundred million consumers.

Membership of The European Union also forced the country to look outward for the first time. De Valera's Arcadian vision of a self-sufficient and insular country was shown up to be utterly unattainable.

But with the economic growth and new worldwide stature came dark questions about the pre-Glasnost period. Suddenly the past practices of church and state were under intense scrutiny. What were the dark forces that held Ireland back? What was all the secrecy and the high walls around Catholic institutions both mental and real all about? The truth would prove truly shocking.

CHAPTER 30

The Strange Death of Catholic Ireland

"The rape and torture of children was downplayed or 'managed'. . . . dysfunction, disconnection, and elitism, narcissism, [is] what dominates the culture of the Vatican to this day."
Irish Prime Minister Enda Kenny before he shut down the Irish Embassy at the Vatican in November 2011

The Jesuit magazine *America* reported in February 2018: "More than 90 percent of Irish Catholics reported attending Mass at least weekly in the early 1970s; recent surveys put that percentage at between 30 and 35 percent in recent years. . . . Attendance at some urban parishes is as low as 2 percent . . ."[112]

How did the collapse of the relationship between the Church and the Irish state come about? It is the story of a revolutionary sea change, wrought in the most part by a massive church effort to deny and conceal the horrific scale of church child abuse.

Even the Irish, whose compliant state in the 1940s essentially allowed the Church to write large tracts of the constitution, could no longer look away. What they saw was an evil unparalleled since the British reaction to the famine and, at its heart of darkness, a Father Brendan Smyth, a figure so destructive and malevolent that he almost brought down the Church and caused an Irish government to fall.

The Church was already feeling uneasy at the dawn of the seventies. McQuaid and his ironclad style of dictatorship was long gone. As Ireland opened up to Europe, the old certainties were slowly giving way.

The bishops still preached with all the fire and brimstone of old, but the congregation was simply not listening as much. As the early '70s dawned, a new economic reality—created by free trade, foreign investment, and European Union membership—took shape. For the first time since the Famine emigration stalled, prosperity was dawning.

In the midst of better times, the Catholic Church suddenly began to unravel at a furious pace, much to the astonishment of almost everyone. Suddenly they were out of cadence with the times, and a suppurating issue, long hidden, was about to explode.

The issue of pedophile priests burst into national and international consciousness in the late '80s and early '90s, but this time bomb was ticking, even during McQuaid's later years in Dublin in the early seventies.

One massive pedophile scandal had been spreading since the 1940s. It did more than any other single event to impact the church's standing.

Arguably, if the case of the psychopathic Father Brendan Smyth had been dealt with firmly by any one of a plethora of church authorities right up to the level of cardinals, the disintegration of the Catholic Church in Ireland would not have happened with such force.

Indeed, if you were looking for the smoking gun that initiated and caused the strange death of Catholic Ireland, you would find it about fifty miles from Dublin in Cavan, the birth county of Archbishop John Charles McQuaid.

Kilnacrott is a tiny place; it means "Church On a Hill." Ironically, it has become infamous all over the world. It was formerly the home of the Norbertine Community, an order founded in the twelfth century that closely follows St. Augustine's teaching of practicing poverty, chastity, and obedience. Augustine had an especially hard time with chastity and celibacy. The Norbertine community would, too.

In the cemetery of Kilnacrott Abbey, near the town of Bally-jamesduff, is a grave like no other, encased in concrete in case the malevolent spirit buried there might somehow escape. It is as if the devil himself were entombed. Smyth was buried here in the dead of night in 1997. The *Irish Times* reported: "Just seven Norbertine priests and a few locals gathered in the gloom, with four *gardaí* in the background, the lights from a hearse illuminating the grave as his coffin was lowered down."[113]

Buried with him was the reputation of the once all-seeing, all-dominant Catholic Church.

What would eventually come out was when it came to choosing between a diagnosed psychopath and vicious pedophile—who was one of their own—and the helpless and tortured children he abused, the Church, including the Irish cardinals, chose the psychopath.

The massive oppression that generations had been willing to suffer, from penal times right up to the famine, for their loyalty to the faith was a thing of the past. When the curtain was pulled back, the pomp and pomposity was revealed in all its ignominy.

A large group of celibate, mostly elderly, men had chosen career over conscience to cover up pedophiles over their innocent victims.

There were countless numbers of the religious orders using and abusing children in that era all across Ireland, but of all of them, Father Brendan Smyth was the ultimate prince of darkness. It is doubtful if any pedophile priest worldwide was such a ferocious predator.

Every other case pales in comparison. After all, he became so infamous that failure to act on his extradition from Northern Ireland to face charges in the Irish Republic forced the collapse of the Irish government of the day.

His Norbertine order later stopped practicing in Ireland. Three other priests of the order were also child abusers. An inquiry revealed there were so many attacks on children that the final total would never be known.

The Abbey where they once resided was set to be torn down in late 2019, but it is still open as of today.

In death, the title of "Father" has been removed from the gravestone of Smyth, leaving just a name, Brendan Smyth, definitely the most notorious priest in Irish history.

But who really was Brendan Smyth, the most infamous of child rapists?

Born in Belfast in 1927, he would destroy forever the perception of the Catholic Church in Ireland as made up of pious religious men and women, rightfully exalted above others carrying on a storied tradition going back to St. Patrick's time over 1,500 hundred years before. Who was this monster?

Psychiatrist Ian Bownes, who observed Smyth in prison in Northern Ireland, labeled him an "incurable psychopath on a scale of one to ten very close to the number ten." Bowens revealed this to an Ulster Television documentary maker, Chris Moore, the journalist who first broke the Smyth story.

An incurable psychopath in priest's clothing is a dangerous animal indeed, but when church elders, including cardinals, rushed to cover up for him and feed the beast, then it had catastrophic consequences.

He brought down an Irish government, as well as an attorney general, and he destroyed two cardinals—Cathal Daly and Sean Brady—when it became clear they had actively covered up for him.

He relentlessly abused hundreds of children in at least six different jurisdictions: Ireland, Northern Ireland, Italy, Scotland, Wales, and the USA. In America, he operated with impunity in Rhode Island, North Dakota, and Boston, always safe in the knowledge that his Irish superiors, who had sent him to America, would not reveal his dirty secret. He was just another Irish priest helping out in America.

He was the iceberg who tore a fatal hole in the reputation of the Irish church when it became public knowledge that this vicious psychopath had been given free rein time and again.

Hundreds of child abuse and rape victims, some as young as four, had their lives ruined.

How many children did Smyth actually abuse?

He told an examining doctor, "Over the years of religious life, it could be that I have sexually abused between 50 and 100 children. That number could even be doubled or perhaps even more."[114] Some experts believe it could run as high as five hundred.

Smyth took advantage of the tenor of the times, especially in the early years of his assaults. Priests in Ireland were minigods, sacred persons. A mother could ask for no greater joy than to have a son as a priest. They were transcendent. A visit to a parishioner's home was a visit by royalty.

Smyth raped and abused children many times, even when their parents were also in the house. Some of those parents refused to believe their own children when they told them of this abuse; they were so deeply embedded in the Church and so admiring of priests that the idea of illicit sex with their children was completely outside their realm of thought.

However, when the truth finally came out, they were deeply embittered when it became evident Smyth could have been stopped in his tracks before he was ever a priest.

There were grave suspicions about him even from the beginning.

He began his studies at the Norbertine Abbey in Cavan. He was vested on September 8, 1945, and professed on September 8, 1947. He studied at the Pontifical Gregorian University in Rome from 1947 to 1951, when he was ordained. He was the first Irish Norbertine to attend the prestigious school, and his star was shining bright.

A letter written by a superior in September 1949 described him as having a "brilliant mind. Studies well and understands."

But as early as the 1940s, there were red-alert warning signs.

In revelations made to the Historical Institutional Abuse (HIA) inquiry in Northern Ireland, conducted by the British government between 2014 and 2016, the truth about the Church and Smyth came tumbling out.

Joseph Aiken, counsel for the inquiry, revealed: "The Norbertine order believes that knowledge of Brendan Smyth's activities exists prior to his ordination yet he was ordained as a priest in any event. A complaint had been made about Smyth when he was a student in Rome in the 1940s. He was accused of abusing a child in the vicinity of the college."[115]

Retired judge Sir Anthony Hart, who led the HIA probe, was told that "advice from a senior cleric in Rome, not to ordain Smyth, had been ignored." That senior cleric was the abbott general of the Norbertines in Rome, who quickly realized Smyth was a dangerous man.

The reason the Abbott General was ignored was the Irish felt it would be a "shame" if the first student the Irish Norbertines sent to Rome failed.

Thus, Smyth was ordained by the Archbishop of Dublin, Archbishop John Charles McQuaid, on July 31, 1951.

It is clear that there remained significant doubts about his suitability. Shortly afterward, a senior priest who knew him sent a strong letter saying the ordination was a terrible mistake. "My letter is hard," he wrote. "I hope my fear is exaggerated."

Obviously, his fears were too modest, as it turned out. The pedophile psychopath would injure, maim, and rape for over forty years after being ordained. Many of his victims committed suicide, most had their lives ruined.

The 1951 decision to ordain him, despite flashing red lights, was a disaster and a huge missed opportunity.

The Norbertines continued to be culpable with successive superiors refusing to act on clear evidence.

For example, in 1963, the Bishop of Wrexham in Wales sent Smyth back home to Ireland because he had sexually abused an altar boy. Smyth had admitted to the allegations made by a ten-year-old boy that he had encouraged the boy "to commit indecent actions," and that in those circumstances he was being sent back to Kilnacrott in disgrace. The Irish Abbott just sent Smyth to America, to Rhode Island, where he wreaked havoc.

Yet nothing was done after he returned from there.

Even as the allegations poured in, his Irish superiors did nothing. In 1984, his last superior, Father Kevin Smith (no relation), who was fully aware of his pedophile acts because of the scale of complaints, made perhaps one of the most absurd statements in the history of police inquiries.

Abbott Smith told police, "I did not realize it was a criminal offence. If I had realized it was a criminal offence, I would have reported it. At that time, I did not know what pedophilia was."[116]

The second chance to stop Smyth in his tracks was even more shocking. In 1975, two young boys in Cavan made strong allegations of abuse while they were altar boys.

Father John Brady, who later became Cardinal Sean Brady, head of the Church in Ireland, was sent to examine the allegations. For years, Brady sought to downplay his role in the three-man panel of inquiry, claiming to be only a note-taker, but clear evidence has emerged he was far more than that, as he was the senior canon lawyer in the group.

One boy, Brendan Boland, has since gone public on his ordeal. He described being abused by Smyth and subsequently facing a barrage of hostile questions from Brady and two other inquisitors, including whether he enjoyed masturbation, the inference being that he enjoyed being abused.

Boland wrote that Brady and the other priests were immediately hostile.

"In my mind's eye they were old men in black. And if they made any effort to be nonthreatening, they failed."

He was asked to describe what Smyth had done and was then asked, "You never got to like it?" to which he replied, "No." Brendan Boland continued: "So now they had established that I masturbated, alone. Again, I felt it put the blame back on me: the blame and the shame. Because if I was masturbating, well, that was because I enjoyed it. And if I enjoyed that, well, then I must have enjoyed being assaulted by Fr Smyth. Follow the logic."[117]

The boy named several other children he knew who were abused or were in danger of being abused. Brady took their names and swore him to secrecy at the end of his testimony.

Brady told the bishop of the diocese; he believed both boys' stories but then did nothing to inform the families of the children who were in grave danger or had already been abused.

Brady subsequently rose to the position of Cardinal Archbishop of Armagh, the most important position in the Irish church. His predecessor, Cardinal Cahal Daly, was one of the bishops Brady had told of the abuse but who had also done nothing.

Both holy men then watched as Smyth was sent away, not to prison, but to Fargo, North Dakota, as a parish priest, free to abuse and use. When he returned to Kilnacrott Abbey in disgrace from Fargo in 1983, he was put in charge of the altar servers and the children's choir.

For eighteen years after Cardinal Brady had been informed in 1975 and accepted that two young boys were raped and others endangered, Smyth was allowed to continue his rampage of rape and destruction of young people.

As for Brady's predecessor, the *National Catholic Reporter* stated in 1994, "Cardinal Cahal Daly knew about Smyth and wrote letters in 1990 and 1992 to one of Smyth's victims and the victim's family, offered sympathy, admitted he knew of the priest's activities and had previously spoken to his abbot, but professed he could do 'nothing more.'"[118]

It only came to a halt when courageous Ulster Television journalist Chris Moore sat down with a distraught West Belfast family who described to him how their beloved "Father Brendan" raped all their four children in the house, sometimes when the parents were home. On several occasions, he raped the children upstairs while the parents were preparing dinner for him downstairs.

This time, Moore, a thorough and respected journalist, was not put off by the attempted cover-ups, the lies and deceits that went all the way to the top. He called it the "Vatican's Boys Club." He unraveled the entire sorry and dreadful career of Smyth and named his protectors. The story caused a sensation.

At last the authorities took action, something they should have done decades earlier. In 1991, they arrested Smyth, who, freed on bond, happily scooted across the Irish border to freedom. He even worked in two hospitals as a chaplain in Cork and Tralee.

The Northern police force, the RUC, now fully aware of his depravity, drew up a carefully considered extradition warrant, knowing the importance of the case as the coverage of the pedophile scandals took root.

There was one last, bizarre twist when the Irish Attorney General Harry Whelehan let the RUC warrant languish for seven long months. Theories ranged from some believing as a conservative Catholic Whelehan was engaging in one last effort to cover up for the church's plain bad management at the attorney general's office, where the official excuse was the warrant had been overlooked.

Either way, Smyth was ordered back north by his superiors, now keen to have the matter dealt with.

He returned and was sentenced to three years on seventeen counts of abuse against five girls and three boys, including the brave children of the Falls Road family, who had told their story to Chris Moore.

Meanwhile, in the Irish Republic, *Taoiseach* Albert Reynolds committed political suicide just six months after winning a historic IRA ceasefire in August 1994 that effectively brought peace to the North—after twenty-six years of massive violence.

Reynolds appointed Attorney General Harry Whelehan to the position of President of the High Court to the consternation of everyone, especially to his coalition partners, the Labour Party, who pointed to the mayhem caused by Whelehan's delay in following up the Smyth extradition request.

Reynolds refused to back down, and the government collapsed. This placed the new peace breakthrough in the North in real jeopardy, as Reynolds had been a key architect of it.

It was Smyth's latest foul act to impact on the political system. He served his time in the North and was then extradited south to face new charges. He was found guilty and sentenced to twelve years.

Rarely had one man done so much to destroy a hallowed institution in any society, anywhere in the world. He was a psychopath to the end. Police who escorted him to court hearings told stories of Smyth peering out of the prison van and becoming visibly excited when he would see a young girl or boy.

The Catholic Church after the scandal of Smyth and the others was unrecognizable from the time of the papal visit by John Paul II in 1979. The pope, in his famous visit in Galway, had talked about a heart of darkness, evil forces that sought to corrupt young people. He could hardly have expected these dark forces were lurking within his own church. Indeed, some were standing beside him as he gave his historic address.

Monsignor John Magee, private secretary to three popes and a powerful figure in the Vatican, had been a key figure in the pope's visit to Ireland. He was made Bishop of Cloyne in Cork in 1987.

There was a belief among many Vatican watchers that he would be back in the Roman Curia before too long. A French religious newspaper speculated he would become head of the Congregation for Divine Worship and the Discipline of the Sacrament, but this was not to be. Instead, Magee found himself embroiled in the pedophile scandals sweeping the church.

In December 2008, Magee was at the center of a cover-up for pedophiles in his own diocese, and he was forced to step aside. The subsequent inquiry lacerated him.

The Cloyne Report, published on July 13, 2011, found that Bishop Magee had falsely told authorities that he had reported all child abusers to them.

The inquiry found differently, that nine allegations out of fifteen were not passed on to the police. Magee apologized.

In an unprecedented attack on a fellow member of the clergy in the diocese, Father Michael Mernagh lashed out at his superior. He described the bishop's apology as "hollow" and told him he should no longer stay in his diocese:

Father Mernagh, an Augustinian, told Bishop Magee he should "remove himself completely from the good people of

North Cork—go back to a monastery of your order and continue to do that penance."

He stated: "What you need to do is to go out in front of the Cathedral in Cobh and there in a purple robe of penance, prostrate yourself for some time, for some days, in fasting and prayer, and be open to hear the criticism and whatever the people and priests and others would have to say."[119]

Stung into finally breaking his silence, the former Bishop John Magee said he apologized "unreservedly" to victims of child sex abuse in the dioceses of Cloyne.

In a statement, he said he would be "very willing" to meet victims and their families privately if they wished: "I also apologised to victims of abuse in this statement and I unreservedly apologise to these victims again today. I publicly apologised to victims of abuse in the Diocese, in Cobh Cathedral, on Christmas Eve 2008," the bishop said.[120]

Published in July, the report into clerical sex abuse also found that Bishop Magee misled the then-minister for children when he informed them guidelines for handling abuse accusations were being complied with: "Given my position of responsibility, I am particularly saddened when I read the accounts of the complainants describing the effects of the abuse, knowing that I contributed to their distress."[121]

The former bishop said he had met some of the victims and listened to their stories.

The people, who were so terribly abused by priests, found the courage to come forward to talk to me, or to my delegate, Msgr [Denis] O'Callaghan who was representing me, and in many cases, we failed them. I am sorry that this happened and I unreservedly apologize to all those who suffered additional hurt because of the flawed implementation of the Church procedures, for which I take full responsibility.[122]

It was too little too late, and a once-bright star in the Vatican, a keeper of papal secrets, was reduced to pleading for forgiveness for his sins. He remains a remote figure in retirement, forever tainted by the cover-up in the Cloyne diocese. For a man who soared so high, who stood at the side of three popes and expected to have a stellar career, it was a shattering end.

As to the other two stars in the firmament on that 1979 day in Galway, first Father Michael Cleary. After he died, the *Sunday World* newspaper had a banner headline revealing he had two children by his teenage housekeeper and that he had practiced exactly the opposite of what he had preached all his life.

Historian James Donnelly of the University of Wisconsin, Madison, summed up Father Cleary's hypocrisy best.

> The Catholic Church could not long survive, in Ireland or anywhere else, if its priests, who take a solemn vow of celibacy, secretly have wives or lovers and sometimes beget children, while at the same time proclaiming that such things as a celibate priesthood and the papal ban on 'artificial' contraception are absolute laws of God.
>
> The hypocrisy involved, whenever revealed, must inflict grievous wounds on the Church, not to mention the psychological harm done to the secret lovers of non-celibate Catholic priests and to any children born of their unions.[123]

Cleary and Magee did indeed inflict deep wounds, but it was Bishop Eamon Casey's admitted pedophilia that made even devout Catholics question their faith.

Casey had been seen as a man of the people, a fallen sinner who had had an affair and a child with a twenty-five-year-old American woman. Given what had been taking place with pedophile priests, his "offense" seemed normal.

Then came this stunning report in the *Irish Times* in March 2019:

Three women made allegations that they were sexually abused
as children by former Bishop of Galway the late Eamonn
Casey and two have received compensation as a result.

In one of the cases, Bishop Casey, who died in March 2017
aged 89, admitted the abuse occurred when he was serving as
a priest in the south England diocese of Arundel and Brighton
[between the nineties and 2005] . . .

Bishop Casey made this admission in the context of
another allegation of child abuse made against him by his
niece Patricia Donovan a short time beforehand in November
2005.[124]

Patricia Donovan alleged Casey had molested her from the age of
five.

It was a stunning revelation about a man whose funeral was
attended by the great and the good of Irish society, including the
president.

Casey bookended the clerical pedophile scandals in Ireland. At
the time of his appearance as the opening warm-up act for Pope
John Paul, he had a secret son, then five years old, and he was post-
humously revealed as a pedophile.

His niece, Patricia Donovan, stated the abuse had begun when
she was five years old and had continued for a decade across three
counties, Kerry, Galway, and Limerick.

In reaction to the Cloyne report—which condemned Magee and
found a series of obfuscations, cover-ups, and plain lies by Magee
and Vatican sources—Irish *Taoiseach*/Prime Minister Enda Kenny
took a very dramatic step and announced the closure of Ireland's
embassy at the Vatican.

Though the stated reason was budget cuts and not a political
one, it smacked of retaliation for the noncooperation of the Vatican
on the pedophile inquiries.

In July, Enda Kenny as *taoiseach* had slammed the Vatican and
publicly blasted what he called the "dysfunction, disconnection and

elitism, narcissism, that dominates the culture of the Vatican to this day."

Kenny was infuriated by an eleven-thousand-word missive, sent by the Vatican, that read as a justification for the cover-ups in Cloyne and elsewhere.

As John Allen, renowned Vatican correspondent for *National Catholic Reporter*, wrote:

> In September, the Vatican issued an usually detailed 11,000-word response to Kenny's criticism. Among other things, it argued that a 1997 letter from a Vatican official to the Irish bishops, warning them that mandatory reporter policies could conflict with church law, was not intended to prevent the bishops from reporting child abuse to the police. Instead, the Vatican said, the point was to make sure that abusers could not evade ecclesial punishment on a technicality.[125]

Nobody believed the Vatican statement. The Irish had run out of patience.

That was because a scandal as big as the pedophile priests had broken in 1999. Father Brendan Smyth was only three years in his grave when another scandalous story around church-run children institutions in the state came to light and exposed the plight of the Magdalene laundry women and their children.

Everything Father Flanagan of Boys Town USA had predicted during his 1946 visit about the Irish penal institutions had come true.

But the trail of tears and the evil nature of religious institutions did not end there. There were further unbelievable stories ready to emerge that would prove the last straw and ended with an Ireland transformed beyond recognition, one that closed down its embassy at the Vatican and was ready to embrace modernism in an astonishing manner.

CHAPTER 31

Suffer Little Children

Children reported "being beaten on every part of their body: the front and back of hands, wrists, legs, back, buttocks, head, face and feet."

From the Ryan Report

Jack Sheehan, an Irish writer and PhD student of history at Trinity College in Dublin—who has studied the issue—wrote that in the mid-twentieth century, more people in Ireland were incarcerated per capita than in the USSR under Stalin.

It is a statistic that begs the question—why such hatred toward the most vulnerable and weak?

The early Catholic Church—Patrick's church—was contemplative, intellectual, curious. The modern church of Archbishop Cullen and his successor McQuaid was Roman-centric, heavily influenced by Jansenism and the prudery and sexual denial of the Victorian era.

This was a corrosive mix that exploded in the 1990s.

After the pedophile priest revelations, questions were finally asked about what was going on behind the closed doors of the Gulag-like schools and convents built and run by the Church with the full backing of the state.

In response there was deceit, lies, bluster, and venom aimed at critics like Father Flanagan from Boys Town USA.

The truth did eventually come out, thanks to one incredibly dedicated journalist, Mary Raftery, a television journalist with RTÉ, the national broadcaster.

In 1990, Raftery created the seminal documentary *States of Fear,* which for the first time exposed a massive cover-up and conspiracy involving almost every industrial school and Magdalene Laundry in Ireland.

The power grab to control almost all the educational institutions, led by the Church and by Archbishop McQuaid, would now come back to haunt them.

The savagery of the treatment of young, often orphaned children, in the industrial schools and the illegal confinement and abuse of thousands of young, unmarried, pregnant women in the Magdalene Laundries, shocked the country. Catholics all over Ireland recoiled in horror and disgust. Raftery became a heroine for exposing the putrid reality of industrial school for tens of thousands of Irish children.

Raftery first became interested in what had happened in industrial schools while working as a journalist in Dublin in the 1980s. She made the acquaintance of an inner-city family where all of the children had come through industrial school and were damaged beyond repair.

As her obituary (she died of cervical cancer in 2012) in the *Irish Independent* noted, "It was the first step on the road to breaking down the wall of silence that had shrouded the State's most horrific secret for decades: the widespread physical and sexual torture of children in industrial schools run by religious orders."

In 1999, she produced *States of Fear*—a series of documentaries that revealed, in her words, "the extremely vicious and sadistic physical abuse, way off the scale, and horrific emotional abuse, designed to break the children."

The country was shattered by the revelations, and the government moved quickly to set up an investigation. The result was "the

Ryan Inquiry," led by Judge Sean Ryan, which was given the task of undertaking a major inquiry into 250 institutions run by the Catholic Church.

The commission's 2,600-page report, which took nine years to complete and was released in May 2009, found that rape, sexual molestation, and beatings were "endemic" in Irish Catholic Church-run industrial schools and orphanages.

The *Guardian* reported: "The nine-year investigation found that Catholic priests and nuns for decades terrorized thousands of boys and girls in the Irish Republic, while government inspectors failed to stop the chronic beatings, rape, and humiliation."[126]

The report noted that police were called to the news conference, amid angry scenes, as victims were prevented from attending.

The *Guardian* explained that "More than 30,000 children, deemed to be petty thieves, truants or from dysfunctional families—a category that often included unmarried mothers—were sent to Ireland's austere network of industrial schools, reformatories, orphanages, and hostels from the 1930s until the last facilities shut in the 1990s."[127]

The BBC reported that the Commission's report had demonstrated beyond a doubt that the entire system treated children more like prison inmates and slaves than people with legal rights and human potential, that some religious officials encouraged ritual beatings and consistently shielded their orders amid a "culture of self-serving secrecy," and that government inspectors failed to stop the abuse.[128]

Children reported "being beaten on every part of their body: the front and back of hands, wrists, legs, back, buttocks, head, face, and feet. Some beatings were administered in public and witnesses reported that they were sometimes made to remove all their clothing for these public beatings."[129]

The weapons used included leather straps and "a variety of sticks and other instruments including ash plants, blackthorn sticks, brush handles, pointers, farm implements, drain rods, rubber tires, fan belts, horse tackle, sliotars [hurling ball], and hurling sticks."[130]

The final conclusions of the inquiry stated:

Physical and emotional abuse and neglect were features of
the institutions. Sexual abuse occurred in many of them, particularly boys' institutions. Schools were run in a severe, regi-
mented manner that imposed unreasonable and oppressive
discipline on children and even on staff . . .

A climate of fear, created by pervasive, excessive and arbi-
trary punishment, permeated most of the institutions and all
those run for boys. Children lived with the daily terror of not
knowing where the next beating was coming from . . .

Sexual abuse was endemic in boys' institutions. . . . The
schools investigated revealed a substantial level of sexual abuse
of boys in care that extended over a range from improper
touching and fondling to rape with violence. Perpetrators of
abuse were able to operate undetected for long periods at the
core of institutions . . .

The situation in girls' institutions was different. Although
girls were subjected to predatory sexual abuse by male
employees or visitors or in outside placements, sexual abuse
was not systemic in girls' schools.

When confronted with evidence of sexual abuse, the
response of the religious authorities was to transfer the
offender to another location where, in many instances, he was
free to abuse again. . . . The safety of children in general was
not a consideration.

Children were frequently hungry and food was inadequate, inedible, and badly prepared in many schools. . . .
Accommodation was cold, Spartan, and bleak. Sanitary provision was primitive in most boys' schools and general hygiene
facilities were poor . . .

The Department of Education dealt inadequately with
complaints about sexual abuse, [which] were generally dismissed or ignored.

Witnesses spoke of being belittled and ridiculed on a daily basis. . . . Private matters such as bodily functions and personal hygiene were used as opportunities for degradation and humiliation. Personal and family denigration was widespread. . . . There was constant criticism and verbal abuse and children were told they were worthless . . .[131]

The impact was stunning. For the first time the public saw the full extent of the poisonous behavior being practiced in Catholic institutions.

The *Irish Times* called the report "a devastating indictment of Church and State authorities," and "the map of an Irish hell."

The sheer scale and longevity of the torment inflicted on defenseless children—over 800 known abusers in over 200 [Catholic] institutions during a period of 35 years—should alone make it clear that it was not accidental or opportunistic but systematic. . . . Abuse was not a failure of the system. It was the system.[132]

Irish president Mary McAleese called the abuse "an atrocious betrayal of love," saying: "My heart goes out to the victims of this terrible injustice, an injustice compounded by the fact that they had to suffer in silence for so long."

The report made the front page of the *New York Times* with the headline "Ireland's Shameful Tragedy."

Raftery was hailed as a hero after her exposure of the abuse. She stated:

We now know there was decades of disgraceful behavior that was absolutely contrary to every single thing [the Church] preached. With this knowledge, it's going to be impossible for people to establish the same relationship of trust with the Catholic Church. I think it has vanished.[133]

It seemed like it finally had—Ireland suddenly looked like one giant concentration camp for helpless children, many of whom had their lives torn apart by perverts and pedophiles.

The following is just an example of one female and one male talking about their experience:

> [Female:] holding onto the bed, she . . . (lay care staff) . . . would tell you to face straight ahead, in your nightdress, she would hit you with a steel coat hanger, other staff would hold up the nightdress. If you got into bed and cried you would have to get out and the same would happen again.
>
> I started wetting the bed. I don't remember wetting the bed before I was about 6 or 7. There were about 30 of us in the dormitory, only a handful of us wet the bed. We had to stay with the younger ones until we stopped wetting the bed and in my case that was about 10 or 11. . . . We had long brown mackintoshes . . . (rubber sheets) . . . under our sheets, I remember pulling the sheets off so you wouldn't wet the sheet, if you wet the mackintosh maybe nobody would notice. We had to bring our wet sheets to the girl in charge who would swipe you across the face with it and bring you into the dressing room for a flogging. I remember trying so hard not to wet the bed. . . . I remember sitting on the toilet and falling asleep, going back to bed and still waking up soaking wet.[134]

Witnesses described the distress they experienced observing their younger siblings being physically punished for bed-wetting.

Many described protecting them from beatings by any means, including pretending that they had wet the beds themselves and taking the punishment instead of their siblings. They also described hiding wet sheets and trying to dry sheets in advance of an inspection. In some instances, witnesses reported swapping their sibling's wet sheet with that of another resident, who was then punished instead:

The girls who wet the bed got beaten. I never wet the bed but
my sister did and my older sister and I used to get up early and
make sure her bed was dry so that she didn't get hit, the babies
who wet the bed got beaten. We would change her bed. I know
it's a horrible thing but we would change the bed with someone
else, so that she did not get hit and if we didn't get time we'd
change her with our own bed and we'd take the beating. We
just didn't want her to get hit, she was only a baby. The punishment was, beaten with a leather strap all over. The nun used to
get a big girl to go around and check what one was wet, what
one was dry. You couldn't save everyone you know.[135]

Six witnesses from one school reported being made to spend the
night outside in the pigsty or locked under the stairs as punishment
for bed-wetting.

The forms of physical abuse reported by male witnesses to the
Committee included punching, flogging, assault, and bodily attacks,
hitting with the hand, kicking, ear-pulling, hair-pulling, head-shav-
ing, beating on the soles of the feet, burning, scalding, stabbing,
severe beatings with or without clothes, being made to kneel and
stand in fixed positions for lengthy periods, made to sleep outside
overnight, being forced into cold or excessively hot baths and showers, hosed down with cold water before being beaten, beaten while
hanging from hooks on the wall, being set upon by dogs, being re-
strained in order to be beaten, physical assaults by more than one
person, and having objects thrown at them.

The report found locations where physical abuse had taken place
included classrooms, offices, cloakrooms, dormitories, showers, in-
firmaries, refectories, the bedrooms of staff members, churches,
work areas and trade shops, fields, farmyards, play/sports areas, and
outdoor sheds.

The worst of the abuses were horrific. The report states:

I had a hiding in the boot room, you had to take your shirt
off, you were completely naked and he . . . (Br X) . . . beat

me with a strap and a hurley stick on the behind and the legs and that.

I was beaten up quite a few times for not making the bed right, I had to go to the boot room. We used to have long night shirts then you know, he . . . (Br X) . . . dragged it off me, naked and whop, he knocked the hell out of me, he knocked the shit out of me . . . he hit with a leather strap with coins in it. One Brother . . . he used a tire he did, a bicycle tire, it used to wrap around your arm. That was for wiping my nose in my sleeve, he didn't like that, it "wasn't a nice thing," he said.[136]

Among some of the strongest abuse claims, one person described how they attempted to tell nuns they had been molested by an ambulance driver, only to be "stripped naked and whipped by four nuns to 'get the devil out of you.'"[137]

Another described how they were removed from their bed and "made to walk around naked with other boys whilst brothers used their canes and flicked at their penis." Yet another was "[t]ied to a cross and raped whilst others masturbated at the side."[138]

The natural progression from the Ryan Report was to examine the other dark blot—the Magdalene Laundries, where dreadful stories had been circulating.

Raftery also helped uncover the truth about the laundries.

The Magdalene Laundries were institutions established in Ireland in the eighteenth century and that continued to operate nationwide until the later twentieth century.

The institutions were established with the purpose of housing Ireland's "fallen women," those who were regarded by the Catholic Church as having strayed from the moral path by engaging in premarital sex, falling pregnant before marriage, or having been a victim of rape or incest.

The treatment of Irish women within the laundry has been a subject of outrage internationally as the abuse and shame experienced by the women, who were often held against their own will, emerged into the public consciousness.

The "fallen women" were at the mercy of the nuns when they went to the laundry. If they were pregnant, their children were almost always sent for adoption soon after birth. There was a lucrative sale of Irish babies to America for thousands of dollars a head. The numbers were reckoned to be five hundred a year in the 1950s. The state had no oversight role whatever of the adoption business.

Thousands of babies were ripped from the breasts of their mothers and given up for adoption. To this day, many of those adopted children seek their birth mothers. A hit Hollywood film called *Philomena* starring Judy Dench was the heart-wrenching, real story of a Magdalene Laundry mother's search for her son.

The women were used as slave labor, with long days spent in the heat of the laundry washing dirty clothes.

Unlike in the industrial school, verbal humiliation was very much to the fore, as one inmate remembered: "I remember a nun telling me that you came from an illegitimate mother. I suppose it was that you were no good and that's why we were there."[139]

Another woman also spoke of her family background as being unkindly referred to. She said that "the nuns looked down on me because I had no father."

Another woman in that same laundry said, "We were never happy. You were lonely." She described how, on the journey to the Laundry, "In the car the nuns were saying I had the devil in me, shaking holy water and saying the rosary in the car."[140]

She had been raised in an industrial school with no known family and also described how a Sister on her entry to the Laundry, in front of all the other women, said, "Tell them where you were brought up and reared."

Another woman, who was in a number of Magdalene Laundries, said that in one of these Laundries the Sisters would make cruel comments about her family background, such as, "What do you think you are, I heard all about your family." This was particularly harmful to the woman concerned as she said, "My father interfered with the bigger girls."

More scandals were to come, seismic aftershocks from the original quakes. But something had begun to change in Ireland, something so raw, so fundamental, so real that it helped sweep away the old and usher in a completely different world. A new Ireland from the ruins of the old suddenly emerged.

It was a jagged vision at first, with no clear purpose or direction. U2 provided a powerful catalyst for change as they lit up the 1980s and 1990s and kicked off a sea change.

But it was a race for political office, one where the winning candidate had once been 100/1 with Dublin bookmakers to win the race, that would signal huge change. For once the bookies had it wrong.

CHAPTER 32

Mrs. Robinson Makes Her Mark

"I find it almost painful to contemplate Mary Robinson. She is radical, literate, a woman, and she's in power. Couldn't she be President of us as well?"
British writer Sean French, New York Times, *February 1993*

In 1989, Mary Robinson called a finish to her political career, deciding not to run for her safe Senate seat, and concentrated instead on the Irish Center for European Law, which she had founded. Having narrowly missed out on a seat in the *Dáil* in 1977, the main chamber in 1977, and being passed over for European Commissioner for Ireland, her political career seemed over.

Indeed, the tide in the country appeared out for a liberal, feminist, Eurocentric, female lawyer.

In 1986, a referendum on allowing divorce was emphatically defeated by 63 percent to 37 percent.

A 1983 attempt to change the laws and decriminalize homosexuality also failed when an Appeals Court ruled that the laws making homosexual conduct criminal were consistent with the Irish Constitution.

The court also held that no right of privacy obtained for even consensual homosexual activity because of the "Christian and democratic nature of the Irish State."

This verdict tarred every gay person as a criminal, even in the case of consensual sex. Ireland seemed hopelessly mired in the past. Robinson, among others, must have wondered if the momentum would come for issues such as gay and women's rights.

Her retirement lasted until the following Valentine's Day in 1990, when former Attorney General John Rogers dropped around to her house for a fateful conversation.

He informed her that the Labour Party wanted her to run for president of Ireland.

This was a job previously held by retired Irish male politicians or, in one case, by a senior judge who quit in disgust after being called a "thundering disgrace" by a leading politician of the time. It was widely viewed as a retirement home and a soft landing for retiring political leaders—which is how men like Eamon de Valera used the office.

Mary Robinson seemed the most unlikely candidate imaginable.

Robinson herself was taken aback. Labour Party leader Dick Spring had given no indication he was thinking of asking her. Indeed, the candidate being spoken of was Dr. Noël Browne, the old warhorse and survivor of the famous clash with Archbishop McQuaid over free healthcare for women and children in 1951.

The president of Ireland is head of state and has the role of signing and approving each law passed by the parliament. If they have questions about it, they can refer it to the Supreme Court.

In addition, the president can decide if the time is not right to call an election. He or she can reject a request from a leader of the government to dissolve the *Dáil*, as previous president Doctor Patrick Hillery had done.

The previous incumbents pre-1990 had done little else, other than, very occasionally, adjudicate such matters and be present when ambassadors presented their credentials. They would show up at state dinners and meet visiting dignitaries.

Robinson envisaged something very different, a people's presidency, where the ordinary people and their concerns and interests could be front and center.

It would be a presidency concerned with bringing a new focus to Irish life and speaking to and for marginalized groups.

As a young woman of just forty-six, Robinson vowed she would speak to a new generation and make the presidency relevant.

"If I entered the race, I could contribute to a new idea of the Irish presidency, an office of head of state with . . . influence, moral influence, and the potential to define the modern Ireland."[141]

Most of all, she wanted a joyous celebration of Irishness, which was a far cry from the gathering of old men, the fussy and tedious state dinners and the interests of the privileged few that defined the old office.

She quoted W. B. Yeats: "I am of Ireland/ Come dance with me in Ireland."

After some much ruminating and intense discussions with friends and family, Robinson decided to run for office. The response was a collective "Who does she think she is?" The bookmakers immediately published odds of 100/1 on her winning. Some thought the odds should be longer.

The political consensus saw her as an unlikely outsider: a high-powered intellectual and human rights lawyer with an elite Trinity College background. She was one of the first Catholics to be educated there. She was not exactly a woman of the people.

Also, as the third largest party, Labour candidates started at a huge disadvantage. Since the birth of the Irish State, the Labour Party had never nominated a candidate to contest the presidential election.

Indeed, there had not been a contested election for president for seventeen years, due to the tight grip de Valera's party, Fianna Fáil, had on the office.

Then there was the gender issue: almost all women in politics at that time were either widows or daughters of male politicians. She was a rara avis, an independent mother and wife, the major breadwinner for her family. During the campaign, Robinson reported being called a "Marxist Leninist Lesbian" by a priest.

Then there was her advocacy for contraception, divorce, women's rights. She was so aggressive in her pursuit of these issues that she had been attacked from the pulpit by her local bishop in Mayo while her parents were present at Mass.

She wanted expert information to be offered to those seeking abortions in Britain, an estimated five thousand a year.

It sounded like an ideal résumé for a candidate for presidency of the left-wing Trinity Students' Union, but for Ireland's highest constitutional office?

Robinson even doubted herself. When asked to run, she stated, "[M]y jaw dropped . . . and I . . . said to myself, No way!"[142]

But widely encouraged by colleagues and friends and, most important, by her husband, Nick, Robinson took the plunge.

It proved to be an inspired decision. It was the beginning of an Irish springtime, the start of a profound change that would wash over the country in the following three decades. Mary Robinson's election was the harbinger of that.

Robinson was the first candidate who believed in a new and reinvented presidency, and a new Ireland, too. The gray men in gray suits had had their day.

As the *Irish Times* wrote in 1997, when she left to become UN High Commissioner on Refugees:

> . . . Mary Robinson emerged from the relative obscurity of the Senate and the Law Library as a tide of demanding change rose through Ireland. It was a tide which sought an end to the sterility of traditional party politics, which rejected the inconsistencies of many of those claiming spiritual authority and which demanded accountability to the people as never before.[143]

Her main opponent was straight out of the de Valera, Fianna Fáil playbook. Brian Lenihan had filled most major Cabinet jobs and was "a safe pair of hands" and loyal supporter of the then-*Taoiseach* Charles Haughey, a deeply divisive figure in Irish politics whose source of great wealth and philandering were a constant source of disquiet.

Fine Gael, the largest opposition party, nominated candidate Austin Currie, a brave Northern Ireland civil rights figure, who did not play well with the Irish electorate.

Robinson drew immediate media attention as the first woman candidate ever to be considered for high office. She made an inspired decision to be true to herself and never disavowed her radical beliefs.

As William Tuohy wrote in the *Los Angeles Times*, "During the campaign, she pulled no punches. She supported liberal positions on the difficult and politically loaded issues of divorce, contraception, homosexuality, illegitimacy, adoption, family law, legal aid, and the right to information on abortion in the overwhelmingly Roman Catholic nation."[144]

She stuck to her plan, refusing to soften her positions, as some advised. She also launched a massive ground campaign of appearing in hundreds of villages, towns, and cities across the country at a time when the two other/opposing candidates had not even been chosen. Her slogan was brief: "A President with a Purpose."

What she encountered was a sub-rosa overwhelming desire for change. She advocated a more caring leadership and a better community spirit, a *meitheal* mentality and approach, based on the old Gaelic tradition of a co-operative labor system where people in rural communities gathered together to help one another. She was also astounded by the number of marginalized groups who showed up just wanting a sympathetic ear.

She found her message resonating and her poll numbers bouncing into a solid second place, but still some distance behind Lenihan.

"Famously frumpy" by her own admission, in terms of clothes and being ignorant of make-up, she got a professional makeover that pleased her and, more important, made her far more telegenic.

Naturally somewhat aloof, she learned to listen to and empathize with the small print of people's lives, thus making a deep impression. She also understood that she was a child of privilege (a doctor's daughter with a Trinity education) compared to most people she encountered and worked hard to bridge that divide.

As she noted in a 2013 interview in the popular Daily Beast website in the US, "I had a somewhat privileged upbringing. We were doctor's children, and we had maids, and we had our nanny, the beloved Nanny Coyne, who not only helped raise me and my four brothers, but came and helped me to raise my children. So I'm aware that I've had supports that not everybody has."[145]

Connecting more and more with people and keeping a far more arduous schedule than her rivals, she was closing the gap, but conservative Ireland wasn't about to unclench its grip so easily. She was widely smeared with claims she was divorced, she was a Protestant (her husband Nick is), had abandoned her children, had abortions, the whole gamut.

Then, like in many political breakthroughs, she caught a huge break. Weeks before the election, Fianna Fáil candidate Lenihan lied that he had sought to interfere when as a government minister he allegedly made a call to President Hillery seeking to influence his decision on how he would act in a looming political crisis—a huge constitutional no-no.

But a university student, studying the presidency, produced a tape of Lenihan admitting he had made such calls during an interview with the presidential contender.

It was crisis time for Fianna Fáil and greatly exacerbated when a deeply conservative minister, Padraig Flynn, a fellow Mayo native, made derogatory statements about Robinson as a mother.

It was straight out of the Archbishop McQuaid "playbook" but hopelessly out of line with the changing climate of the times.

He stated she had "a newfound interest in family, being a mother and all that kind of thing . . . but none of us, you know, none of us who knew Mary Robinson very well in previous incarnations ever heard her claiming to be a great wife and mother."[146]

The giant marching sound was the tens of thousands of women appearing at polling places, changing their vote overnight as the Flynn remarks misfired.

On November 7, 1990, the unthinkable happened, and Mary Robinson was elected president.

Her remarks on election night were historic, especially as she claimed that it was the group power of women that made her election possible:

> Today is a day of victory and valediction. Even as I salute my supporters, as Mary Robinson, I must also bid them farewell as president-elect. They are not just partisans, but patriots too. They know that as president of Ireland I must be a president for all the people, but more than that, I *want* to be a president for all the people.
>
> Because I was elected by men and women of all parties and none, by many with great courage who stepped out from the faded flags of the Civil War and voted for a new Ireland, and above all by the women of Ireland, *Mná na hÉireann*, who instead of rocking the cradle rocked the system, and who came out massively to make their mark on the ballot paper and on a new Ireland.[147]

The words were welcomed everywhere.

In her inauguration speech on December 3, 1990, she also honed in on the Irish Diaspora, the seventy million worldwide who had ancestral links to Ireland, millions of them Irish-born but forced to emigrate in order to survive economically:

> Beyond our State there is a vast community of Irish emigrants extending not only across our neighbouring island—which has provided a home away from home for several Irish generations—but also throughout the continent of North America, Australia, and of course Europe itself. There are over 70 million people living on this globe who claim Irish decent. I will be proud to represent them.

> And I would like to see Áras an Uachtaráin, my official
> residence, serve on something of an annual basis—as a place
> where our emigrant communities could send representatives for
> a get-together of the extended Irish family abroad.[148]

Those were inspirational words of welcome/inclusion for many
Irish-born immigrants, who felt abandoned by the home country
once they left. They were owed this recognition. In the '30s, '40s,
'50s, and '60s, emigrant remittances allowed many dirt-poor Irish
families to survive.

She went further and promised a lamp in the window of her official residence, Áras an Uachtaráin, as a symbol of lighting the way
home for returning migrants.

As president, she lived up to her advance billing. She made a
statement right away about her priorities. As her personal advisor,
Bride Rosney, told the *New York Times*:

> She was in power two weeks when she went to Sunday Mass—
> traditionally the President goes to private Mass at the private
> chapel in the official residence—in the most deprived area in
> Dublin, called Ballymun. She just turned up there in order to
> attract attention to their situation. She can invite people to
> come and meet her and tell her what their problems are. She
> can't make statements without Government approval, but she
> can sit and listen. That is what she will do.[149]

She was seen as part of a new world wave. Peace was coming to
Northern Ireland, an uneasy peace but a lasting one; the Berlin Wall
had come down in 1989, and the subsequent flowering of democ-
racy in the Eastern European states seemed to be part of this new
world. In South Africa and the Middle East peace moves—like those
in Ireland—began to bear fruit, and in Ireland, Mary Robinson was
creating a new paradigm in the oldest, most conservative country in
the Western World.

Someone named Francis Fukuyama wrote a ridiculously optimistic book with "The End of History" in the title, and for a moment the pre-9/11 world believed it.

In Ireland, Robinson threw open Áras an Uachtaráin to the poor and deserving, as well as the good and the great, including GLEN the Gay and Lesbian Equality Network (de Valera's ghost surely quailed).

She paid a powerful visit to Rwanda in the aftermath of a terrible holocaust and broke down at a subsequent press conference, a rare departure from a famously "cool" president, but one that gained the world's attention for Rwanda's plight.

Her popularity soared into the nineties in approval rating: she was the most popular politician in the history of the state when she left office a few months prematurely to take up the position of the UN High Commissioner for Refugees. Her impact on the job was plain to see as another woman, Mary McAleese, followed her and continued her work of outreach. Years later, McAleese, who has a gay son, was a resounding voice in the battle for same-sex marriage.

Robinson was like the summer wind blowing change. One of the biggest cultural events during her presidency was the staging of the internationally acclaimed *Riverdance*.

The brainchild of producers Maya Doherty and John McColgan, with Bill Whelan's inspired musical score, and performed superbly by renowned American dancers Michael Flatley and Jean Butler, *Riverdance* encapsulated this change in microcosm.

Historically, Irish dance, with its rigid hands clenched by the sides and stiff, unmoving upper body, was as sexy as two mole rats mating—the rigidity of the Irish dance encapsulated the subjugation of sexuality.

The *Riverdance* creators blew all that up, and the sexy movement, alluring music, and drumbeat of the frantic foot-tapping became a worldwide phenomenon.

With Irish politics producing a Mary Robinson and Irish dance liberated, what would come next in the new Ireland?

It did not take long to find out.

CHAPTER 33

Hello Divorce and Good-bye Jailing Gays

"I think the demise of the Church and the various scandals that they became involved in, particularly around child abuse, did change mindsets in Ireland."

Irish Prime Minister Leo Varadkar in an interview with me in 2017

In the wake of the successful election of Mary Robinson, the liberal agenda was at last on the map, and first up was removing the ban on divorce from the constitution and decriminalizing homosexual behavior.

Divorce was a lot easier to sell to the Irish heartland by 1995, yet it barely succeeded when a referendum to allow very limited divorce was voted on.

"Hello Divorce, Bye Bye Daddy" was the cutting edge slogan of the antidivorce side in 1996. It turned out the scare tactics nearly worked.

The referendum vote on divorce was very close, with 50.28 percent in favor and 49.79 percent opposed. Divorce had been banned outright in the Irish Constitution since its adoption in 1937. There was an earlier referendum on liberalizing the divorce laws in 1986, which the Irish people voted strongly against by a 25 percent margin.

By the time of the 1995 divorce referendum, Ireland was the only country in Europe where divorce was still illegal, an indication of the strong if waning influence the Catholic Church still held.

As a *New York Times* article published four days before the vote explained, there were massive public campaigns by both sides leading up to the vote in 1995.

John Bruton, the *taoiseach* at the time, viewed it as imperative that Ireland amend its constitution to allow divorce and worried that another "No" vote would damage Ireland's already reactionary image and increase tensions in Northern Ireland linked to the Catholic Church's sway on Irish society.

He encouraged the Irish people to vote "Yes" in a passionate radio address:

> The essence of the Catholic faith is particularly that it shows forgiveness. It would be very wrong not to allow our law to express forgiveness to those whose consciences allow them to remarry . . .
>
> Is it the Ireland we like to present to the world as a place that has very strong beliefs but doesn't need to enforce them by law, that welcomes people with a different point of view and treats them well? Or an Ireland that's so afraid it has to use the criminal and civil law to enforce a particular set of beliefs?[150]

Church officials and antidivorce advocates brought an equally fierce campaign, with warnings that divorce was "un-Catholic" and would lead to instability in Irish society. It portrayed farmers' spouses as especially vulnerable because the farmer could throw them off the land if divorced. It was a clear ploy to win the rural vote, and it almost succeeded.

Thomas Flynn, who was Bishop of Achonry at the time, indicated that Catholics who got divorced or remarried could be denied sacraments such as communion and confession. However, the Church did affirm that it would not be a sin for Catholics to vote yes, as long as they did so in good conscience.

On November 24, 62.15 percent of Ireland's registered voters turned out to cast their ballots and approved the 15th Amendment to the Irish Constitution by a margin of slightly more than .5 percent. The amendment was signed into law on June 16, 1996.

"It was a very close run thing. Rejection would have set back the progressive agenda by years," said *Irish Times* columnist Eddie Holt.

Two years previously in 1993, the final chapter in decriminalizing homosexuality was closed.

It had taken ten years since the commencement of the 1983 case asking the European Court to overturn an Irish court verdict that homosexual activity was criminal. It was a major moment in Irish life.

The 1983 case was taken by Trinity professor, later Senator David Norris, the tireless, if lonely, campaigner for gay rights who wrote to his lawyer, later president Mary Robinson, explaining his reasons why she should take the case.

> About the age of 13/14 I first noticed that feelings which were quite natural . . . to me were not shared by my closest companions. . . . I discovered to my horror that other people did not share my ability to respond to my own sex . . . [it] always came back to the same two points: that my nature was both sinful and criminal . . .
>
> [T]he idea of being a criminal without even knowing it [under the 1885 British act criminalizing homosexual behavior] was much more disturbing as it was not a matter of opinion but a political fact. . . . I became de facto . . . a member of the criminal classes liable to punishment and disgrace . . . I was shocked to discover that the very laws [1885 Act] under which he [Oscar Wilde] had suffered so many years before still applied to Ireland.[151]

The Irish courts had rejected his efforts to decriminalize despite the fact that Britain had done so in 1967, but he had one last forum, the European Court of Human Rights in Strasbourg, which was the final arbiter under European law.

Article 8 of the European Commission on Human Rights stated that everyone had the right to respect for his private and family life.

The Irish government opposed it, saying that the fact that Norris had never been arrested for gay activities proved that the state was using its "discretion powers in the protection of morals" well and not interfering.

However, the European Court disagreed with the government, saying there was no justification for retaining the laws covering the rights of the state to interfere in the private life of a citizen.

It was a historic day in October 1988, that the European Court found Ireland in breach of Article 8.

The *Irish Times* editorial noted: "The time has come for change. It is a sad state of affairs that once again, it had to be forced on us by the European Court."

It was not until 1993 that the law was passed by the Irish parliament and signed by President Mary Robinson, the tireless campaigner for the issue. It must have been one chicken she was glad to see come home to roost.

Kieran Rose, the head of the Gay and Lesbian Equality Network, said, "The passage of the Bill in June 1993 was a watershed in the lives of gay and lesbian people in Ireland. No longer were Irish people to be treated as criminals, just because of who they were."

"The passage of the Bill was one of the most important steps in the liberation of gay people in Ireland," said Rose. "It led to new generations of lesbian and gay people able to live their lives more openly."[152]

The LGBTQ community had finally begun to become visible. The killing of gay man Declan Flynn in Fairview Park in 1982 and the ridiculous lack of a prison sentence for the gay bashers had forced the gay community's hands. The first public demonstration was held and attracted one thousand marchers. The consciousness about the gay rights issue was brought home following that killing.

Even before the Flynn killing, some early pioneers—in addition to Norris—had spoken out.

In February 1977, well-known journalist Cathal O'Shannon featured members of the gay community in a program about their lives, the first of its kind on RTÉ, the national broadcasting company.

The reaction was very positive. *Hibernia* magazine noted:

If the Tuesday Report did nothing else for the homosexual it did, at least attempt to explode this particular myth (homosexuals are sick, weak and depraved human beings). Here was a group of normal, decent and intelligent people who just happened to be sexually orientated towards members of their own sex. They did not choose to be what they are—who does?

And all they were demanding was the right to live their own lives in their own way without interference from the State, or anyone else. This is the same right that any heterosexual would demand—and get. So where's the problem? You may well ask.

It is not often these days that one can lavish praise on RTÉ, especially in the area of current affairs programmes, but in this case they deserve to be congratulated. The programme was a winner.[153]

Only four of the forty calls received by the program were negative. Even in the late '70s, there was a quiet acceptance of gay rights among many Irish.

After the European Court decision in 1988 and its enactment in 1993, the gay community began to lobby for more significant changes.

Two critical factors were apparent: hollowed out by the sex scandals, the Church had greatly weakened in the Mary Robinson era, and the role of the European Court of Human Rights in liberalizing Irish law was extremely impactful.

The European Court provided a liberal counterpoint to the far more conservative Irish courts and impacted Ireland profoundly, especially in areas such as free legal aid, family and women's rights, and the rights of minorities.

The biggest winner, however, was the gay rights lobby that began the long march to equality.

It was a feel-good era in Ireland in the mid-'90s to 2008. The Celtic Tiger was born, and the Irish economy expanded at an average rate of 9.4 percent between 1995 and 2000.

Full employment ensued, immigrants came home, major American companies expanded their Irish bases.

With the economic change, which lasted eventually until 2008, came a social liberalism that was also fueled by migration to Ireland from EU countries—the Polish, Latvian, and Spanish added to an eclectic mix and a sense of a new Ireland.

The joke was you couldn't find an Irish bartender anymore. The Temple bar area of Dublin, hard by the River Liffey, became Ireland's social hub, Left Bank, and West Village all at once.

As the good times rolled, the rigid social conventions began to peel off in the new Internet age.

Gay rights became a fashionable cause, an idea that would have seemed absurd a few decades before when public toilets were the place for many gays to meet.

The Green Party was the first major political party in government to commit to same-sex marriage. They were the junior partner in the 2007-to-2011 government with Fianna Fáil.

However, Green Party head John Gormley told disappointed LGBT groups following the election that there was no hope of their more conservative Fianna Fáil partners accepting same-sex marriage and that civil partnership would be the best they could do.

His comments created a firestorm within the gay community, with more moderate groups willing to accept it as a stepping stone while more militant groups wanted to fight on for same-sex marriage.

The published bill in 2009 did not help heal the wounds.

That was despite Minister for Justice and Law Reform Dermot Ahern saying: "This is one of the most important pieces of civil rights legislation to be enacted since independence. Its legislative advance has seen an unprecedented degree of unity and support within both Houses of the Oireachtas."[154]

A ban on adopting children was especially criticized, as well as the second-class status of the union compared to marriage.

A civil partnership was presented to the Cabinet on June 24, 2009, and was published on June 26, 2010. It was half a loaf.

The bill was signed into law by President Mary McAleese on July 19, 2010. But no one was fooled. The biggest battle of all, the Everest of the LGBTQ movement, was same-sex marriage agreed by popular vote.

No country in the world had ever voted for it, though it had been enforced through judicial and parliamentary ways in others.

But in Ireland a referendum was needed to change the constitution. The cynics said it would never be done. The world was about to find out if they were right.

CHAPTER 34

The Same-Sex Marriage Battle Begins

"Marriage may be contracted in accordance with law by two persons without distinction as to their sex."
Wording of same-sex marriage constitutional amendment to be voted on by the Irish people on May 22, 2015.

D e Valera and Archbishop McQuaid's 1937 Irish Constitution was creaking and leaky by the turn of the century. Hugely controversial issues, such as divorce, same-sex marriage, and women's equality, urgently needed to be dealt with, and the constitution was not fit for this purpose.

Recognizing the issue, the *Oireachtas* (Parliamentary) Joint Committee on the Constitution recommended a Citizen's Assembly on Electoral Reform.

As Doctor Matthew Wall of Swansea University explained in *Journal.ie*: "The idea first developed in the Canadian province of British Columbia (BC) in 2003 was to recruit ordinary citizens to recommend changes to the province's electoral system. This was an ambitious project—electoral systems are complex and the topic required extensive learning on the part of the citizen participants."[155]

After the 2011 election, the Fine Gael–Labour Government had as part of their joint platform pledged to "establish a Constitutional

Convention to consider comprehensive constitutional reform, with a brief to consider, as a whole or in subgroups, and report on, within twelve months, the following:

- Review of the *Dáil* electoral system
- Reducing the presidential term to five years and aligning it with the local and European elections
- Provision for same-sex marriage
- Amending the clause on women in the home and encouraging greater participation of women in public life
- Removing blasphemy from the Constitution
- Possible reduction of the voting age
- Other relevant constitutional amendments that may be recommended by the Convention
- The constitutional convention came together for the first time under respected Chairman Tom Arnold, CEO of the Irish charity, Concern[156]

It met for the first time on December 1, 2012, and was in situ right up to March 31, 2014. It had one hundred members: a chairman, twenty-nine members of the *Oireachtas*, four representatives from Northern Ireland political parties, and sixty-six randomly selected Irish citizens chosen from the electoral register.

The change to the constitution on same-sex marriage was one of the suggested areas for consideration. While the convention could only recommend and not mandate, the government was duty-bound to consider its recommendations.

This convention performed an invaluable service by removing discussions from raw politics and giving elected representatives a deep perspective on what the general public was thinking.

(One can only imagine how much better the Brexit debate would have been in Britain if the Irish model for dealing with contentious issues was used.)

In 2013, the convention dealt with the issue of same-sex marriage from April 12 to April 14.

Pro- and anti-same-sex marriage representatives faced off before the Constitutional Convention members at the Grand Hotel in Malahide, an upscale seaside suburb near Dublin.

The atmosphere was tense. Here was the first step . . . or a spectacular failure if the convention voted down its being sent to the government.

As related in the book *Ireland Says Yes,* written by several same-sex marriage activists, first up for the pro-same-sex marriage side was advocate Claire O'Connell, who stated bluntly, "My parents are two women. Marriage equality would mean that my parents could get married just like anyone else's parents. No one could ever tell us again we are not a family."

It was an emotional testimony and a direct blow at the heart of the issue: should two people who love each other be allowed to marry, irrespective of gender?

Next up were the ecclesiasticals, led by Bishop Leo O'Reilly, who talked about unforeseen consequences that could arise from allowing same-sex marriage.

Breda MacDonald from the No side argued that we would be the "first generation in history to be asked if the roles of mothers and fathers [would] be considered irrelevant in the bringing up of children[.]"[157]

Powerful testimony was heard from an elected member of the *Dáil*, a gay man named Jerry Buttimer who stated, "I want to marry the person I love, to enhance and enrich my life."[158]

An array of heavyweight figures weighed in on both sides, but a clear pattern emerged. Personal stories were more compelling than moral or legal issues.

A study of voters by the Yes side clearly pointed out that the winning position for "Yes" was a "live and let live" mind-set; the voter realized that a "Yes" vote would have no impact on his or her life and felt what people did privately was of no concern to them.

Over two days, the arguments went back and forth, but it was clear that the Yes side arguments were more emotional and personal, while the No side ones consisted of moral and legal admonitions that carried lesser weight.

When it came time to vote, an astonishing 79 percent of the Constitutional Committee members voted in favor of asking the government to allow a public vote to change the constitution and to legalize gay marriage. Even the most optimistic Yes side advocates had not anticipated that kind of margin of victory. It looked like something fundamental had changed in the Irish mind-set.

It was a huge victory for the same-sex marriage side, but two very tough issues remained: getting the government to agree to hold what promised to be a divisive referendum and then winning that vote.

Following the convention approval, strong pressure was placed on the government to agree on a referendum date. It was eventually agreed that people would go to the polls on May 22, 2015.

The Yes side got an incredible media boost when Ireland's leading drag queen, Rory O'Neill, a.k.a. Panti Bliss, a highly respected figure in the gay community, went on live TV in January 2014 and blasted homophobia in the Irish media, naming names.

He said, "Get out of my life. I mean, it astounds me. There are people out there in the world who devote large amounts of time and energy to stop people achieving happiness." [Applause]

There was a massive reaction, and RTÉ was successfully sued for libel. Shortly afterward, Panti Bliss took to the stage at the famed Abbey Theater after a performance of James Plunket's *A Risen People*, a play about the 1913 lockout of union workers by employers.

Her speech went viral, attracting over one million YouTube viewers. She spoke as part of the Abbey's "Noble Call" series.

The speech was described as "the most eloquent Irish speech" in almost two hundred years by *Irish Times* leading columnist Fintan O'Toole and garnered the support of Dan Savage, RuPaul, Graham Norton, Stephen Fry, Madonna, and others.

It stated in part:

Hello. My name is Panti and for the benefit of the visually impaired or the incredibly naïve, I am a drag queen, a performer, and an accidental and occasional gay rights activist.

And as you may have already gathered, I am also painfully middle-class. My father was a country vet, I went to a nice school, and afterwards to that most middle-class of institutions—art college. And although this may surprise some of you, I have always managed to find gainful employment in my chosen field—gender discombobulation.

So the grinding, abject poverty, so powerfully displayed in tonight's performance, is something I can thankfully, say I have no experience of.

But oppression is something I can relate to. Oh, I'm not comparing my experience to Dublin workers of 1913, but I do know what it feels like to be put in your place.

Have you ever been standing at a pedestrian crossing when a car drives by and in it are a bunch of lads, and they lean out the window and they shout "Fag!" and throw a milk carton at you?

Now it doesn't really hurt. It's just a wet carton and anyway they're right—I am a fag. But it feels oppressive.

When it really does hurt, is afterwards. Afterwards I wonder and worry and obsess over what was it about me, what was it they saw in me? What was it that gave me away? And I hate myself for thinking that. It feels oppressive and the next time I'm at a pedestrian crossing I check myself to see what is it about me that "gives the gay away" and I check myself to make sure I'm not doing it this time.

Have any of you ever come home in the evening and turned on the television and there is a panel of people—nice people, respectable people, smart people, the kind of people who make good neighborly neighbors and write for newspapers. And they are having a reasoned debate about you.

About what kind of a person you are, about whether you are capable of being a good parent, about whether you want to destroy marriage, about whether you are safe around children, about whether God herself thinks you are an abomination, about whether in fact you are "intrinsically disordered."

And even the nice TV presenter lady who you feel, like you know, thinks it's perfectly ok that they are all having this reasonable debate about who you are and what rights you "deserve."

And that feels oppressive.

Have you ever been on a crowded train with your gay friend and a small part of you is cringing because he is being SO gay and you find yourself trying to compensate by butching up or nudging the conversation onto 'straighter' territory? This is you who have spent 35 years trying to be the best gay possible and yet still a small part of you is embarrassed by his gayness.

And I hate myself for that. And that feels oppressive. And when I'm standing at the pedestrian lights I am checking myself.

Have you ever gone into your favorite neighborhood café with the paper that you buy every day, and you open it up and inside is a 500-word opinion written by a nice middle-class woman, the kind of woman who probably gives to charity, the kind of woman that you would be happy to leave your children with? And she is arguing so reasonably about whether you should be treated less than everybody else, arguing that you should be given fewer rights than everybody else.

And when the woman at the next table gets up and excuses herself to squeeze by you with a smile you wonder, "Does she think that about me too?"

And that feels oppressive. And you go outside and you stand at the pedestrian crossing and you check yourself and I hate myself for that.

Have you ever turned on the computer and seen videos of people just like you in faraway countries, and countries not far away at all, being beaten and imprisoned and tortured and murdered because they are just like you?

And that feels oppressive.

Three weeks ago I was on the television and I said that I believed that people who actively campaign for gay people to be treated less or differently are, in my gay opinion, homophobic. Some people, people who actively campaign for gay people to be treated less under the law, took great exception at this characterization and threatened legal action against me and RTÉ. RTÉ, in its wisdom, decided incredibly quickly to hand over a huge sum of money to make it go away. I haven't been so lucky.

And for the last three weeks I have been lectured by heterosexual people about what homophobia is and who should be allowed to identify it . . . . people who have never experienced homophobia in their lives, people who have never checked themselves at a pedestrian crossing, have told me that unless I am being thrown in prison or herded onto a cattle train, then it is not homophobia.

And that feels oppressive . . .

I do . . . believe that almost all of you are probably homophobes. But I'm a homophobe. It would be incredible if we weren't. To grow up in a society that is overwhelmingly homophobic and to escape unscathed would be miraculous. So I don't hate you because you are homophobic. I actually admire you. I admire you because most of you are only a bit homophobic. Which all things considered is pretty good going.

But I do sometimes hate myself. I hate myself because I f*cking check myself while standing at pedestrian crossings. And sometimes I hate you for doing that to me.

But not right now. Right now, I like you all very much for giving me a few moments of your time. And I thank you for it.[159]

The speech lifted the rafters and set the tone for the entire debate. Panti Bliss became an overnight sensation.

The road to victory was clear for the Yes side: just get gay people to tell the truth about their lives and hope their stories bring out the "better angel" side of voters. At the launch of the "Yes Equality" group, a father spoke very movingly about holding his lesbian daughter in his arms for hours as she cried after telling him she was gay. The room was struck silent. Hardly the rah-rah of a normal campaign liftoff, but far more effective.

They (the "Yes Equality" group) also engaged shrewd political operatives to ensure that the messaging was presented correctly.

The slogan on posters, "I'm Voting Yes, Ask Me Why," was immediately inclusive. When they detected from opinion polls that a potential problem voters had related to was about whether church weddings would be downgraded, they moved quickly to reassure that the issue only related to civil marriage.

As the book *Ireland Says Yes* explained, they realized that it was especially important to get women in the forty-to-sixty age bracket on their side. Many of these were considered to be too young to be over-reactionary but yet too old to be reached successfully on social media.

Short of Mary Robinson, the Yes camp had the next best thing: her successor, Mary McAleese, who had served two terms in office and whose son Justin was gay.

McAleese, like Robinson, had enjoyed stellar poll numbers as she left office. Though profoundly Catholic, she had been one of the founders of the "Campaign for Homosexual Law Reform" in the 1970s. She had form, as the Irish say.

One of the best orators in Ireland, the former journalist and law professor was the most powerful advocate the Yes campaign had. Internal polls showed all sections of the community trusted both her and her husband, Martin, a highly respected and significant player in the peace process.

A big problem for the Yes campaign was lack of funds. Donations could only come from Irish citizens, and the cap was about three thousand dollars. In contrast, the No campaign seemed well funded. Volunteerism helped close the gap.

Door-to-door canvassing, undertaken by thousands of volunteers all over the country, was a particularly good way to meet undecided voters.

Some canvassers experienced homophobia. One canvassing crew in a midlands Irish town was chased off by a woman sprinkling holy water on them, but in the main, the personal contact was a tremendous way to show that the Yes canvassers were just ordinary people who believed in their cause.

Social media was crucial, but despite huge support for the Yes campaign, many young people were not registered to vote.

One particularly successful tactic undertaken was the mobilizing of a bus loaded with canvassers driving all over Ireland. There was an amazing response in country areas and small towns, with local politicians coming out to be photographed with the bus, a sure sign that Yes was doing very well.

The Yes bus traveled almost ten thousand miles in a month, stopping at locations all over the twenty-six counties in Ireland. It was the surprise hit of the campaign.

Tremendous personal revelations and contributions were made.

Ursula Halligan, one of the best-known and respected journalists in Ireland, felt she finally had to "come out" after seeing the huge effort being put in. She did do in a profoundly moving op-ed in the *Irish Times*.

Halligan came out as gay, stating that at age seventeen she had fallen hard for a girl in her class and wrote in her diary: "There have been times when I have even thought about death, of escaping from this world, of sleeping untouched by no-one forever. I have been so depressed, so sad, and so confused."[160]

She called for and believed a "Yes" vote was "the most Christian thing to do."

She said that as a woman who spent decades not telling the truth about her own sexuality, she felt she had to do so now for the sake of the younger generation. Her honesty made an amazing impact, but another person who had "come out" made an even more profound impact on voters. His decision to go public made world news.

CHAPTER 35

Leo Varadkar Reveals a Secret

"I am a gay man."

Leo Varadkar

There had been an even bigger revelation in January 2015, when the rising star of the Irish government, Leo Varadkar, son of an Indian migrant doctor and a Waterford mother who was a nurse, "came out" on Irish radio.

Interviewed by Miriam O'Callaghan, Varadkar—Ireland's then-minister for health, himself a doctor by profession—before entering politics and just thirty-six on the day of the interview, put his entire political career on the line by announcing he was gay. It was a huge risk that could have finished him politically.

A decade earlier, this admission would almost certainly have meant he was finished.

He stated, "Well, you know I'm a very private person and I still am. I keep my private life to myself and that's going to continue. I always think that friends and family are off-bounds. I went into politics, they didn't. But I am a gay man—it's not a secret, but not something everyone would necessarily know, but it isn't something I've spoken publicly about before now."[161]

In the green room, his handlers breathed a huge sigh of relief. Varadkar had called a meeting of top staff earlier that week to discuss the issue, in light of a number of media outlets nosing around and most of all because of the upcoming referendum.

Varadkar, an intensely private person, had clearly wrestled with the issue for some time. Tall and handsome with sharp political instincts, he was clearly bound for the top—if his gay orientation did not damage him.

But with tabloid papers snapping at his heels and a same-sex marriage referendum coming up, he knew he needed to act.

He called his boss, Prime Minister Enda Kenny, and told him he was going to "come out." Kenny, who was strongly in favor of the same-sex referendum, was supportive and urged him to go ahead. The die was cast.

He signaled to his top staff he would do it on his thirty-sixth birthday that coming Sunday on the highly popular Miriam O'Callaghan show. At the last moment, he almost got cold feet, and the interview was well advanced before he delivered his truth that he was gay and wanted the referendum to pass because: "I'd like to be an equal citizen in my own country."

It was a profound statement from a rising politician, the son of an immigrant, with a secret about his sexuality to hide.

In 2017, Varadkar sat for a joint interview with me and Maureen Dowd of the *New York Times* in his government office. In June of that year, he had become prime minister, defying all odds.

He discussed his complicated childhood and his decision to come out:

> I [Maureen Dowd] asked him if he had spent years hiding his sexuality. "Of course, yeah," he said. "I would have kept my private life very private. Maybe didn't have much of a private life as well. You know, a lot of people sort of turn themselves into their careers, and that's something I definitely did, both as a doctor and a politician.

"When confronted with those little questions that people ask, understandably, 'Are you seeing anyone?' 'Do you have a girlfriend?' well, I suppose I'd be very cagey. I'd just say, 'No,' or 'I'm not one to answer those kind of questions.'"

But "once I'd sort of come out to myself," he said, a cloud was lifted. "The biggest thing I say to anyone—and a lot of people would ask me for advice before they come out—is that I don't regret it for a second. And a lot of the fears that you have are very much your own fears. And the vast majority of people don't really care. It's a matter of passing interest. You know, your friends and family, the people who really love you, will always support you no matter what, and those that don't, you probably don't need anyway."

I asked about his mother being afraid that when he came out he would be beaten up on the street or lose his seat or get roughed up by opponents.

"Yeah, yeah, she was," he said. "And I suppose, like most Irish moms, and I imagine American moms as well, she'd be very protective. I think, at that point, she would have preferred that I kept it to myself and kept it as something private. But I was very conscious that a referendum was coming up on marriage equality. That was really the catalyst for me. And as a government minister, you know, I couldn't go out there advocating a change in the Constitution and somehow pretend that it didn't really affect me or that it wasn't something that I wasn't taking personally.

"And I do remember discussions that I would have had with other politicians, and the one that really stuck with me was the one with another minister who was very supportive of marriage equality and who talked about being generous to 'them.' And so it was 'them.' And I thought I needed to tell my colleagues that I was one of 'them.'"

He laughs. "We're here among you, lots of us. And secondly, the line about it being generosity. It's actually something that we should have. So if I wasn't willing to show leadership on this, then I was in the wrong business."[162]

The media and public reaction to his coming out was overwhelmingly positive and augured well for the referendum. He was one of the most senior politicians in Ireland, a man destined for the highest office in the land, and he had just revealed his most vulnerable aspect: that he was a gay man.

And the sun had risen and set, and people got on with their lives, and soon it was a nonstory.

But the rapidly approaching referendum was a different matter that everyone predicted would be nip and tuck. Modern Ireland or old Ireland, who would speak the loudest?

CHAPTER 36

The Eve of Vote

"A yes vote costs the rest of us nothing, a no vote costs our children everything."

Mary McAleese, former Irish president

There was one central truth that both sides believed in as the polling day drew close: no one should believe the polls.

It seemed as though every poll taken had the Yes side well ahead, but the caveats were huge.

As with the real level of support for Donald Trump in 2016, both sides suspected the "No" vote was being undercounted. It was feared that in the privacy of the polling booth, many would push the No lever.

It was based on assumptions of unconscious bias, of reluctance to tell a pollster you were voting against gay rights, and the traditional conservatism of the Irish people.

Given votes like Brexit, where hardline Brexit supporters did not show their hand until referendum day, nobody was taking the Irish same-sex marriage polls at face value.

That was despite a clearly lackluster No campaign. The opposition group, launched as "Mothers and Fathers Matter," never got off the ground and made what many considered a major error by highlighting a handful of gay men who believed they should not be allowed to marry.

Their banners and posters showed a mother, father, and baby with the tagline "Children Deserve a Mother and Father."

The response to that from the Yes side was children deserve two loving parents, whether they be the same sex or heterosexual.

Then there was the Church. The bishops used many of the same tactics that had almost kept divorce at bay in the 1996 referendum, mobilizing at parish level across the country.

The bishops' pastoral statement, *The Meaning of Marriage*, advised the faithful that "to redefine the nature of marriage would be to undermine it as the fundamental building block of our society. The Church seeks with others to reaffirm . . . that marriage should be reserved for the unique and complementary relationship between a woman and a man from which the generation and upbringing of children is uniquely possible."[163]

Bishops encouraged everyone to read *The Meaning of Marriage*, which was available in churches in more than 1,300 parishes throughout the island.

Once upon a time, that could have been enough, but "the day that God proposes and the bishop disposes" was well over in Ireland. The famous network, based on the instructions from on high in 1,300 parishes, was no longer effective.

Indeed, there was one remarkable moment when Father Martin Dolan told parishioners in his Dublin church that while he had been told to preach the No gospel, he was urging them to vote Yes, and furthermore, he was coming out as a gay man himself. The reaction was a standing ovation.

The most effective argument was that civil partnership was enough, as all the necessary rights were protected. That was the only No side message that resonated.

Noel Whelan, a leading light on the Yes side, *Irish Times* columnist, and political strategist supreme, spoke directly and very effectively on the civil partnership versus marriage argument in a

Times column, defining the significant differences between the two and helping defuse that issue.

The Iona Institute, a significant right-wing Catholic think-tank group, also set about undermining the "Yes" vote by asking awkward questions about adoption and surrogacy issues. Again, it failed to catch fire, a complex argument amid what most people saw as a simple proposition on same-sex marriage, Yea or Nay.

Meanwhile, the Yes side continued to implement their personal stories strategy. World champion runner Eamonn Coghlan spoke movingly about his son being gay. *Irish Times* columnist Una Mullally spoke about her battle with colon cancer and the inability of her partner to have full visiting and consultation rights.

All polling indications were for a massive Yes win. A 72 percent "Yes" vote was predicted in a *Sunday Business Post* poll on May 1, just three weeks from polling day. That seemed conclusive, but there were still very few taking it for granted.

That was because a series of live television debates, which would be watched by millions, still had to be aired, and there was plenty of time left to lose ground.

But the debates revealed a country that seemed ready to make a historic change, and the live debates did not move the needle.

The Barack Obama "Yes We Can"–type campaign on the Yes side had firmly caught the imagination. On May 15, the *Irish Times* published its final poll and predicted a massive 70 percent to 30 percent victory for Yes. The race seemed over.

Adding momentum was the "Home to Vote" movement: young immigrants streamed home to vote from far-flung countries such as South Africa, Australia, the US, and, closer to home, Britain. Due to Ireland's ban on overseas voting, they had to physically present themselves at a polling station. Their Twitter accounts of their journeys home became viral sensations as members of Ireland's lost tribes returned one more time to add to the surreal atmosphere before the vote.

Momentum was clearly gathering, and a moving speech by former president Mary McAleese, which attracted a capacity audience on the eve of polling day, cemented this momentum.

> We who are parents, brothers and sisters, colleagues, and friends of Ireland's gay citizens know what they have suffered because of second class citizenship. The referendum is about them and them alone. A "yes" vote costs the rest of us nothing, a "no" vote costs our children everything.[164]

A tremendous round of applause followed. The question now was, would her heartfelt plea hit home?

CHAPTER 37

"Walking on Air"

"A great day for a revolution."
Voter outside a Drogheda polling station

May 22, 2015, D-Day, dawned bright and sunny. The world media had descended as never before on Ireland. No country in the world freely voted to support same-sex marriage.

The fact that Ireland could be the first was dumbfounding.

"I voted for myself even though I wasn't on the ballot," one gay man stated exuberantly outside a Dublin polling station.

An example of the interest was #voteyes; according to Twitter, it was the top trend worldwide. On its home page, Google chirped, "Google supports marriage equality, #Proud to Love." Facebook included an "I've voted" icon on its Irish page.

A clip of emigrants taking a boat home from London went viral as they sang the haunting ballad "She Moved Through the Fair," the last line of which brought tears: "It will not be long now until our wedding day."

Pundits compared it to Italia '90, the year Irish soccer fans went wild as their team made completely unexpected progress to the World Cup quarter-final. This was turning into a gay Mardi Gras.

221

Instead of the green of Irish flags and bunting, the rainbow colors flew.

It seemed from all indications that people had taken Nobel poet Seamus Heaney's advice, which became his epitaph: "Walk on Air against Your Better Judgement."

They walked on air all over Ireland, especially in the critical Dublin constituencies. The long-awaited tide was surging for equality.

Colin Farrell tweeted his support, so did Ellen DeGeneres, so did Martina Navratilova and Stephen Fry.

David Norris, the pioneer politician who first stood up for gay rights, became emotional when talking about what a "Yes" vote would mean.

In 1993, he and Mary Robinson had won a landmark case in the European Court decriminalizing homosexuality. Now just twenty-two years later, an incredible victory beckoned.

"I've just gone 75 years old, and for the majority of my life I was a criminal," says Norris. "So it's nice to go from being a criminal to being able to marry a man . . ."[165]

He pointed out Ireland would be the first country in the world to legalize same-sex marriage through a popular vote.

Suddenly, it was happening in real time. As soon as the ballot boxes were opened, the "Yes" votes spilled out—and not just in Dublin, but all over the country.

From Donegal to Cork and Galway to Dublin, in small hamlets and large cities, in byways and cities off highways, they voted for same-sex marriage.

In Donegal, one of Ireland's most conservative counties, a 60–40 percent vote against divorce had swung around to 51–49 percent for gay marriage, an incredible turnaround in less than two decades.

In total, the BBC reported 1,201,607 people voted in favor of same-sex marriage, while 734,300 voted against. It was a 62 percent to 38 percent massacre on a 60 percent turnout. The much-maligned pollsters had got it right.

Irish Prime Minister Enda Kenny said Ireland, though a "small country," sent "a big message for equality" around the world.

Irish Deputy Prime Minister and Labour leader Joan Burton added: "The people of Ireland have struck a massive blow against discrimination."

She quoted the late American politician and LGBTQ rights activist Harvey Milk, who was shot dead by a homophobe: "Hope will never be silent."

David Norris was mobbed when he arrived at Dublin Castle. His pioneering had made it possible for this incredible day, but he was philosophical rather than triumphant: "The battle is not over. There are countries throughout Africa and Asia in which it is terribly dangerous to be gay," Norris said. "It's wonderful. It's a little bit late for me . . . I've spent so much time pushing the boat out that I forgot to jump on, and now it's out beyond the harbor on the high seas. But it's very nice to look at."[166]

Out of forty-three constituencies, only the largely rural Roscommon-South Leitrim had a majority of "No" votes.

The atmosphere inside and outside Dublin Castle, where the votes were being counted, was incredible, as the thousands gathered to watch the vote tallies roll in. As the official announcement was made, the vast throng began singing *Amhrán Na bhFiann*," the Irish National Anthem. Suddenly it seemed a more inclusive anthem than ever with its plea for men and women to rise up.

J. K. Rowling, Hillary Clinton, Ian McKellen, and David Cameron were among those tweeting congratulations.

The Church struck a sour note with Cardinal Parolin, the secretary of state, the equivalent of Vatican prime minister, calling it a "defeat for humanity."

Cardinal Parolin stated:

This result left me feeling very sad but as the Archbishop of Dublin [Diarmuid Martin] pointed out, the Church will have to take this reality on board in the sense of a renewed and strengthened evangelization. I believe that we are talking here not just about a defeat for Christian principles but also about a defeat for humanity.[167]

One Irish bishop described it as like a bereavement.

Archbishop Eamon Martin was more even: The changed social and political climate in Ireland "brings new pastoral realities for the Catholic Church which presents us with fresh challenges. We need not be daunted by these challenges, nor stand around like the first disciples staring into the sky."[168]

The message on Earth could not have been clearer. Leo Varadkar, gay minister for health, called it a "social revolution" and stated it was days like this that he got into politics for.

He said the vote showed that the "traditional cultural divide" between rural and urban areas had vanished.

"This is really Ireland speaking with one voice in favor of equality," he told Irish broadcaster RTÉ.

Catholic Archbishop of Dublin, Diarmuid Martin, said, "[I]f this referendum is an affirmation of the views of young people, then the Church has a huge task in front of it . . ."

Political scientist Jane Suiter, evaluating the victory, wrote in the *Washington Post* that "in the war of words the Yes side proved far superior":

Mirroring the Obama campaign's 50 states strategy, the Yes campaign ran aground campaign with teams in every constituency. It focused on providing messaging for the mainstream and not just the LGBT community. Their strategy was to go after every vote, not just the supportive base. By the last Sunday, five days before polling day they had knocked on every door in every urban center. This sent out a very successful get out the vote campaign across all constituencies as well as on social media in the closing days of the campaign.

The No campaign focused on traditional family values with messages such as "Children Need a Mother and a Father." Given the lived reality of many Irish families today, this likely resulted in a backlash in communities with large numbers of single-parent families. Anecdotally, canvassers found that there was resentment against this perceived slight.[169]

The victory caused a worldwide aftershock. Same-sex marriage groups in Germany and Austria sought a similar referendum vote. The *New York Times* ran the page one headline, "Irish Vote to Approve Gay Marriage, Putting Country in Vanguard."

Alex White, the government's minister for communications, said: "This didn't change Ireland—it confirmed the change. We can no longer be regarded as the authoritarian state we once might have been perceived to be. This marks the true separation of church and state."

Gerry Adams, president of Sinn Féin, said: "There are two Irelands, the elite Ireland and the hidden Ireland. And today the hidden Ireland spoke."[170]

Even as the Yes side celebrated, it was clear that there was one issue that continued to create a deep cleavage like same-sex rights. It involved not two consenting men or women, but a far different set of rules over when, if ever, an Irish woman could have a legal abortion in Ireland. That battle was now joined.

CHAPTER 38

A Gay Prime Minister

"But I stand here as the leader of my country, flawed and human, where I am judged by my political actions and not my sexual orientation, my skin tone, gender or religious beliefs."

Leo Varadkar

A gay man, the son of a migrant, was elected *taoiseach* on June 2, 2017, an incredible feat for a thirty-eight-year-old, the youngest Irish leader ever. Twenty-five years earlier he could have been jailed for his sexuality.

After the victory on same-sex marriage, it was another incredible advance for Ireland and for the astonished watching world.

It was the gay *taoiseach* angle that won the headlines worldwide. No other country in the world had a gay prime minister with the exception of Luxembourg, who had an openly gay man in charge of the country.

The *New York Times* led with the headline "Gay Lawmaker, Leo Varadkar, Is in Line to Be Ireland's Prime Minister."[171]

AFP ran with the headline "Ireland's first gay prime minister enters office."

It reported: "Although regarded as relatively liberal on social issues such as gender equality and abortion rights, Varadkar has been criticized by opposition parties for his right-wing economic views."[172]

The *Guardian* lead stated: "Ireland's first gay prime minister Leo Varadkar formally elected."

The article continued: "The former GP, son of an Indian father and Irish mother, faces a number of challenges as he takes over the only EU country that has a land border with the UK as it prepares for Brexit. . ."[173]

The *Telegraph* had the headline "Ireland elects first gay prime minister Leo Varadkar."

It reported: "Mr. Varadkar, a qualified doctor, only revealed he was gay months before Ireland became the first country in the world to back same-sex marriage in a referendum in May 2015. He has been in a relationship with another medic for about two years."[174]

Only the *Irish Times* led with the age angle: "Leo Varadkar becomes youngest ever *Taoiseach*."[175]

Varadkar's rise to the top had been meteoric since first being elected to the *Dáil* from a Dublin constituency in 2007. Six foot, three inches tall, handsome, brown-skinned, a doctor with an exotic past and bright as a button, he stood out quickly and caught the zeitgeist as Ireland moved ever closer to a multicultural society.

He entered the *Dáil* around the time of the collapse of the Celtic Tiger, which was due to extraordinary shenanigans by Irish banks, lending recklessly and creating a golden circle of insiders who were, in common parlance, "laughing all the way to the bank." The biggest property bubble collapse in history was on the cards, some experts warned but they were not listened to. At its economic peak, half as many homes were being built in Ireland as were being constructed in Britain, fifteen times its size.

Mary Robinson stated to the *New York Times*, "The Celtic tiger ultimately was a huge foolishness. The banks borrowed and lent money irresponsibly, and the developers developed irresponsibly. It's quite fair to heavily criticize the lack of political oversight."[176]

The *New York Times*, in 2005, described Ireland as the "Wild West of European finance."[177] The government was offering huge tax incentives to buy homes, and the reckless level of debt and lack of oversight could not be explained.

Eventually, the crash came, and Ireland survived only by borrowing $100 billion from the EU and the International Monetary Fund.

Saddled with massive debt, the economy was in a tailspin by the 2011 general election, and the outgoing Fianna Fáil/Greens coalition was as popular as bedbugs.

The election was a massacre for Fianna Fáil, who went from seventy-one seats to twenty, while the Greens were totally wiped out. It seemed the two great institutions of Ireland, church and state, were in danger of imminent collapse.

In the new government, Varadkar was immediately promoted to minister for enterprise, a pivotal role, marking him out as a key contender in any future leadership contest. He was later appointed as minister for tourism and then minister for health.

He had clear leadership ambitions. He took an intensive course on the Irish language, a smart move for any leadership contender, and he had successfully held a variety of high-profile portfolios.

His party, Fine Gael, barely hung on to power in the 2016 election by being propped up by an arrangement with the opposition, Fianna Fáil.

It was clear Kenny's leadership days were numbered. He was in his midsixties, and a younger generation was clamoring for change.

By 2017, Enda Kenny had become enmeshed in a police whistle-blower scandal, where honest cop Maurice McCabe had revealed massive corrupt practices within the police force that bled into a government cover-up. Two justice ministers and a police commissioner would ultimately resign, and the party was in a state of complete disarray.

The time was ripe for two young contenders, Varadkar and Simon Coveney, foreign minister, to inform Kenny they could win a vote of no confidence against him within the parliamentary party.

Kenny had no option but to stand aside. It was clear he had become a political liability.

At the heart of Varadkar's support for leadership were Dublin members of the party who wanted a young, dynamic leader from the capital city and county where a massive 1.3 million people lived.

Coveney was considered the candidate from rural Ireland. In the end, the Dublin surge easily won the day, and Varadkar was elected by the Fine Gael Party as party leader and *taoiseach*.

In his speech of acceptance, he specifically singled out Kenny's courage in bringing about a same-sex marriage referendum allowing Varadkar the opportunity to reveal his gay status: "His leadership also enabled me to become an equal citizen in my own country only two short years ago and to aspire to hold this office, an aspiration which I once thought was beyond my reach, at least, if I chose to be myself."[178]

Varadkar certainly had enough to occupy him on getting into office with the Brexit disaster speeding down the tracks.

He won high praise in Ireland for his cool handling of the topic, in contrast to Theresa May's panic mode.

He secured the backing of his European partners, who remained resolute in standing by the agreement that there could be no return to a physical Irish border after Britain departed the EU.

The issue of being gay came back into the headlines around St. Patrick's Day in Washington, where the Irish leader is usually hosted for a St. Patrick's breakfast by the vice president. In this case, Irish-American Mike Pence, a noted critic of gays, would be Varadkar's host.

This 2018 breakfast went so well that Varadkar promised he would bring his partner, Matt Barrett, with him in 2019. It was a far cry from the de Valera days!

Barrett accompanied in 2019 and was received warmly by Pence. In his deft remarks, Varadkar referred to the fact that American political leaders had often inspired him in their outreach to diversity.

Varadkar's partner, Matt Barrett, sat watching expressionless— as did Pence.

It helped inspire me to run for office. I also knew at the time that I lived in a country where if I tried to be myself, at the time I would have ended up breaking laws.

But . . . I stand here as the leader of my country, flawed and human but judged by my political actions and not my sexual orientation, my skin tone, gender, or religious beliefs.

I don't believe my country is the only one in the world where this story is possible. It's found in every country where freedom and liberty are cherished.[179]

In his *New York Times* interview with Maureen Dowd, Varadkar had revealed how he would, in advance, size up the situation with Pence. Would he engage in deep dialogue with him?

Yeah, I would. . . . My experience of the very successful marriage equality referendum here was that if you want to convince people to change their minds, it's not by shouting at them or lecturing them or attacking them personally or degrading them. That's not how you change hearts and minds.

And I certainly look forward to meeting him. I'd like to hear about his stories and his Irish connections, which he seems to be proud of, and maybe tell him a bit about my story, too.[180]

With elegant wording like that, an abundance of talent, and the honesty to address his sexuality early on, it was no great surprise the son of an Indian immigrant made it to the top of the greasy pole in Irish politics. But it was still an incredible achievement.

He cherished his Indian roots, and it would be coincidentally Savita Halapannavar—a daughter of India, a beautiful young woman—who would be at the center of Ireland's next grave crisis and constitutional battle and Varadkar's toughest-ever domestic political battle.

Most Irish people thought they would never see the day that an abortion referendum would succeed. But by 2018, it was no longer your father's Ireland.

CHAPTER 39

"Ireland Murders Pregnant Indian Dentist"

"This is a Catholic country; we don't allow abortion here."
Irish midwife to Savita Halapannavar as she lay dying
after a pregnancy gone wrong

Soon after he was elected, *Taoiseach* Leo Varadkar made clear he would hold a referendum on the right to abortion for Irish women. Varadkar knew the Eighth Amendment to the Constitution had led to tragic outcomes and desperately needed to be addressed. There was also the fact that women were seeking illegal ways around the abortion ban.

Independent.ie broke down part of what he said as follows:

He said "women from every county are risking their lives" by obtaining abortion tablets through "the post."

"Abortion is not a black and white issue; it is a grey area" but we can't continue to "criminalize our sisters and friends" he said.

But there will be "restrictions" said Mr. Varadkar of the likely legislation.

Abortion tablets won't be available "over the counter."

But he said if the referendum is passed, abortion will "no longer be an article for the constitution."[181]

The Eighth Amendment to the Irish Constitution, the one at the heart of the abortion issue, was passed on September 7, 1983, by a 67 to 33 percent majority.

It meant, in practical terms, that a woman had three choices if she had an unplanned pregnancy, even as a result of rape or incest:

The first was to illegally import the abortion pill from overseas. The second option was to travel for an abortion to Britain, where it had been legal since 1967. The third was to allow the pregnancy to continue and give birth to the baby against her will.

The pregnant Irish woman did not have available what was legally allowed in twenty-five of the twenty-eight EU countries—a termination in her own country, by lawful and medically professional means.

The passage of the 1983 referendum seemed to shut the door on that last option forever.

Abortion was already a criminal act in Ireland, but pro-life groups feared, as in the *Roe v. Wade* decision in the US, that somehow abortion could be legalized through the courts. It was a time when abortion laws in many countries were being liberalized.

The proponents of the Eighth Amendment wished to insert a clause into the Constitution where the rights of the unborn baby and the pregnant mother were the same. There would be no equivocation on that. Threatened suicide, or any such condition, would not change the ban against abortion, the only exception being when the life of the mother was in mortal danger. But if that were the case and a fetal heartbeat could be heard, it was bound to create an existential question for the doctors concerned. By aborting with a heartbeat present, the doctor could risk criminal prosecution.

It was a poorly devised amendment, one bound to lead to massive complications as doctors and legislators tried to define in "referendum parlance" how life was to be saved in a hypothetical critical situation.

However, this "hypothetical" question became a real situation in 1991 with the Miss X case, which showed how emotional amendments make bad common-sense laws. Miss X, who was fourteen, was raped by her neighbor and went to England for an abortion. The attorney general became aware of her case and informed her parents they were acting in a criminal manner under the 1983 Amendment, which grants equal rights to the fetus, if they allowed their daughter to abort the baby.

The young girl returned home in a suicidal state of mind and subsequently lost one ruling before the Irish Supreme Court eventually ruled in her favor. As it turned out, she miscarried.

The Miss Y case in 2014 was equally tragic. A foreign national, who was raped and became pregnant in a war zone, ended up in Ireland seeking asylum. She tried to go to England for an abortion but was refused entry. Even when she became suicidal, she was still forced to have the child—who was then given up for adoption.

The 1983 Amendment was clearly problematic, and a later provision—allowing abortion in the case of suicidal tendencies—clearly did not work, as the Miss Y case proved.

Between the time of the Miss X and Miss Y cases, a catastrophic event occurred that dramatically changed the views of the Irish people on abortion.

The woman in question was born in India, the same country as Leo Varadkar's father, and just like the Varadkars', her life story, too, made a massive impact on Ireland. *Irish Times* journalist Kitty Holland delved deeply into the case in the course of her research for a superb book on the topic: *Savita: The Tragedy That Shook a Nation.*

Savita Andanappa Yalagi was born on September 1981 in Bagalkot, a city of 112,000 residents, some three hundred miles from its provincial capital of Bangalore in northwest India. She was beloved as the only girl—she had two brothers.

"She was always funny, always smiling and always the little ruler," her mother told Holland. "We knew she would be a ruler of the house the moment she was born." She was also the precious little sister of her brothers, Santosh and Sanjeev, who were hugely protective of her. "They would do anything she asked."

Andanappa, her father, traveled widely in his job as an electrical engineer with Karnataka Electricity Board. Her mother, Akhmedevi, remembers her as "very fond of dancing."

The family moved to Belgaum, 120 miles or so away, where Savita's father got a better job. She proved to be a brilliant student in the local school.

Her mother recalls, "She loved science and wanted to be a dentist."

After graduating in dentistry in 2004, Savita did a year's internship with a dentist in Belgaum and would have stayed in the city but for meeting her future husband, Praveen Halappanavar, whom she met through a matrimonial website (as is customary for many Indians).

"With the girls, they marry and they accompany their husbands, so that is why she went to Ireland. If she had not gone there would be no problem. She would have worked easily in Belgaum," her father said.

Praveen had been living in Galway for two years working at the Boston Scientific plant, which makes medical devices.

They decided to get married during a meeting in April 2008, and the wedding was arranged there and then. "She was so happy that day," says her father, smiling.

They arrived in Ireland in 2008 and set up home in a rented apartment—later in a house—and settled into a vibrant expat Indian social scene. Savita visited dental clinics "to observe" in preparation for her exams to enable her to practice in Ireland.

Savita passed her Irish board exams and registered, as a fully-fledged dentist in Ireland, on July 11, 2012. That same month, she discovered she was pregnant. Three months later in October, her first gynecological scan showed no complications. The baby was due on March 30, 2013. She decided to delay practicing until after the baby was born.

"She was so happy." Her parents visited and remembered. "She loved Ireland and the peace there. She was happy."

The Halappanavars were celebrating with an early baby shower because her parents were visiting, when Savita felt the sharp pain she had been feeling in her pelvis getting worse. Up to that point, her parents remembered, "Savita was on top of the world. We were so excited, all talking about the baby."

That night she couldn't sleep. The pain she had had in her lower back for the previous few months was worse than usual and was radiating around her pelvis. At about 9 a.m., Praveen phoned the maternity ward at University Hospital Galway.

"I spoke to a midwife and explained what was happening and she said to come on in. So we told her parents we were going to the hospital."

On Sunday, October 21, 2012, at 9:35 a.m., Savita and her husband, Praveen, attended the gynecological ward at University Hospital Galway without an appointment. She presented with sharp back pain.

She was assured it was just back pain and was sent home, but she was told to come back if it got worse.

It did, and she returned later that day after she felt "something coming down" in her stomach. She was in great pain.

The midwife believed she was miscarrying, and doctors agreed.[182]

Journal.ie reported that "even with the partial miscarriage there was still a fetal heartbeat and under Irish law the doctors claimed they could do nothing given the equal life amendment to the constitution, passed in 1983."[183]

Of course, with the fetus being nonviable on its own at that stage of pregnancy, it was a ridiculous assessment.

A midwife told her as she struggled in pain that she couldn't have an abortion, as "This is a Catholic country."

Holland reported:

Just after midnight on Monday, 22 October, Savita began vomiting violently and had a spontaneous rupture of membranes—that is that the bag of membranes around the fetus had burst and the fluid . . . had leaked out.

By 8:20 a.m., she was experiencing bleeding but her pain had eased. At this time, the consultant discussed the risk of infection and sepsis with her, explaining the need to continuously check for a fetal heartbeat.[184]

At the same time the following day, Savita and Praveen asked about using medication to induce the miscarriage. Since the outcome was inevitable, they did not want a protracted waiting time.

The doctor kept telling her that as long as there was a heartbeat, they could not perform what they called an abortion.

For three days, they refused her request. Eventually she contracted sepsis and plunged into a death spiral.

Her husband remembered a nurse running to him and asking if he could be with Savita as she was dying.

> [T]he nurse came running. . . . She, she just told me to pray and she took me near Savita and she said, "Will you be OK to be there during her last few minutes?" I said, "Yes; I want to" . . .
>
> It was all in their hands, and they just let her go. How can you let a young woman go to save a baby who will die anyway? Savita could have had more babies.
>
> What is the use in being angry? . . . I've lost her. I am talking about this because it shouldn't happen to anyone else. It has been very hard to understand how this can happen in the 21st century.[185]

The story was reported across the world and became a sensation. One headline stood out. On November 16, the main story on the *India Times* website was "Ireland Murders Pregnant Indian Dentist."[186]

It was clear that the newspaper had a point.

It was also clear there could be no more Savitas. Her death and the circumstances around it shocked the nation and the world. The fact that the fetus was nonviable but Savita was still forced to undergo tremendous pain and eventually die incensed people.

The inquiry into her death heard evidence from the hospital consultant:

> At interview the consultant stated: "Under Irish law, if there's no evidence of risk to the life of the mother, our hands are tied so long as there's a fetal heart." The consultant stated that if risk to the mother was to increase then a termination would have been possible, but that it would be based on actual risk and not a theoretical risk of infection "we can't predict who is going to get an infection."[187]

The parsing and analysis was clear: Savita died because of a ludicrous law barring a termination on a nonviable fetus.

There were no quick fixes. Abortion was still the third rail of Irish politics, but the Eighth Amendment was fatally flawed. A referendum to overturn the Eighth took five years to organize as constitutional arguments raged as to working and legal consequences.

The result of the same-sex marriage referendum in 2015 buoyed the "Repeal the 8th" group, and finally a referendum date was set for May 25, 2018.

Savita's father, from India, pleaded with the people to vote for no more Savitas.

"I hope the people of Ireland remember my daughter, Savita, on the day of the referendum and that what happened to her won't happen to any other family," Andanappa Yalagi told the *Guardian* newspaper by phone from his home in Karnataka in southwest India.

He said his daughter's death at the age of thirty-one had devastated the family. "It's still very emotional after five years. I think about her every day. She didn't get the medical treatment she needed because of the eighth amendment. They must change the law."[188]

Just as in the case of the same-sex marriage referendum, there was no guarantee that this referendum would be passed (and that the law would be changed). It was untested ground.

CHAPTER 40

The Drive to Repeal the Eighth Amendment

"I hope the people of Ireland remember my daughter, Savita, on the day of the referendum and that what happened to her won't happen to any other family."

Andanappa Yalagi

Following on in 2016, from the success of the same-sex marriage referendum in 2015, the then-*Taoiseach* Enda Kenny set about creating the correct conditions for the passage of a vote to repeal the Eighth Amendment.

That Eighth Amendment read, "The State acknowledges the right to life of the unborn and, with due regard to the equal right to life of the mother, guarantees in its laws to respect, and, as far as practicable, by its laws to defend and vindicate that right."[189]

The Amendment copper-fastened the rights of the fetus as the same as the mother. The Savita Halapannavar case revealed the fatal flaw in the wording of the Eighth.

Ironically, Peter Sutherland, Ireland's attorney general at the time the Eighth was passed in 1983, strongly opposed the wording and stated it would "lead inevitably to confusion and uncertainty."

Sutherland was concerned that the wording meant that a doctor faced with a case where the life of the mother and the child were equally at risk would come to the "only lawful conclusion . . . that he could do nothing, absolutely nothing which infringed on either right."[190]

His concerns went unheard. The anti-abortion groups in Ireland in 1983 were very powerful and aided in large part by American funding and involvement. The anti-amendment forces were thin on the ground and were famously branded as "wife-swopping sodomites" at one anti-abortion group rally.

Bernadette Bonar, one of the founders of the pro-life Amendment lobby, told how the pro-amendment group had first met in a pub. "The five of us met in a Dublin pub. We knew we had to do something to stop abortion coming into the county. We had lost the fight against contraception, and one thing was certain: we couldn't afford to lose this one."[191]

They didn't, winning in spectacular style by 67 percent to 33 percent. It was 1983, and Savita Halappanavar was an unknown two-year-old toddler in India.

The Eighth Amendment was thus added to the Irish Constitution. The anti-abortion language used clearly suggested the necessity for punishment. Abortion was a criminal offense. Indeed, women caught with the abortion pill were liable for jail terms of fourteen years.

Over the next thirty-five years, Peter Sutherland's fears were realized, and the Amendment continued to haunt due, in no small way, to the lack of clarity in its wording.

For instance, many women were illegally importing the abortion pill from Britain, and they risked a fourteen-year jail term, plus the danger of major medical complications by taking the abortion pill unsupervised.

"I think it's only a matter of time before someone hemorrhages or bleeds to death after taking these pills unregulated," Leo Varadkar told broadcaster RTÉ. "Let's not wait for this to happen."

The decision, made in 2016 to push for repeal of the Eighth, was a bold step for Kenny, a rural TD whose constituency in Mayo was far more conservative than most.

Kenny and Varadkar saw the work of the constitutional convention on the same-sex marriage referendum as absolutely vital. Kenny described its role as "outstanding."

An abortion amendment was a different animal, however, and Kenny confided to his associates that he felt it had to be handled just right at the beginning if a vote to delete the Eighth were to be successful.

By midsummer 2016, amid the euphoria and celebration of the 100th anniversary of Easter 1916, Kenny placed his plan before his Cabinet colleagues. The Cabinet approved another meeting of the Constitutional Convention to hear the merits and demerits. Kenny correctly guessed a positive recommendation there would go a very long way in ensuring victory. The deliberations were not being held in a vacuum. The Tuam Babies story had grabbed headlines all over the world and continued to do so.

In 2012, thanks to a dedicated amateur historian in the town of Tuam, some thirty miles from Galway, Catherine Corless presented convincing evidence that babies and young children from the local orphanage had been buried in a mass grave. There was a steady flow of new and damaging stories almost every week up to 2018, almost all of which reflected very badly on the church and state. In 2017, the *New York Times* featured a lengthy piece on its front page titled "The Lost Children of Tuam."

It was the story that would not go away.

This Associated Press story was carried worldwide in 2017: "A mass grave containing the remains of babies and young children has been discovered at a former Catholic orphanage in Ireland, government-appointed investigators announced Friday in a finding that offered the first conclusive proof following a historian's efforts to trace the fates of nearly 800 children who perished there."[192]

It put the Church on the defensive again, as stoutly as it had been in covering up for Father Brendan Smyth. It made their interventions in issues such as abortion rights appear downright brazen given their own history of callous and criminal behavior against defenseless children and babies.

An insight into the brutal fate suffered by children consigned to orphanages like the Tuam one can be gleaned from the following statement made by a medical doctor:

"A great many people are always asking what is the good of keeping these children alive? I quite agree that it would be a great deal kinder to strangle these children at birth than to put them out to nurse."[193]

That was Doctor Ella Webb, June 18, 1924, speaking about illegitimate children in care in Ireland at the time.

Elaine Byrne, a columnist with the *Sunday Business Post* in Ireland, discovered the quote as she researched how on Earth up to eight hundred children had been allowed to die and then had their bodies stuffed into a septic tank by the Bon Secours Sisters in Tuam, County Galway.

Her answer is clear; it was condoned and covered up by the political, religious, and medical establishments at the time. They were like God's little executioners when it came to children out of wedlock.

The sin of having sex outside marriage was all-encompassing. The progeny of such sex was the devil's spawn.

Confirmation now exists that a mass grave of little children existed near the former Catholic orphanage. The Mother and Baby Homes Commission found an underground structure divided into twenty chambers containing "significant quantities of human remains."

One in four of those little children born out of wedlock would die within a year of birth. As stated in *Irish Central*, in Dr. Webb's time, a commission found that: "The illegitimate child being proof of the mother's shame is in most cases sought to be hidden at all costs. The child becomes an encumbrance on the foster mother who has no interest in keeping it alive."

The mortality rate for these children admittedly was 25 percent on average over the years, but only 7 percent for the "normal" children of married parents. A 1935 report unearthed by Byrne states, "Doubtless the great proportion of deaths in these cases is due to congenital debility, congenital malformation and other antenatal causes traceable to the conditions associated with the unfortunate lot of the unmarried mother."[194]

There you had it. A child out of wedlock was the fault of the clearly morally and physically corrupted single mother. The official Irish state had ruled.

No wonder the poor orphans were allowed to die of neglect. The Irish state and church, it appears, let them die by the hundreds.

As Catherine Corless, the noble campaigner who against all the odds and cover-ups exposed the Tuam babies scandal, stated, "The county council knew at the time there were remains there, the local guards knew, the religious knew. And yet it was all nicely covered up and forgotten about."

DNA analysis of selected remains confirmed the ages of the dead ranged from thirty-five weeks to three years old and that they were buried chiefly in the 1950s, when the overcrowded facility was one of more than a dozen in Ireland offering "shelter" to orphans, unwed mothers, and their children. The Tuam home closed in 1961.

Catherine Corless tracked down death certificates for nearly eight hundred children. Eighteen, she discovered, actually died of starvation.

"Everything pointed to this area being a mass grave," said Corless.

The Church or state had no valid response, as they had not for pedophiles or selling babies to America without the mother's consent (it is estimated up to a one thousand babies a year were sold from Tuam alone).

Issues such as the "Tuam babies" and weekly stories of high-level cover-ups of pedophiles meant the Church had lost all moral influence as they girded up for the battle over abortion. Even the good priests and bishops found themselves tarred.

An unthinkable development, the legalization of abortion, was about to be voted on, but the Church was too mired in its own scandals to properly mobilize.

The Yes side in the Abortion debate had learned well from the same-sex marriage debate, which showed that personal stories could and would trump all the theological and moral appeals of the No side.

After the election, 39 percent of "Yes" voters stated that a conversation or knowledge about someone they knew personally who had an abortion had influenced their vote.

Notwithstanding such personal stories, *Taoiseach* Enda Kenny felt clarity was the key to the successful passage of the amendment.

"There needs to be a real discussion here, and people would want to know if you're going to take that (The Eighth Amendment) out of the Constitution, what are you going to replace it with?" he asked.

He and his successor, Leo Varadkar, felt the strategy had to be just right. Same-sex marriage between two consenting adults was an easier sell than introducing abortion into what recently had been the most conservative country in the Western hemisphere. The fact was that abortion was an incredibly difficult issue on both sides.

Kenny knew the intricacies and warned his Cabinet at the first meeting on the topic that if a referendum were to be held right now, "it would not be passed."

But Kenny's hunch was also that after Savita, Miss X, and Miss Y, the country was ahead of the political class, if the right tactics and message were utilized. Support had to come from the ground up, which is why, in the first instance, the imprimatur of the Constitutional Convention was vital.

His instinct was right. The Constitutional Convention was convened. The *Irish Times* reported that "Ninety-nine men and women gathered over five weekends in Malahide, Co Dublin, and heard from 40 experts in medicine, law, and ethics and six women directly affected by the amendment."[195] (The 100th person was the chairman, a distinguished judge, Mary Laffoy.)

The delegates would acquire incredible knowledge and an "almost uniquely comprehensive understanding" of abortion, Laffoy stated.

Given that, the result of their deliberations was astonishing: an extraordinary 87.3 percent wanted the amendment removed from the Irish Constitution, and 64 percent wanted no restrictions on abortions in the first twelve weeks of pregnancy.

The outcome was far more liberal than anyone had expected. It also showed the inability of the Catholic Church and its acolytes, such as the Knights of Columbus, to muster its base in opposition on arguably the most important issue of all to them.

From the convention, the recommendations went to the Oireachtas Committee dealing with constitutional referendums.

They met and backed up the Citizen's Constitutional Convention vote.

The *Times* reported: "Led by Fine Gael Senator Catherine Noone, it would eventually mirror the decision of those 99 citizens, with the majority of TDs and Senators voting in favor of unrestricted abortion up to 12 weeks, and for access to terminations in the case of fatal fetal abnormality or where the life or health of the mother was at risk."[196]

The committee concluded its work in December 2017. Leo Varadkar had replaced Kenny as *taoiseach* in June of that year. The last great battle between secular and religious forces in Ireland was now set. Varadkar just needed to announce the date. It was game on.

CHAPTER 41

"The Old Ireland Is Gone"

"I grew up in an Ireland that was so different. It's not just another country, it's another planet."

Ailbhe Smyth, Repeal the 8th Amendment Leadership Member, on the referendum result

The path to the referendum date had not been all smooth. Debate in the national parliament on the abortion referendum was fraught, as conservative members attacked the proposed referendum bill. Health Minister Simon Harris led the debate for the government.

"I hope that as a country we can no longer tolerate a law which denies care and understanding to women who are our friends, our sisters, our mothers, our daughters, our wives."

Hildegarde Naughton of Fine Gael, previously against removing the Eighth, changed her mind after being educated about the abortion pill being allegedly effective for ten weeks. "Abortion pills are being taken in Ireland and if we do nothing, some women in the not-too-distant future will rupture their uteruses and die," she said.

There was one sensational development. Michael Martin, leader of the main opposition party Fianna Fáil, announced he was in favor of abortion up to twelve weeks. His own party at their annual convention had voted three to one against repealing the amendment.

He stated: "While I have supported different proposals to clarify the law and to address the threat to the life of the mother I have been broadly in favor of the law as enabled by the Eighth Amendment."

His decision was also influenced by the easy availability of the abortion pill. "Equally it is clear that the reality of the abortion pill means we are no longer talking about a procedure which involves the broader medical system. However," he added, "I believe we each have a duty to be willing to question our own views, to be open to different perspectives, and to respond to new information . . . I will vote accordingly."

This admission of support from the leader of the party founded by Eamon de Valera, whose constitutional ban on abortion was being ripped asunder, was a huge boost for the Yes side. The unseen factor was the abortion pill importance. Irish women were using it, and it was apparently effective up to twelve weeks. So why should the much safer type of abortion, with medical assistance, not be approved?

Leo Varadkar announced that the referendum would be held on May 25, 2018. Ireland "already has abortion, but it is unsafe," he said. "Women from every county are risking their lives" by obtaining abortion tablets through "the post."

The 1983 abortion referendum was one of the nastiest political campaigns in Irish history, but the 2018 campaign was conducted with far more restraint. Perhaps it was out of respect for the memory of Savita, whose face appeared on Yes posters throughout the last few weeks of the campaign. As *Irish Times* writer Harry McGee noted:

"The Savita case was never too far away from people's minds during the eight weeks."[197]

Ivana Bacik, a Labour Party senator and women's rights activist, also pointed to Savita's death as a major factor.

Writing in the *Guardian,* she stated that the reaction to the Savita and Miss X cases meant that "public opinion had thus shifted towards supporting repeal of the constitutional ban and for legal abortion to take place in Ireland."[198]

Maureen Dowd, star columnist of the *New York Times*, who was in Dublin to cover the story, wrote:

"This country is in the midst of an excruciating existential battle over whether it should keep its adamantine abortion statute, giving an unborn baby equal rights with the mother. Under the Eighth Amendment, abortions are illegal, even in cases of rape or incest. The only exception is when it is believed that the mother will die. Anyone caught buying pills online to induce a miscarriage faces up to 14 years in prison."[199]

Archbishop Eamon Martin, primate of Ireland, issued a plea not to remove the Eighth from the Constitution.

"When you go inside the voting booth on 25 May, pause and think of two lives—the life of the mother and the life of her baby—two hearts beating; two lives which are both precious and deserving of compassion and protection," Martin said.

He continued, "The Eighth Amendment recognizes the equality of life of a mother and her unborn baby," and said women's lives "are precious, to be loved, valued, and protected."

But he said babies' lives are also "precious, to be loved, valued, and protected."

Martin also said abortion was not a Catholic issue, but one of human dignity steeped in "reason as well as in faith," and is a value for "people of all faiths and none."[200]

The Pro Life Campaign issued its own statement headlined "Life Equality, Keep the 8th":

Each human being regardless of age, gender, disability, race, status in society, possesses a profound, inherent, equal, and irreplaceable value and dignity. Abortion advocates want the unborn child to be an exception to this rule. To do this they resort to the ploy of denying the humanity of the unborn.

The sign of a truly civilized society, however, is one that welcomes *everyone* in life and protects *everyone* in its laws.

Equality includes *Everyone*.[201]

As noted, the Church went quiet as the debate heated up. The topic of abortion should have been catnip to them, but, as the Jesuit magazine *America* noted:

> "A notably muted voice during the debate . . . has been that of the Catholic Church in Ireland . . . its moral authority weakened by years of revelations about the sexual abuse of children by its clergy, the Irish Church, many say, has taken a low-profile role on the vote."[202]

The lack of a vigorous church response certainly impacted the campaign. Yet the Church was like Banquo's ghost at Macbeth's coronation banquet, with the sins of the past still resonating in the public mind.

The abortion campaign was also heavily influenced by a scandal involving Irish women getting false all-clears from pap smears conducted by a company in Texas that had been employed by the Irish health service on the grounds of saving money. Many women would subsequently die because of these horrifying misreads.

Many Irish female voters perceived this as another example of neglect of women's issues by the government.

On the pro-life side, two arguments were being made. The first, that a provision allowing abortion, in the case of a risk of a mother's suicide, meant the abortion could happen up to six months; the second, that the vast majority of Down syndrome babies were being aborted in Britain. The Yes answer was there was no way to identify a Down baby in the first twelve weeks—a claim the No side denied.

However, when it came to expert testimony on the overall issue, there was far more buy-in on the repeal side by doctors and surgeons. This became particularly important during the televised debates, when complex issues around abortion were examined.

There were also the lessons learned from the same-sex marriage victory: personal stories worked, they worked especially on social media, and they worked when shared with close friends and families. Tales of incest, rape, pedophile attacks, and taking night boats and trains to London for abortions all came spilling out.

Following the vote, 40 percent who voted "yes" said their vote had been influenced by personal contact with a woman or women who shared their stories with them.

As voting day approached, the interest from the world media was beyond belief, and the global press descended on Ireland.

Would Ireland once again defy its own history and rigid Catholic past to allow abortion?

As the *Irish Times* noted: "[T]his extraordinary referendum campaign seeped into Irish public consciousness on doorsteps, in the streets, in the media, or on the airwaves . . . right up to polling day."[203]

The overall result was too close to call. The general sense was there would be a Dublin/rural split with the more conservative country voters disapproving. There was a large undecided vote.

The final opinion polls showed the gap closing with the repeal group ahead, but there was widespread speculation of "shy" "No" voters not admitting they would vote against repeal.

Then came the moment of truth.

On May 25, 2018, the Irish voters spoke loudly and vociferously, and they voted for abortion up to twelve weeks with no restrictions. Sixty-six percent voted for, 34 percent against.

Even the most optimistic repeal advocates had not dared to dream of such a big win.

The *Taoiseach* Leo Varadkar welcomed the result.

"What we have seen today is the culmination of a quiet revolution [that has been taking place] for the past 10 or 20 years." Still, it was a bittersweet victory.[204]

Savita Halappanavar's father, full of emotion, told the *Observer* newspaper "I have no words to express my gratitude to the people of Ireland."

"I'm really overwhelmed and proud," Dominique McMullan, 31, told the *Guardian* while wiping away tears. "With the marriage equality referendum and this, we are leading the way—we are a new country. The old Ireland is gone."

The *Guardian* headline read: "Ireland votes by landslide to legalize abortion."

Every constituency except for Donegal voted to repeal. There was no city/rural divide.

In Dublin, a large mural of Savita Halapannavar became a symbolic pilgrimage site with hundreds leaving notes and candles.

Dominque McMullan had made her way there, too.

"I came down especially to pay tribute," McMullan said. "It's brilliant that this has happened, but we can't forget the people who died because of our laws."[205]

W. B. Yeats's words "All changed, changed utterly" spring to mind.

A new generation had changed Ireland, from a hidebound, narrow, and insular country to one of the most liberal and admired in the world. This was the reality that would greet Pope Francis during his August visit. Between two popes, John Paul II and Francis, and their visits to Ireland forty years apart, the country had changed beyond all recognition, as Francis was about to learn.

CHAPTER 42

The Past Is Another Country

"We ask for forgiveness for the abuses in Ireland, abuses of power and conscience, sexual abuses on the part of qualified members of the Church."

Pope Francis during his Irish visit in August 2018

At 10:30 a.m., on the bright summer morning of August 25, 2018, Pope Francis arrived in Dublin Airport.

The pope was in Ireland to take part in a world family Congress and to try and heal the open wounds of the Church abuse scandals.

Unlike the visit of Pope John Paul II in 1979, which was marked by triumphal processions throughout the country and where 2.7 million people turned out to greet him at Mass rallies, this visit was profoundly different in tone and response.

Just three months earlier, abortion had been legalized by a stunning referendum win of 66 percent to 34 percent. In 2015, same-sex marriage had also been passed by a similar margin.

Meanwhile, Mass attendance had dropped to a mere 35 percent (18 percent in Dublin) down from 90 percent during the visit of John Paul II in 1979. Hopes among church leaders in Ireland that the Francis visit would spark a renewed interest in the Church were quickly dashed.

Francis, an enormously popular figure worldwide, learned quickly that the past was another country and the Ireland of 1979, which had seen an estimated 2.7 million flock to see Pope John Paul, no longer existed.

A large group of protestors in 2018 greeted Francis, marching through Dublin, demanding full accountability by the Irish bishops. Such a protest would have been unthinkable in 1979.

Father Michael Cleary and Bishop Eamonn Casey, who led the rapturous welcome in 1979 for John Paul II, were now both dead with their reputations in tatters as a result of the revelations of their ignominious activities: it was child abuse in the case of Casey and his denial of his son Peter's existence for many years, and in Cleary's case the fathering of a child with his seventeen-year-old housemaid. Cardinal Tómas Ó Fiaich, who had been primate of all Ireland during the pope's visit, was the last cardinal to pass with an unsullied reputation. His successors, Cardinal Cahal Daly and Cardinal Sean Brady, had been unmasked for their roles in covering up for the arch pedophile and psychopath Father Brendan Smyth.

Meanwhile, from his retirement residence in Cork, Bishop John Magee must have contemplated what might have been.

As private secretary to John Paul II, he had been the key figure behind the triumphal papal visit to Ireland in 1979, a cleric with a very promising future. Now, almost forty years later, he was in retirement and disgrace for his own handling of pedophilia cases.

At the end of his stay, Francis celebrated Mass in Dublin's Phoenix Park, where the large cross, illegally erected for John Paul, still stood and where the largest crowd in the history of Ireland, over one million, had gathered in 1979.

In a clear case of pathetic fallacy, the rain poured down on Francis.

There were literally hundreds of thousands of empty spaces where the crowds should be. The official attendance estimate from the Office of Public Works was 152,000, while more than 475,000 had been expected to attend. Pope John Paul had attracted over one million to his Mass in Phoenix Park. The numbers did not lie.

That September day in 1979 was the zenith of the power of the Catholic Church in Ireland.

John Paul had hardly departed when the rot set in for the church. By the time of the visit of Francis, a compassionate and beloved man, there was little hope that anything could be done to salvage the Church's reputation.

The Irish people, too, had risen up, and fearless men and women had stepped forward to tell the searing truth behind the magisterium of the institutional church. As a nation of storytellers, the Irish are unsurpassed, and now as a nation of truth-tellers, they were unbeatable.

The Irish had embarked on a long journey for truth. There were massive obstacles and diversions, mistruths and empty promises on the way, but somehow, like a weary river, the truth had found its way safely to the sea.

It wasn't your father's Ireland anymore; now it was a more humane, understanding country where power was exercised by the will of the people and not hidden hands. It is finally a more just society.

Somewhere, Father Flanagan is smiling. In 2012, he got the Church recognition he deeply deserved and was declared a Servant of God, a step toward sainthood. His incredible work recognized at last. No doubt Archbishop McQuaid turned in his lonely grave.

Endnotes

1   John Fay, "Boys Town founder Fr. Flanagan warned Irish Church about abuse," Irish Central, July 13, 2016, https://www.irishcentral .com/news/boys-town-founder-fr-flanagan-warned-irish-church -about-abuse-46390952-237644371.

2   "Fr Flanagan and industrial schools," *History Ireland*, https:// www.historyireland.com/20th-century-contemporary-history/ fr-flanagan-and-industrial-schools.

3   Ibid.

4   Fay, "Boys Town founder."

5   The *Irish Times, Do they think we're eejits?: A selection of Mary Raftery columns 2003–2009* (Dublin: The Irish Times Limited, 2013), chap. "No doubts at stance of Fr, Flanagan," https://www .irishtimes.com/polopoly_fs/irishtimes.eBooks.DTTWE.pdf!/menu /standard/file/Do%20they%20think%20we%27re%20Eejits.pdf.

6   "BOYS TOWN FOUNDER AND ABUSE," *Irish Times*, February 21, 2020, https://www.irishtimes.com/opinion/letters/boys-town-founder -and-abuse-1.1051271.

7   Petula Martyn, "Glin: The Limerick councillor who shouted 'stop'," *Limerick Leader*, May 8, 2009, http://www.alliancesupport.org/news /archives/002863.html.

8   Mary Raftery, "No doubts at stance of Fr Flanagan," *Irish Times*, September 9, 2014, https://www.irishtimes.com/opinion/no-doubts -at-stance-of-fr-flanagan-1.1156859.

9   Fay, "Boys Town founder."

10   John Fay, "On This Day: Father Flanagan, founder of Boys Town, is born in Ireland," *Irish Central*, July 13, 2019, https://www .irishcentral.com/roots/history/father-flanagan-boys-town-founder.

11   Michael O'Regan, "Obituary: Eamonn Casey," *Irish Times*, March 13, 2017, https://www.irishtimes.com/news/social-affairs/religion-and -beliefs/obituary-eamonn-casey-1.3008779.

12   Irish Central Staff, "Bishop Eamon Casey raped his niece (5) and assaulted other children," *Irish Central*, March 26, 2019, https ://www.irishcentral.com/news/bishop-eamon-casey-raped-assaulted -children.

13   Fintan O'Toole, "Why is the story of Fr Michael Cleary still the subject of denial?," *Irish Times*, July 1, 2014, https://www.irishtimes .com/news/social-affairs/religion-and-beliefs/why-is-the-story-of-fr -michael-cleary-still-the-subject-of-denial-1.1850600.

14   "Dark secrets of a charismatic cleric: Rollercoaster career of Bishop Eamonn Casey," *Independent.ie*, December 10, 2019, https://www .independent.ie/irish-news/dark-secrets-of-a-charismatic-cleric -rollercoaster-career-of-bishop-eamonn-casey-37961946.html.

15   John Paul II, "Apostolic Journey to Ireland Holy Mass for the Youth of Ireland," Galway, County Galway, September 30, 1979, http ://www.vatican.va/content/john-paul-ii/en/homilies/1979/documents /hf_jp-ii_hom_19790930_irlanda-galway-giovani.html.

16   Patsy McGarry, "Controversial private secretary to three popes subject of disturbing revelations," *Irish Times*, July 14, 2011, https://www .irishtimes.com/news/controversial-private-secretary-to-three-popes -subject-of-disturbing-revelations-1.599206?mode=sample&auth -failed=1&pw-origin=https%3A%2F%2Fwww.irishtimes .com%2Fnews%2Fcontroversial-private-secretary-to-three-popes -subject-of-disturbing-revelations-1.599206.

17   Niall O'Dowd, "What secrets does disgraced Bishop Magee take to the grave?," *Irish Central*, March 27, 2010, https://www.irishcentral .com/opinion/niallodowd/what-vatican-secrets-does-disgraced -bishop-john-magee-take-with-him-89340797-238024831.

18   John L. Allen Jr., "Secretary to three popes has vivid memories," *National Catholic Reporter*, April 5, 2015, http://www.national catholicreporter.org/update/conclave/pt040505a.htm.

19   Peter Costello, "A diplomatic view of Bishop John Magee," *The Irish Catholic*, January 4, 2014, https://www.irishcatholic.com/diplomatic -view-bishop-john-magee.

20   Gerard Howlin, "Congress reduced to niche affair," *Irish Examiner*, June 8, 2012, https://www.irishexaminer.com/viewpoints/analysis /congress-reduced-to-niche-affair-196626.html.

21   Barry Sheppard, "Inflaming sectarian passions' The Eucharistic Congress of 1932 and the North of Ireland," *The Irish History*, July 7, 2016, https://www.theirishstory.com/2016/07/07/inflaming-sectarian -passions-the-eucharistic-congress-of-1932-and-the-north-of -ireland/#.Xe_gwzNKiM9.

22   "Pope and ceremony: how the 1932 Congress melded church and State," *Irish Times*, January 2, 2012, https://www.irishtimes.com /life-and-style/people/pope-and-ceremony-how-the-1932-congress -melded-church-and-state-1.1063510?mode=sample&auth -failed=1&pw-origin=https%3A%2F%2Fwww.irishtimes .com%2Flife-and-style%2Fpeople%2Fpope-and-ceremony-how-the -1932-congress-melded-church-and-state-1.1063510.

23   "Haughey blamed for sex smear against Hillery," *Independent.ie*, December 13, 2008, https://www.independent.ie/irish-news/haughey -blamed-for-sex-smear-against-hillery-26499151.html.

24   Cahir O'Doherty, "A tale of two popes: Recalling John Paul in Ireland as Francis visits," *Irish Central*, August 25, 2018, https://www .irishcentral.com/opinion/cahirodoherty/papal-visits-ireland-francis -john-paul.

25   "Flashback to 1979: Remembering when Pope John Paul II came to Ireland," *Irish Times*, August 25, 2018, https://www.irishtimes .com/news/social-affairs/religion-and-beliefs/flashback-to-1979 -remembering-when-pope-john-paul-ii-came-to-ireland-1.3608010.

26   Nuala McCann, "Remembering when the Pope came to Ireland," *BBC*, September 16, 2010, https://www.bbc.com/news/uk-northern -ireland-11222063.

27 "On the day the Pope flew in, we were looking for an excuse to party," *Independent.ie*, December 4, 2016, https://www.independent .ie/life/on-the-day-the-pope-flew-in-we-were-looking-for-an-excuse -to-party-35260909.html.

28 Kim Bielenberg, "Ecstatic welcome for charismatic John Paul II," March 12, 2017, https://www.independent.ie/life/ecstatic-welcome -for-charismatic-john-paul-ii-35517209.html.

29 Ibid.

30 Ibid.

31 Ibid.

32 Ibid.

33 Ibid.

34 Liam O'Dwyer, "How A Gang of Irish Lads Protected the Pope from the Dignitaries," *Regina*, https://reginamag.com/john-paul-ii-ireland/.

35 Dean Ruxton, "Pope hysteria in 1979: 'I made 5,000 sandwiches, and sold only 2,000'," *Irish Times*, August 15, 2018, https://www .irishtimes.com/news/social-affairs/religion-and-beliefs/pope-hysteria -in-1979-i-made-5-000-sandwiches-and-sold-only-2-000-1.3596321.

36 Conor Gallagher, "Gay community recalls dark days before decriminalization," *Irish Times*, November 30, 2016, https://www .irishtimes.com/news/social-affairs/gay-community-recalls-dark -days-before-decriminalisation-1.2886652?mode=sample&auth -failed=1&pw-origin=https%3A%2F%2Fwww.irishtimes .com%2Fnews%2Fsocial-affairs%2Fgay-community-recalls-dark -days-before-decriminalisation-1.2886652.

37 Ibid.

38 Rictor Norton (Ed.), *Homosexuality in Eighteenth-Century England: A Sourcebook*. Updated July 28, 2019, http://rictornorton.co.uk /eighteen/.

39 Cahir O'Doherty, interviewed by Niall O'Dowd.

40 Gallagher, "Dark days."

41 Ibid.

42 Maggie O' Kane, "The night they killed Declan Flynn."

43   Amarra Mohamed, "Pride in Pictures: Dublin hosts a 10 day festival for Pride," *LGBTQ Nation*, June 7, 2019, https://www.lgbtqnation .com/2019/06/pride-pictures-dublin-hosts-10-day-festival-pride/.

44   Louisa McGrath, "It's Time to Acknowledge the Lesbians Who Fought in the Easter Rising," *Dublin Inquirer*, November 25, 2015, https://dublininquirer.com/2015/11/25/it-s-time-to-acknowledge-the -lesbians-who-fought-in-the-easter-rising.

45   Diarmaid Ferriter, "Diarmaid Ferriter: Abortionist Mamie Cadden was no Vera Drake," *Irish Times*, January 27, 2018, https://www .irishtimes.com/opinion/diarmaid-ferriter-abortionist-mamie-cadden -was-no-vera-drake-1.3369632.

46   Nell McCafferty, *A Woman to Blame: The Kerry Babies Case* (Ireland, Attic Press: 2010).

47   Sinead O'Carroll, "Twenty years on: a timeline of the X case," *Journal.ie*, February 6, 2012, https://www.thejournal.ie/twenty-years -on-a-timeline-of-the-x-case-347359-Feb2012/.

48   Kitty Holland, "Timeline of Ms Y case," *Irish Times*, September 4, 2014, https://www.irishtimes.com/news/social-affairs/timeline-of-ms -y-case-1.1951699.

49   Ibid.

50   Mary Robinson, *Everybody Matters: My Life Giving Voice* (New York: Bloomsbury Publishing, 2014), chap. 5, 71.

51   Ibid., 27.

52   T. Ryle Dwyer, "'This is not a proper person we should have entertaining here' - How Jayne Mansfield inflamed the Kerry church," *Independent. ie*, April 23, 2017, https://www.independent.ie/entertainment/movies /this-is-not-a-proper-person-we-should-have-entertaining-here-how -jayne-mansfield-inflamed-the-kerry-church-35645774.html.

53   Ibid.

54   Ibid.

55   *Irish Central* Staff, "German name for royal baby Archie revisits troubling Nazi links," *Irish Central*, May 13, 2019, https://www .irishcentral.com/opinion/niallodowd/german-name-for-royal-baby -archie-revisits-troubling-nazi-links.

56 John Cooney, *John Charles McQuaid: The Ruler of Catholic Ireland* (New York: Syracuse University Press, 2000), 69.

57 "Dáil Éireann debates, Vol. 91 (9 July 1943)," *Houses of the Oireachtas,* July 9, 1943, https://www.oireachtas.ie/en/debates/debate /dail/1943-07-09/8/?highlight%5B0%5D=jews&highlight%5B1%5 D=jews&highlight%5B2%5D=jews.

58 Edna O'Brien, "Causing a commotion," the *Guardian,* April 18, 2008, https://www.theguardian.com/books/2008/apr/19/featuresreviews .guardianreview2.

59 James Kelly, "Happy birthday Edna O'Brien, one of Ireland's finest writers," *Irish Central,* December 15, 2018, https://www.irishcentral .com/culture/entertainment/happy-birthday-edna-obrien-irish-writer.

60 Rachel Cooke, "Edna O'Brien: 'A writer's imaginative life commences in childhood'," the *Guardian,* February 5, 2011, https://www.theguardian .com/books/2011/feb/06/edna-obrien-ireland-interview.

61 Ibid.

62 Susan O' Grady, "20 Great Interviews: Edna O'Brien," *Irish* America, October/November 2005, https://irishamerica.com/2005/10/20-great -interviews-edna-obrien/

63 Patricia Harty, "Mother, Life, Landscape, and the Connection," *Irish America,* February/March 2007, https://irishamerica.com/2007/02 /mother-life-landscape-and-the-connection/.

64 "Confession of St. Patrick," *Christian Classic Ethereal Library,* chap. vi, https://www.ccel.org/ccel/patrick/confession.vi.html.

65 Ibid.

66 *Irish Central* Staff, "Three million people in the world are descended from one Irish High King," *Irish Central,* May 17, 2019, https ://www.irishcentral.com/roots/three-million-descended-irish-high-king.

67 *Out of Mist: Celtic Christianity* (Mainz, Germany, Pedia Press), 69.

68 "Confession of St. Patrick," vi.

69 Geoffrey Keating, *The History of Ireland, Volume 2* (London: Irish Texts Society, 1906), 319, https://play.google.com/store/books/detail s?id=eeMGAAAAYAAJ&rdid=book-eeMGAAAAYAAJ&rdot=1.

70 Simon Schama, "Invasions of Ireland from 1170–1320," *BBC*, February 2, 2017, http://www.bbc.co.uk/history/british/middle_ages /ireland_invasion_01.shtml.

71 Richard Huscroft, *Tales From the Long Twelfth Century: The Rise and Fall of the Angevin Empire* (Great Britain: Yale University Press, 2016), 88–90.

72 *Calendar of Letters, Despatches, and State Papers Relating to the Negotiations Between England and Spain, Volume 1 2,* Edited by G. A. Bergenroth (London: H.M. Stationery Office, 1866), 19, https ://play.google.com/store/books/details?id=PWIVCeGyAIAC&rdid=b ook-PWIVCeGyAIAC&rdot=1.

73 T. W. Moody, F. X. Martin, F. J. Byrne, *A New History of Ireland: Volume III: Early Modern Ireland 1534–1691* (New York: OUP Oxford, 2009), 66.

74 Colin Murphy, *The Priest Hunters: The True Story of Ireland's Bounty Hunters* (Dublin, Ireland: O'Brien Press, 2013).

75 John O'Beirne Ranelagh, *A Short History of Ireland* (Cambridge, Great Britain: Cambridge University Press, 1994), 83.

76 N. C. Fleming. *Ireland and Anglo-Irish Relations since 1800: Critical Essays: Volume 1: Union to the Land War* (New York: Routledge, 2017), II.

77 Ignatius Murphy, *The Diocese of Killaloe 1800–1850* (Dublin: Four Courts Press,1992), 80.

78 Ross Douthat, "The Tragedy of Irish Catholicism," *New York Times,* December 1, 2019, https://douthat.blogs.nytimes.com/2009/12/01/the -tragedy-of-irish-catholicism/.

79 Ibid.

80 Ibid.

81 Anonymous, *Ireland: her wit, peculiarities, and popular superstitions: with anecdotes, legendary and characteristic* (Nabu Press, 2013).

82 Timothy Daniel Sullivan, *Recollections of Troubled Times in Irish Politics* (Dublin: Sealy, Bryers, & Walker, 1905), 84.

83 Ryle Dwyer, "Charles Stewart Parnell felt full brunt of the Church over his personal life," *Irish Examiner,"* October 6, 2016, https ://www.irishexaminer.com/viewpoints/analysis/charles-stewart

-parnell-felt-full-brunt-of-the-church-over-his-personal-life-424349.
html.

84 James Joyce, *The Best of James Joyce* (New York: Simon and Schuster, 2013), "The Death of Parnell."

85 Prof. Oliver P. Rafferty SJ, "The Catholic Church and the Easter Rising." *RTÉ*, https://www.rte.ie/centuryireland/index.php/articles/the-catholic-church-and-the-1916-rising.

86 Brian Maye, "A defiant bishop—An Irishman's Diary on Edward O'Dwyer, Limerick and 1916," *Irish Times*, May 16, 2016, https://www.irishtimes.com/opinion/a-defiant-bishop-an-irishman-s-diary-on-edward-o-dwyer-limerick-and-1916-1.2648520?mode=print&ot=example.AjaxPageLayout.ot.

87 Gregory Castle, *Modernism and the Celtic Revival* (Cambridge: Cambridge University Press: 2001), 4.

88 James Connolly, *James Connolly: Selected Writings* (London: Pluto Press, 1997), 66.

89 Shane Kenna, "1916: Crisis of faith led to a new baptism for Thomas MacDonagh," *Irish Examiner*, March 21, 2016.

90 Niall O'Dowd, "Gerry Adams on what must never be forgotten about Easter 1916 Rising," *Irish Central*, April 2, 2018, https://www.irishcentral.com/opinion/gerry-adams-1916-easter-rising.

91 Gerry Adams, "Gerry Adams on what must never be forgotten about Easter 1916 Rising," interview by Niall O'Dowd, *Irish Central*, April 8, 2018, https://www.irishcentral.com/opinion/gerry-adams-1916-easter-rising.

92 Ibid.

93 David McCullagh, "David McCullagh: Was de Valera's mother telling the truth about his parentage?," *Journal.ie*, November 12, 2017, https://www.thejournal.ie/readme/david-mccullagh-was-devaleras-mother-telling-the-truth-about-his-parentage-3688639-Nov2017/.

94 Tim Pat Coogan, *De Valera: Long Fellow, Long Shadow* (London: Head of Zeus Ltd., 2015), chap. 1.

95 Ibid.

96 Cooney, *John Charles McQuaid.*

97   Conor Fitzgerald, "'The Ireland That We Dreamed Of,' and the 'Ireland That We Got,'" *Medium*, March 26, https://medium.com /@fitzfromdublin/the-ireland-that-we-dreamed-of-and-the-ireland -that-we-got-211af132db80.

98   Thomas Flanagan, *The End of the Hunt* (New York: The New York Review of Books, 2016).

99   "The Catholic Church and the writing of the 1937 constitution," *History Ireland*, https://www.historyireland.com/20th-century-contemporary -history/the-catholic-church-and-the-writing-of-the-1937-constitution/.

100 Luddy, Maria. "A 'SINISTER AND RETROGRESSIVE' PROPOSAL: IRISH WOMEN'S OPPOSITION TO THE 1937 DRAFT CONSTI- TUTION." *Transactions of the Royal Historical Society* 15 (2005): 175–95. doi:10.1017/S0080440105000307.

101 Ibid.

102 *Irish Independent*, May 7, 1937.

103 Donal Ó Drisceoil, "Letters show McQuaid's astounding arrogance," *Irish Examiner*, December 19, 2012, https://www.irishexaminer.com /ireland/letters-show-mcquaids-astounding-arrogance-218068.html.

104 Joey Joyce, "February 17th, 1947: Protecting young from university, dancing and books," *Irish Times*, February 17, 2010, https://www .irishtimes.com/opinion/february-17th-1947-protecting-young-from -university-dancing-and-books-1.623043.

105 Ibid.

106 Noel Browne, *Against the Tide*.

107 Douglas Dalby, "Irish Archbishop Who Died in '73 Is Linked to Abuse," *New York Times*, December 8, 2011, https://www.nytimes .com/2011/12/09/world/europe/former-irish-archbishop-tied-to -sexual-abuse.html?auth=login-email.

108 Éibhear Walshe, *Sex, Nation, and Dissent* (Cork: Cork University Press, 1997).

109 *Economic Development* (Dublin: Department of Finance, 1958), 5.

110 Maureen Dowd interview with the author, Niall O'Dowd.

111 Paul Donnelly, "How foreign firms transformed Ireland's domestic economy," *Irish Times*, November 13, 2013, https://www.irishtimes

.com/business/how-foreign-firms-transformed-ireland-s-domestic -economy-1.1593462.

112 James T. Keane, "The uncertain future of Catholic Ireland," *America Magazine*, February 23, 2018, https://www.americamagazine.org/arts -culture/2018/02/23/uncertain-future-catholic-ireland.

113 Patsy MgGarry, "Norbertines' time in Ireland caused unspeakable damage," *Irish Times*, April 8, 2017, https://www.irishtimes.com /news/social-affairs/religion-and-beliefs/norbertines-time-in-ireland -caused-unspeakable-damage-1.3040703.

114 Lesley-Anne Mckeown, "Paedophile priest Brendan Smyth told doctor he may have sexually abused hundreds of children, inquiry hears," *Iirish Mirror*, June 22, 2015, https://www.irishmirror.ie/news /irish-news/crime/paedophile-priest-brendan-smyth-told-5931556.

115 Lesley-Anne Mckeown, Suspicions about notorious paedophile priest Brendan Smyth existed before he was ordained," *Independent.ie*, June 22, 2015, https://www.independent.ie/irish-news/news/suspicions-about -notorious-paedophile-priest-brendan-smyth-existed-before-he-was -ordained-31321873.html.

116 Gerry Moriarty, "Abbot accused of lying about Fr Brendan Smyth," *Irish Times*, June 23, 2015, https://www.irishtimes.com/news/ireland /irish-news/abbot-accused-of-lying-about-fr-brendan-smyth-1 .2260429.

117 Brendan Boland, Darragh Macintyre, *Sworn to Silence: A Young Boy. An Abusive Priest, A Buried Truth*. (Dublin: The O'Brien Press, 2014), chap. 5.

118 A.W. Richard, "Priest Sex Abuse Case Stirs Political Storm in Ireland; Norbertine Fr. Brendan Smyth," *National Catholic Reporter*, December 2, 1994, http://www.bishop-accountability.org/news3/1994_12_02 _Richard_PriestSex_Brendan_Smyth_1.htm.

119 Cathy Hayes, "Priest launches astonishing attack on Bishop Magee over child abuse," *Irish Central*, August 23, 2011, https://www .irishcentral.com/news/priest-launches-astonishing-attack-on-bishop -magee-over-child-abuse-128235198-237407731.

120 "Bishop apologises over Cloyne," *Irish Times*, August 22, 2011, https
://www.irishtimes.com/news/bishop-apologises-over-cloyne
-1.882195.

121 "Bishop John Magee statement," *Irish Times*, August 23, 2011.

122 Ibid.

123 "Hypocrisy and Fr Michael Cleary," *History Ireland*, https://www
.historyireland.com/20th-century-contemporary-history/hypocrisy
-and-fr-michael-cleary/.

124 Patsy McGarry, "Bishop Eamonn Casey accused of sexually abusing three
women as children," *Irish Times*, Mar 25, 2019, https://www.irishtimes
.com/news/social-affairs/religion-and-beliefs/bishop-eamonn-casey
-accused-of-sexually-abusing-three-women-as-children-1.3838299.

125 John L. Allen Jr. "Ireland closes Vatican embassy," *National Catholic
Reporter*, November 3, 2011, https://www.ncronline.org/blogs/ncr-today
/ireland-closes-vatican-embassy.

126 Henry McDonald, "'Endemic' rape and abuse of Irish children in
Catholic care, inquiry finds," *the Guardian*, May 20, 2019, https
://www.theguardian.com/world/2009/may/20/irish-catholic-schools
-child-abuse-claims.

127 McDonald, "'Endemic' rape."

128 "Irish church knew abuse 'endemic'," *BBC*, May 20, 2009, http
://news.bbc.co.uk/2/hi/europe/8059826.stm.

129 "The end of a decade of inquiry," *Irish Times*, May 16, 2009, https
://www.irishtimes.com/news/the-end-of-a-decade-of-inquiry
-1.764983.

130 Ibid.

131 "The Commission Report," *Child Abuse Commission*, http://www
.childabusecommission.ie/rpt/ExecSummary.php.

132 "The savage reality of our darkest days," *Irish Times*, May 21,
2009, https://www.irishtimes.com/opinion/the-savage-reality-of-our
-darkest-days-1.767385.

133 David Batty, "Pope's letter to Irish Catholics disappoints child abuse
survivors," *the Guardian*, March 20, 2010, http://religiouschildabuse
.blogspot.com/2010/11/selection-of-responses-to-popes.html.

134 "Record of abuse (female witnesses), *Child Abuse Commission*, chap. 9, http://www.childabusecommission.ie/rpt/03-09.php.

135 Ibid.

136 Record of abuse (male witnesses), Child Abuse Commission, chap. 7, http://www.childabusecommission.ie/rpt/pdfs/CICA-VOL3-07.pdf.

137 "The psychological adjustment of adult survivors of institutional abuse in Ireland Report submitted to the Commission to Inquire into Child Abuse." *Child Abuse Commission*, chap. 3, http://www.childabusecommission.ie/rpt/05-03A.php#ftn.id1.

138 Ibid.

139 Gavan Reilly, "In their own words: Survivors' accounts of life inside a Magdalene Laundry," *Journal.ie*, February 5, 2013, https://www.thejournal.ie/magdalene-laundry-report-survivors-quotes-784082-Feb2013/.

140 "Voices from the laundries," *Irish Times*, February 5, 2013, https://www.irishtimes.com/news/voices-from-the-laundries-1.1254776.

141 Robinson, *Everybody Matters*, 127.

142 Ibid., 124.

143 "THE ROBINSON YEARS," *Irish Times*, March 13, 1997, https://www.irishtimes.com/opinion/the-robinson-years-1.51829.

144 William Tuohy, "Ireland's President Beat All Odds to Win: Elections: Robinson is a feminist and a political outsider, and she's sympathetic to Protestants. Voters chose her anyway," *LA Times*, November 11, 1990, https://www.latimes.com/archives/la-xpm-1990-11-11-mn-6255-story.html.

145 Katie Baker, "*Mary Robinson: Climate Change's Gender Gap,*" *Daily Beast*, https://www.thedailybeast.com/mary-robinson-climate-changes-gender-gap.

146 Robinson, *Everybody Matters*, 138.

147 Ibid., 139.

148 "Inaugural Speech," Given by Her Excellency Mary Robinson, President of Ireland, in Dublin Castle on Monday, December 3, 1990, https://prelectur.stanford.edu/lecturers/robinson/inaugural.html.

149 Sheila Rule, "Dublin Journal; New President Sees a 'New Ireland'; Could She Be a Startling Beginning?," *New York Times*, December 27,

1990, https://www.nytimes.com/1990/12/27/world/dublin-journal
-new-president-sees-new-ireland-could-she-be-startling-beginning
.html.

150 James F. Clarity, "Premier Urges Irish to Vote for Legalizing of
Divorce," *New York Times*, November 20, 1995, https://www.nytimes
.com/1995/11/20/world/premier-urges-irish-to-vote-for-legalizing-of
-divorce.html.

151 Robinson, *Everybody Matters*, 115.

152 Christine Bohan, "Today marks the 20th anniversary of the decriminal-
isation of homosexuality," *Journal.ie*, June 24, 2013, https://www
.thejournal.ie/anniversary-decriminalisation-homosexuality-ireland
-963902-Jun2013/.

153 Patrick Galvin, "A Gay Dog," *Hibernia*, March 4, 1997.

154 "Ahern Welcomes Coming Into Law of Civil Partnership and Certain
Rights and Obligations of Cohabitants Act 2010," *Department of
Justice and Law Reform*. 17 July 2010.

155 Dr. Matthew Wall, "Column: Change we can believe in? Ireland's
Constitutional Convention has delivered," *Journal.ie*, July 23, 2013,
https://www.thejournal.ie/readme/column-change-we-can-believe
-in-ireland%E2%80%99s-constitutional-convention-has-delivered
-1003278-Jul2013/.

156 Programme for Government 2011–2016 (Department of An Taoiseach,
2011), 17.

157 Gráinne Healy, Brian Sheehan, Noel Whelan, *Ireland Says Yes: The
Inside Story of How the Vote for Marriage Equality Was Won* (Sallins:
Merrion Press, 2016), chap 1.

158 Ibid.

159 Una Mullally, *In the Name of Love: The Movement for Marriage
Equality in Ireland: An Oral History* (Ireland, UK: The History Press,
2014).

160 Ursula Halligan, "Ursula Halligan: Referendum led me to tell truth
about myself," *Irish Times*, March 15, 2015, https://www.irishtimes
.com/opinion/ursula-halligan-referendum-led-me-to-tell-truth-about
-myself-1.2212960.

161 Irish Bishops' Conference, "The Meaning of Marriage," *Catholic Culture*, https://www.catholicculture.org/culture/library/view.cfm?recnum =10767.

162 Cliodhna Russel, "Mary McAleese says 'the only children affected by this referendum will be Ireland's gay children'," *Journal.ie*, May 19, 2015, https://www.thejournal.ie/mary-mcaleese-same-sex-marriage-2 -2111104-May2015/.

163 Irish Bishops' Conference, "Meaning of Marriage."

164 Cliodhna Russel, "Mary McAleese."

165 Aoibhín Bryant, "ON THIS DAY: Ireland voted in the same-sex marriage referendum," *Hot Press*, May 22, 2019, https://www.hotpress.com /culture/day-ireland-voted-sex-marriage-referendum-22773642.

166 Henry McDonald, "Ireland becomes first country to legalise gay marriage by popular vote," *Guardian*, May 23, 2015, https://www .theguardian.com/world/2015/may/23/gay-marriage-ireland-yes-vote.

167 Paddy Agnew, "Vatican calls Irish referendum a 'defeat for humanity'," *Irish Times*, May 26, 2015, https://www.irishtimes.com/news/social -affairs/religion-and-beliefs/vatican-calls-irish-referendum-a-defeat -for-humanity-1.2226957.

168 Michael Kelly, "Dublin archbishop: Church needs 'reality check' after marriage vote," *Archdiocese of Baltimore*, May 26, 2015, https ://www.archbalt.org/dublin-archbishop-church-needs-reality-check -after-marriage-vote/?print=pdf.

169 Jane Suiter, "How equality campaigners got Ireland to vote for same sex marriage," *Washington Post*, May 23, 2015, https://www .washingtonpost.com/news/monkey-cage/wp/2015/05/23/how -equality-campaigners-got-same-sex-marriage-in-ireland/.

170 Danny Hakim, Douglas Dalby, "Ireland Votes to Approve Gay Marriage, Putting Country in Vanguard," *New York Times*, May 23, 2015, https://www.nytimes.com/2015/05/24/world/europe/ireland-gay -marriage-referendum.html?login=email&auth=login-email.

171 Ed O' Loughlin, "Gay Lawmaker, Leo Varadkar, Is in Line to Be Ireland's Prime Minister," *New York Times*, June 2, 2017, https ://www.nytimes.com/2017/06/02/world/europe/leo-varadkar-ireland -prime-minister.html.

172 "Ireland's first gay prime minister enters office," *AFP*, June 14, 2017, https://www.businessinsider.com/afp-irelands-first-gay-prime-minister-enters-office-2017-6.

173 Henry McDonald, "Ireland's first gay prime minister Leo Varadkar formally elected," *Guardian*, June 14, 2017, https://www.theguardian.com/world/2017/jun/14/leo-varadkar-formally-elected-as-prime-minister-of-ireland.

174 *Telegraph Reporters*, "Ireland elects first gay prime minister Leo Varadkar," June 14, 2017, https://www.telegraph.co.uk/news/2017/06/14/ireland-elects-first-gay-prime-minister-leo-varadkar/.

175 Michael O'Regan, Marie O'Halloran, "Leo Varadkar becomes youngest ever Taoiseach," *Irish Times*, June 14, 2017, https://www.irishtimes.com/news/politics/leo-varadkar-becomes-youngest-ever-taoiseach-1.3119285.

176 Mary Robinson, "Mary Robinson Doesn't Need to be Popular," interview by Andrew Goldman, *New York Times*, March 22, 2013, https://www.nytimes.com/2013/03/24/magazine/mary-robinson-doesnt-need-to-be-popular.html.

177 Brian Lavery, Timothy L. O'Brien, "For Insurance Regulations, Trails Lead to Dublin," *New York Times*, April 1, 2005, https://www.nytimes.com/2005/04/01/business/worldbusiness/for-insurance-regulators-trails-lead-to-dublin.html.

178 Emma Graham-Harrison, "Irish abortion vote is remarkable political victory for Leo Varadkar," *Guardian*, May 29, 2018, https://www.theguardian.com/world/2018/may/29/irish-abortion-vote-remarkable-political-victory-leo-varadkar.

179 "Leo Varadkar says sexuality should not be an issue in judging politicians," *Press Association*, March 14, 2019, https://www.timesandstar.co.uk/news/national/17501556.leo-varadkar-says-sexuality-should-not-be-an-issue-in-judging-politicians/.

180 Maureen Dowd, "Move Over DiCaprio and da Vinci—Here's Ireland's Leo," *New York Times*, September 9, 2017, https://www.nytimes.com/2017/09/09/opinion/sunday/leo-varadkar-ireland-dowd.html.

181 Shona Murray, Kevin Doyle, "Leo Varadkar reveals abortion referendum will be held in May," *Independent.ie.*, January 29, 2018, https://www.independent.ie/irish-news/politics/leo-varadkar-reveals-abortion-referendum-will-be-held-in-may-36543756.html.

182 Kitty Holland, *Savita: The Tragedy That Shook a Aation* (London: Random House, 2013), 13–182.

183 Sinead O'Carroll, "Savita Halappanavar: Her tragic death and how she became part of Ireland's abortion debate," *Journal.ie*, April 29, 2018, https://www.thejournal.ie/eighth-amendment-4-3977441-Apr2018/.

184 Ibid.

185 Holland, *Savita: The Tragedy*, 84.

186 Vandita Agrawal, "Ireland Murders Pregnant Indian Dentist," *India Times*, November 16, 2012, https://www.indiatimes.com/europe/ireland-murders-pregnant-indian-dentist-47214.html.

187 Harriet Sherwood, "Remember Savita: father's plea for voters to end Ireland's abortion ban," *Guardian*, May 23, 2018, https://www.theguardian.com/world/2018/may/23/ireland-abortion-referendum-savita-father-galway.

188 Sherwood, "Remembe Savita."

189 "Eighth Amendment of the Constitution Act, 1983," *Irish Statute Book*, http://www.irishstatutebook.ie/eli/1983/ca/8/schedule/enacted/en/html#sched-part1.

190 "Peter Sutherland's 1983 advice on the Eighth Amendment," *Irish Times*, January 13, 2018, https://www.irishtimes.com/news/social-affairs/peter-sutherland-s-1983-advice-on-the-eighth-amendment-1.3353263.

191 "Repeal the 8th (thread)," *Politics.ie*, August 20, 20116, https://politics.ie/threads/repeal-the-8th-second-thread.265646/page-305.

192 Shawn Pogatchinik, "Experts find mass grave at ex-Catholic orphanage in Ireland," *AP*, March 3, 2017, https://apnews.com/879a13dc886c458eb2a1b89bfdd2cc22.

193 Niall O'Dowd, "Tuam Babies: 'It would be . . . kinder to strangle these children at birth,' said doctor," *Irish Central*, August 22, 2017, https://www.irishcentral.com/news/tuam-babies-it-would-be-kinder-to-strangle-these-illegitimate-children-at-birth.

194   Niall O'Dowd, "Woman at center of Tuam babies story reveals her own sad past to NY Times," *Irish Central*, October 28, 2017, https ://www.irishcentral.com/news/woman-at-center-of-tuam-babies -story-reveals-her-own-sad-past-to-ny-times.

195   Jennifer Bray, "The year conservative, Catholic Ireland lost its mojo," *Irish Times*, December 29, 2018, https://www.irishtimes .com/news/politics/the-year-conservative-catholic-ireland-lost-its -mojo-1.3735535.

196   Ibid.

197   Harry McGee, "How the Yes and No sides won and lost the abortion referendum," *Irish Times*, May 27, 2018, https://www.irishtimes.com /news/politics/how-the-yes-and-no-sides-won-and-lost-the-abortion -referendum-1.3509924.

198   Ivana Bacik, "Ireland has changed utterly: the cruel eighth amendment is history," *Guardian*, May 26, 2018, https://www.theguardian.com /commentisfree/2018/may/26/ireland-has-changed-utterly-the-cruel -eighth-amendment-is-history.

199   Maureen Dowd, "Scarlett Letter in the Emerald Isle," *New York Times*, May 19, 2018, https://www.nytimes.com/2018/05/19/opinion /sunday/ireland-abortion-referendum.html.

200   Archbishop Eamon Martin of Armagh, "Ireland: Love Them Both– Pastoral message from the Primate of All Ireland," *Independent Catholic News*, May 20, 2018, https://www.indcatholicnews.com /news/34938.

201   "Election focuses attention on eighth amendment enshrining abortion law," *Irish Times*, February 15, 2016, https://www.belfasttelegraph .co.uk/news/republic-of-ireland/election-focuses-attention-on-eighth -amendment-enshrining-abortion-law-34455042.html.

202   *America* Staff "Catholic leaders notably quiet as Ireland debates and votes on abortion," *America Magazine*, May 25, 2018, https://www .americamagazine.org/politics-society/2018/05/25/catholic-leaders -notably-quiet-ireland-debates-and-votes-abortion.

203   McGee, "How the Yes and No."

204   William Booth, Isaac Stanley-Becker, "Ireland votes to overturn its abortion ban, 'culmination of a quiet revolution,' prime minister says,"

Washington Post, May 26, 2018, https://www.washingtonpost.com /world/europe/ireland-votes-to-repeal-its-ban-on-abortion/2018/05/26 /fb675fa8-603b-11e8-b656-236c6214ef01_story.html.

205	Henry McDonald, Emma Graham-Harrison, Sinead Baker, "Ireland votes by landslide to legalise abortion," *Guardian*, May 26, 2018, https://www.theguardian.com/world/2018/may/26/ireland-votes-by -landslide-to-legalise-abortion.